PRIMA GAMES WE ARE STRATEGY

FREE eGUID

Enter this code at primagames.com/code to unlock your FRE

D1296667

PU5H-FBZH-UGAE-YVJE

Bonus content for this eGuide includes:

► **INTERACTIVE AREA MAPS**

Mobile Friendly: Access your eGuide on any web-enabled device.

Searchable & Sortable: Quickly find the strategies you need.

Added Value: Strategy where, when, and how you want it.

HECK OUT OUR eGUIDE STORE AT PRIMAGAMES.COM!

All your strategy saved in your own personal digital library!

BECOME A FAN OF PRIMA GAMES!

Subscribe to our Twitch channel twitch.tv/primagames and join our weekly stream every Tuesday from 1-4pm EST!

Prima GAMES

www.primagames.com

CONTENTS

WELCOME
BACK TO MARS

The UAC facilities have been overrun by demons and there's only one man that can help. In response, the lone DOOM Marine is activated in the hope that it isn't too late. You play as the powerful soldier, collecting an arsenal of weapons required to defeat the monsters on Mars and in Hell. Discover the cause of the disaster and figure out a way to right the wrong.

This guide provides you with everything you need to defeat the demons and sever the connection between Mars and Hell. A full walkthrough of the Campaign includes maps and every secret location. Details on all weapons, runes, and upgrades prepare you for the demon onslaught. Instructions on how to unlock all 13 Classic Maps also offer a brief description of how to solve them.

Our complete coverage of DOOM Multiplayer features detailed maps and everything you need to know about the weaponry, hack modules, challenges, and more. We even show you how to get up and running with the SnapMap and create your own DOOM experience.

BASICS

:X THE HUD

The HUD or Heads Up Display, is home to all the information you need while fighting through the demon hordes of DOOM. For extra objective information while playing, press (D-PAD DOWN) to reveal the current objective and challenges for the level.

1. **CURRENT OBJECTIVE:** This marks the current objective that you need to complete in order to progress in the level.

2. **NAVIGATION:** Navigation stays at the top of the screen at all times. Acting much like a compass, it helps give you the general direction of objectives.

3. **COMBAT RATING:** This shows your overall progress to more weapon upgrade points. Killing demons adds progress to the meter.

4. **HEALTH:** Your health appears on the bottom-left of the screen below your current amount of armor.

5. **ARMOR:** Armor is indicated above your health. If you have no armor, the meter is grayed out until you get more.

6. **ACQUIRED KEYS:** Your currently acquired keys are located to the right of your health and armor bars. Depending on the level, these are represented by key cards or skulls.

7. **EQUIPMENT:** Your equipment is located on the bottom-right of the screen to the left of your active gun. The currently equipped item is highlighted, while any other available option is grayed out.

8. **AMMO:** All ammo is located on the bottom-right of the screen next to your equipped weapon. The number and white bar next to your weapon represent the amount of ammo remaining for that specific weapon. A red set of bars below the weapon indicates the amount of Chainsaw ammo you have, while a green set of bars shows the amount of BFG ammo remaining.

9. **MISSION CHALLENGES:** To quickly view the challenges, press (D-PAD Down) and they all appear on the right side of the screen. This is an extremely helpful tool for quickly checking your progress for each challenge in a level.

SHARED AMMO

Several weapons (Shotgun/Super Shotgun, HAR/Chaingun, Plasma/Gauss Rifle) share an ammo bank, so running out of ammo with one causes the other to be empty, as well.

:X MENUS

Pressing (Menu/Options) pauses your game and takes you to the Dossier screen. Use (LB/L1) and (RB/R1) to navigate between the different sections of the Dossier.

MISSION

The Mission menu is the first and main section of the Dossier. Opening the mission tab shows you the map, in its current state of exploration, as well as the Challenges and Secrets that can be unlocked when traversing level to level. Interacting with an AutoMap Station gives you full access to the map for each level and displays the different types of secrets that can be unlocked, as well as their locations on this menu.

ARSENAL

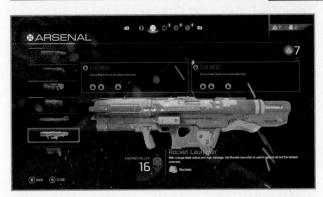

The Arsenal menu is the second section of the Dossier. Opening the Arsenal tab allows you to view all of the weapons you have currently unlocked, as well as functional descriptions and total enemies killed.

This serves as the weapon HUB for you through the campaign experience and the area where you can upgrade and customize each different weapon with the modifications of your choosing.

PRAETOR SUIT

The Praetor Suit menu is the third section of the Dossier. Opening the Preator Suit tab allows you to spend research tokens acquired from Elite Guards, and view the current state of your Argent Cell routing, improved by finding Argent Cells.

You can spend your tokens on one of five different areas that increase the abilities of your Preator Suit: Environmental Resistance, Area-Scanning Technology, Equipment System, Powerup Effectiveness, and Dexterity.

RUNES

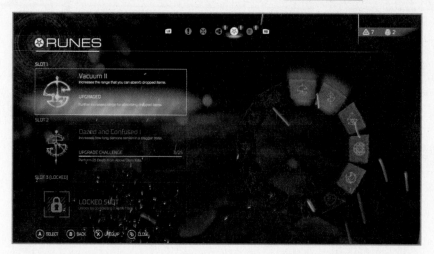

The Runes menu is the fourth section of the Dossier. This tab becomes available to you after the first Trial Stone has been encountered and completed.

Completing Trial Stones unlocks the detailed Rune for you to equip. There are several to acquire and you can equip up to three at a time. Each Rune has a challenge related to the powers it gives, so try them all and harness them at their maximum strength!

CODEX

The Codex is the fifth and final section of the Dossier. This tab continually fills with information about DOOM and the world around the Doom Marine.

The Codex populates as you encounter new demons and weapons, and scour the levels for Data Logs. The more acquired throughout the game, the more you understand the world around you. Find all the Data Logs to put together the pieces leading up to the awakening of the Doom Marine.

:X MOVEMENT

Movement is key to survival in DOOM. To move around the world, use (Left Stick) and (Right Stick) to aim. There's no Sprint button in DOOM, so moving the (Left Stick) all the way in any direction causes you to move at full speed.

JUMPING AND CLIMBING

A standard jump is accomplished by pressing A/X. After finding the Jump Boots, you can jump once more while in the air by pressing A/X again.

When jumping toward any accessible ledge, you automatically pull yourself up and over it.

:X PICKUPS & COLLECTIBLES

Different pickups are scattered around the levels of DOOM. Pickups such as Argent Cells, Field Drones, and Elite Guards provide upgrades to the Doom Marine, while Data Logs further your understanding of the story before you are awakened.

ARGENT CELL

Find Argent Cells throughout the game to obtain orbs of Argent Energy. Overload the Preator Suit with Argent Energy to upgrade maximum Health, Armor, or Ammo capacity of The Doom Marine!

AUTOMAP STATION

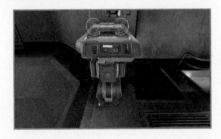

Scattered throughout the DOOM campaign, these stations download the map data for the specific level where you find it.

Accessing the Dossier after acquiring AutoMap Data exposes explorable space.

DATA LOG

Accounts of general DOOM lore that can be found throughout the single player campaign. Keep your eyes open for these to unlock codex entries and learn more of the story that DOOM has to offer.

COLLECTIBLES

Hidden throughout all levels of DOOM, you may find these Collectibles to unlock bonus content in the Extras menu. There are several to collect! Can you find them all?

ELITE GUARD

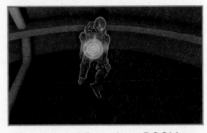

Security personnel charged with protecting the Lazarus Project and maintaining order throughout the Argent facility. Find Elite Guards scattered throughout DOOM to obtain Research Tokens for upgrading the Praetor Suit.

FIELD DRONE

Often referred to as "Droppers," these drones were developed by the UAC to autonomously receive and deliver ordered parts. Find them throughout the campaign to add mods to The Doom Marine's weapons!

CLASSIC MAP LEVER

Carefully hidden throughout the world, these levers unlock a Classic Map secret. Don't leave a corner untouched until you find them all!

TRIAL STONE

Ancient stones scattered throughout the world that transport The Doom Marine to a different dimension to complete a challenge. Complete the challenge to unlock a Rune for The Doom Marine to equip and increase his powers!

:X COMBAT

DOOM revolves around intense combat against horde after horde of demons.

WEAPONS

While you are always "armed" with your melee ability (R3), the real power lies in the guns, equipment, and chainsaw. For a full breakdown on all the weapons, visit the Weaponry section of this guide!

WEAPON WHEEL

To activate your weapon wheel, hold down RB/R1, then use the Right Stick to decide which weapon you would like to select.

When the weapon wheel is up, time slows down, allowing you extra time to select weapons. To quickly swap between your last two weapons, just tap RB/R1.

CHAINSAW

The chainsaw can kill most enemies without help from any other weapons.

Press X/Square to activate your chainsaw, then use LT/L2 to rev it up and RT/R2 to attack. Killing an enemy with the chainsaw causes them to spew out ammo from their corpse.

BFG

The BFG is a powerful weapon that delivers streams of supercharged Argent plasma to multiple targets and is somewhat self-guiding. To equip the BFG, press Y/Triangle.

Firing the BFG is as easy as aiming and pressing RT/R2. Use this weapon against groups of enemies to make the most of each shot as ammo is rare.

EQUIPMENT

There are three different types of equipment in the game. To cycle through your available options, press DPAD-Right or DPAD-Left.

FRAG GRENADE

Your standard grenade, it does explosive damage in a small radius. Basically it goes "Boom!"

HOLOGRAM

Activating the Hologram spawns a clone of the Doom Marine to distract the Demons while you get into a better position to fight.

SIPHON GRENADE

When thrown, the Siphon Grenade spawns a dome that steals health from all enemies inside. All health stolen immediately heals the player.

GLORY KILLS

Glory kills are a great way to finish off enemies and keep your health up.

When enemies lose enough health, they enter a crippled state and begin to flash blue. Move in close until you see them start to flash orange, then press the Melee button to perform a Glory Kill. These always drop health.

There are multiple types of Glory Kills. Attack a crippled enemy from above, behind, and head-on to perform each variety.

MULTIPLAYER

Looking for some intense PvP action? Check out the multiplayer side of DOOM. There are six different modes that take place on nine unique maps.

CLAN ARENA: Kill enemy players to win. Victory is awarded to the first team that wins three rounds.

DOMINATION: Control the zones to win. Victory is awarded to the first team to reach the score limit or have the higher score when the timer expires.

FREEZE TAG: Freeze enemies and thaw your teammates. Victory is awarded to the first team to win three rounds.

SOUL HARVEST: Kill enemies and capture their souls. Victory is awarded to the first team to reach the soul count limit.

TEAM DEATHMATCH: Kill enemies to win. Victory is awarded to the first team to reach the kill limit or have more kills when time expires.

WARPATH: Control the moving zone to win. Victory is awarded to the first team to reach the score limit or have the higher score when time expires.

For complete maps of each multiplayer level, as well as tips to help you dominate the competition, check out the Multiplayer section of this guide.

SNAPMAP

Have a good idea for a DOOM Co-op, Single Player, or Multiplayer experience? Check out the SnapMap mode!

SnapMaps allow you to set your imagination free in the DOOM universe. For all the details, check out the SnapMap section of this guide.

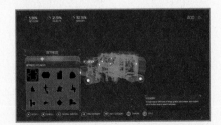

THE UAC

MAIN OBJECTIVE	Find the Resource Ops Entrance
NEW WEAPONS/EQUIPMENT	Pistol, Combat Shotgun, Frag Grenade
NEW MONSTERS	The Possessed, Imp, Possessed Soldier

COLLECTIBLES

COLLECTIBLE	UNLOCKS
Blueguy	Combat Shotgun Model
Classicguy	Imp Model

CLASSIC MAP Doom II - Entryway

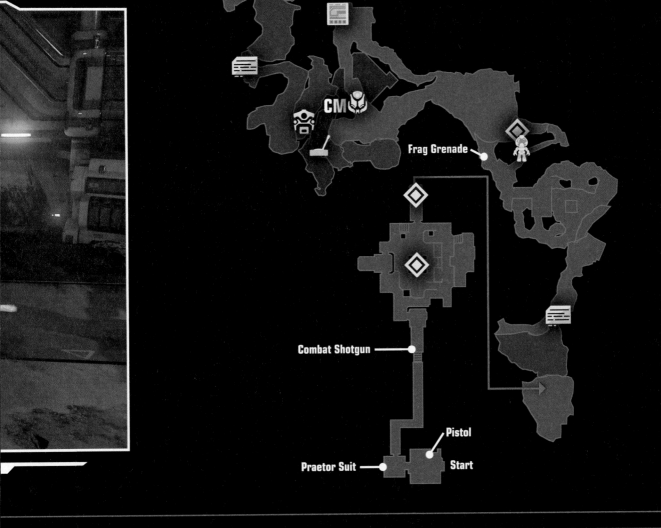

CM

Frag Grenade

Combat Shotgun

Pistol

Praetor Suit

Start

FIND THE SITE 03 EXIT

A demonic invasion has hit the UAC facility on Mars, destroying everything and everyone. You play as the Doom Marine who finds himself chained up in a crypt—coming to, just in time, as three demons converge on your location.

After eliminating The Possessed, use the console next to the exit to begin a playback of an echo recording, then proceed through the door and approach the armor ahead. Interact with the Praetor Suit to slip inside and receive a message from Dr. Samuel Hayden, the UAC Mars Director. Get used to his voice as he guides you through Mars and Hell.

NEW WEAPON
PISTOL

MODIFICATIONS: Charged Energy Shot

The Pistol is a sidearm with limitless ammo that is most effective against weaker targets. Use it whenever high damage is unnecessary, saving the more powerful guns for tougher foes.

MISSION DETAILS

If you ever get lost, access the Mission page in your Dossier. This shows the AutoMap, current objectives, Mission Challenges, and exploration items. The box in the lower-right corner displays the exploration items that you've found. Items appear on the map as you get close, so use this to your advantage to collect these valuable assets.

Continue through the open door until you reach another group of monsters. Take down the first with a Glory Kill and then eliminate the rest. At the top of the steps, grab the **Combat Shotgun** from the corpse and open the door.

GLORY KILLS

Dealing damage to demons causes them to stagger, which is indicated by a blue highlight. Move into close range and when the highlight turns orange, then press the Melee button to perform a Glory Kill. Attack demons from any angle, including from above, to perform different Glory Kills. Glory Killing demons always drops health.

NEW WEAPON
COMBAT SHOTGUN

MODIFICATIONS: Charged Burst, Explosive Shot

Effective at medium and close range, the Shotgun is a versatile weapon for most encounters.

DESTROY THE GORE NEST

An Imp drops from the ceiling. These guys pose a bigger threat than The Possessed as they toss projectiles your way. Step to the side to avoid taking damage and take it down. Continue into the next room to find more Imps. Kill them before stepping up to the Gore Nest. Interact with it to destroy it, but be ready for a big fight. This action attracts a large group of Imps. Stay on the move as you take them all out. Keep an eye out for health, armor, and ammo in the area. Once the coast is clear, the door at the far end opens to reveal the exit.

FIND THE RESOURCE OPS ENTRANCE

Your primary goal in this mission is to find the Resource Ops entrance so that the satellite can be realigned. Exit Site 03 via the elevator ahead. This ends the introduction to the campaign and sends you out to the surface of Mars.

Drop off the cliff, then proceed through the narrow path and grab the **Data Log** on the ground ahead. These Data Logs can be found throughout the missions of DOOM and give you a better idea of what's happening at the UAC facility. Access your Codex in the Dossier to read them.

Just ahead, Possessed Soldiers join weaker foes—The Possessed and Imps. The Shotgun makes quick work of these guys, but stay on the move as the Imps lob projectiles your way. Look out for red barrels that explode when shot. Use them to eliminate nearby foes, but avoid getting caught in the blast. Climb onto the upper walkway and follow it to a gate, which unlocks once the demon threat has been eliminated.

SECRETS

With the prologue out of the way, the maps begin to open up with multiple routes to your objective. It's always good to explore outside of the main path, as there are numerous secrets in each mission. Secret areas, Collectibles, Elite Guards, Field Drones, powerups, armor, Data Logs, and health stations are hidden throughout the environment. Keep your eyes open as you move toward your destination.

FIND BLUE ACCESS KEY

Turn right and follow the narrow passage as it ends at a big crate. Find the blue keycard on a corpse just on the other side. Now you can return to the gate and proceed toward Resource Operations.

BLUEGUY

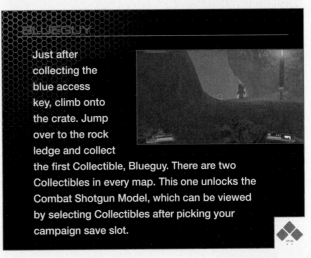

Just after collecting the blue access key, climb onto the crate. Jump over to the rock ledge and collect the first Collectible, Blueguy. There are two Collectibles in every map. This one unlocks the Combat Shotgun Model, which can be viewed by selecting Collectibles after picking your campaign save slot.

FIND THE RESOURCE OPS ENTRANCE

There's a **Frag Grenade** with some armor and shotgun shells just inside the next area. Test your new equipment on the small group of The Possessed below before hopping down. More demons join you as you move through the next area, so mow them down as they do so.

NEW EQUIPMENT
FRAG GRENADE

Frag Grenades are the first piece of equipment you acquire. Pressing the Use Equipment button triggers the explosive. Lob them into groups of enemies to get the most out of this weapon. There are only three equipment items in the game. Once you have more to choose from, press the Next Equipment and Previous Equipment buttons to switch between them.

Instead of moving down the hill, take the right path into a cavern. Clear out the monsters inside and then access the terminal in the far corner. An **AutoMap Station** can be found in every mission, so be on the lookout. It fills in the entire map, giving you a better idea of where you're going. Finding this station unlocks Area-Scanning Technology in Praetor Suit Upgrades.

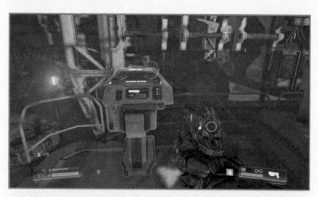

WEAPON UPGRADE POINTS

By completing Mission Challenges, finding secrets, and increasing your Combat Rating you earn Weapon Upgrade Points. Once a point is earned, it can be spent to improve your current weapon mods. Visit the Arsenal tab in the Dossier to spend available points. You can also view your current Mission Challenges and discovered secrets in the Mission tab of the Dossier. Check out the Weapons chapter for full information on each available modification.

Turn left and move to the far ledge. Watch out as demons may attack from below. Feel free to spend some time picking them off from the higher vantage point. Interact with the **Elite Guard** who leans against the wall.

ELITE GUARDS AND PRAETOR SUIT TOKENS

Elite Guards can be found throughout the missions of DOOM. Interacting with these corpses earns a Praetor Suit Token. Accessing the Praetor Suit tab of your Dossier allows you to upgrade a variety of the Praetor Suit's capabilities. Here, you can spend these tokens on available upgrades and view requirements to unlock remaining categories. If finding the Exploration items is important to you, Item Awareness is a good upgrade to start out with.

Drop down, finish off any remaining demons, and continue to the right. A **Field Drone** is visible ahead, moving further to the right. Jump across the gap and follow the bot. Interact with it to earn a Weapon Modification. Each time you find one of these drones, you must select a modification for one of your weapons. It can then be upgraded with Weapon Upgrade Points. At the moment you can only select the Combat Shotgun, but later you must make the decision of which gun to improve.

CLASSIC MAP:
DOOM II - ENTRYWAY

After finding the Elite Guard and dropping to the surface, proceed down the path and descend another level. Look at the map and spot the Field Drone icon on an upper ledge. If you've already approached this drone, it has moved further ahead. A crate blocks an entrance just below its original location. Turn around and find an opening in the cage on the left, then enter and pull the lever inside. This removes the blockage, revealing the first Classic DOOM Map. Move in to find Possessed Soldiers standing guard. This unlocks the DOOM II: Entryway map. Access it from the Main menu by selecting your save slot and then Classic Maps.

CLASSIC MAPS

There's a piece of a Classic DOOM map hidden in every mission! Finding it unlocks the ability to play it by visiting the Classic Maps menu. Access this menu after selecting your Campaign save slot. A lever must be pulled before you can try these maps and they are usually extremely well hidden, so keep an eye out as you explore Mars and Hell.

Before proceeding forward, turn around, drop to the lower level, and search a dock to find another **Data Log**, as well as other helpful assets. Return to the Field Drone and proceed toward the objective.

At first you only meet The Possessed, but as you move further ahead, tougher demons join the fight. Avoid getting surrounded. Start picking them off immediately and steadily clear the monsters out as you continue into a narrow valley. Watch out for the Imps as they quickly move up and down the ledges. From here, you can climb up the right ledges and cut through the tunnel or jump over to the left side and follow a narrow path along the cliff side.

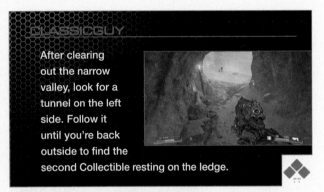

CLASSICGUY

After clearing out the narrow valley, look for a tunnel on the left side. Follow it until you're back outside to find the second Collectible resting on the ledge.

Fight your way through the demons, collecting the items along the way. Once the threat has been eliminated in the next open area, climb the machinery on the right side and continue up to the left. Before entering, turn around and search the carts on the tracks ahead to find hidden armor, health, and ammo. Once you're ready, follow the objective into the building and up the stairs. Interact with the console ahead to exit the facility and complete the first mission.

RESOURCE OPERATIONS

MAIN OBJECTIVE	Discover the Cause
NEW WEAPONS/EQUIPMENT	Chainsaw, Plasma Rifle, Heavy Assault Rifle
NEW MONSTERS	Possessed Engineer, Possessed Security

CHALLENGES

CHALLENGE	DESCRIPTION
Two-fer	Kill 2 of The Possessed with one trigger pull from the Shotgun.
Variety is the Spice of Death I	Perform 5 different Glory Kills on The Possessed.
Quite the Explorer	Find 3 Secrets.

COLLECTIBLES

COLLECTIBLE	UNLOCKS
Doomguy	Doom Marine Model
Bronzeguy	Heavy Assault Rifle Model

CLASSIC MAP DOOM - Hangar

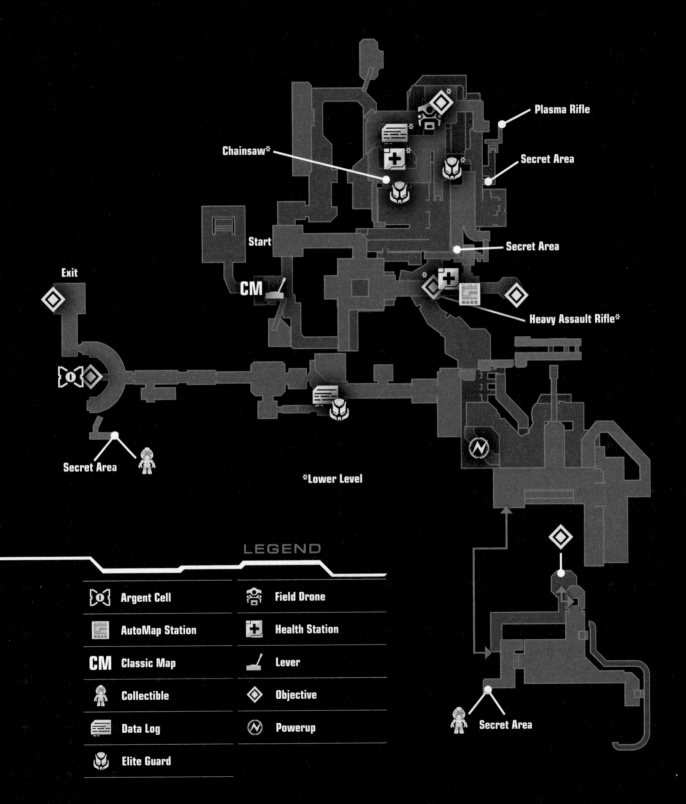

Plasma Rifle

Chainsaw*

Secret Area

Secret Area

Start

Heavy Assault Rifle*

Exit

Secret Area

*Lower Level

Secret Area

LEGEND

🔲	Argent Cell	🤖	Field Drone
🗺	AutoMap Station	➕	Health Station
CM	Classic Map	🔨	Lever
🧍	Collectible	◈	Objective
▤	Data Log	🅝	Powerup
👹	Elite Guard		

RESTORE FACILITY POWER

Climb the steps and follow the corridor into a depot. The Possessed wander all around the start of this mission. Take advantage of the situation to earn the first and second Mission Challenges. Pull open the door on the left and continue through the hall to find a control center.

MISSION CHALLENGES

Mission Challenges are activated when a mission begins, and completing them rewards you with Weapon Upgrade Points. You can view the requirements and track progress in the Mission tab of the Dossier. Keep these challenges in the back of your mind as you play, looking for opportunities to complete them.

Before interacting with the console, turn around and spot the maintenance access above the hall. Jump to the ledge and follow it to the

right to find a secret area and a nice armor boost. Return to the computer and interact with it to reset the power. Unfortunately, a manual release is required to get the satellite aligned.

GAIN SATELLITE ARRAY ACCESS

Descend the steps and interact with the **AutoMap Station** on the left. Return to the main room and approach the Maintenance Bay Door controls on the far leg of the lift. Use it to open the door. Soften up one of The Possessed below and then perform a Glory Kill from above to add to the second challenge.

Follow the walkway around the outside of the room, picking off the demons along the way. Continue along the path all the way around and pry open the jammed door. A new monster is

introduced inside. Take out the Possessed Engineer first, as it explodes when killed. This can be used to your advantage to weaken and eliminate nearby foes, but the detonation can cause serious damage if it gets too close.

CLASSIC MAP
DOOM - HANGAR

After dropping through the Maintenance Bay Door, move to the far corner of the room, climb onto the crates, and grab the armor. Follow the railing to the right and jump over to the ledge on the left. Climb up to find the lever. Pull it to open the door below, then drop down and enter the Classic Map room. Defeat the Possessed Soldiers and collect the armor inside.

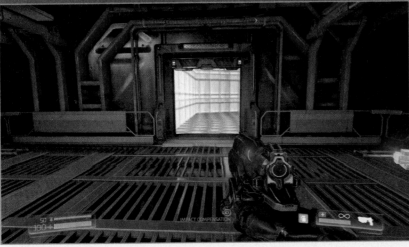

Follow the corridor to a big room that's chock-full of demons. Pull out your Shotgun and start knocking them out. Monsters attack from both sides of the gap, so be ready to make the jump to the other side. When facing a large group of enemies, always look for ways to break line of sight. There isn't a mechanic in DOOM to duck behind cover, but putting an object between you and them can make the difference in a battle.

Once the demons have been eliminated, move around to the far side from the entrance and grab the **Data Log** on the workbench. Look for an accessible console to the left and press the Stop button to halt the elevator on the far wall. Use these to reach the upper platform. Walk out onto the crane and jump over to the ledge on the left. Enter the office to find armor and an alternate route to the locker room. Otherwise, a door near the Data Log is also open.

NEW WEAPON
CHAINSAW

Pull the **Chainsaw** out of the corpse ahead. This is an extremely valuable melee weapon, taking out any enemy with one swipe. Be conservative, though, as it requires the extremely rare fuel. Use the Health Station if needed, then exit via the far door.

FIND YELLOW ACCESS KEY

Wipe out the demonic presence in the Cargo Station to cancel the lock down. Approach the Dish Access door at the far end to find out you need yellow access to get through. Interact with the console to begin an echo-recording playback. Climb onto the nearby stack of crates to reach the upper level, watching out for the containers that move from right to left.

Before continuing toward the objective, follow the maintenance access to the right to find armor and fuel. Return to the previous location and drop inside the next room to find the Security Station. Unfortunately, it also requires yellow access.

DESTROY THE GORE NEST

Move down the next hall and open the jammed door to find another Gore Nest. Wipe out the demons, destroy the nest, and then eliminate the usual suspects that show up. Be ready with the Chainsaw if things get tough. Once the room has been cleared, approach the elevator on the bottom level and call it with the console.

Ride it up and then follow the walkway to find a **Field Drone**. Next, move down the left hall to find the Yellow Keycard. Enter the maintenance access and eliminate the demons as you continue ahead. Drop through the hatch at the other end to conveniently return to the Cargo Station and the yellow access gate.

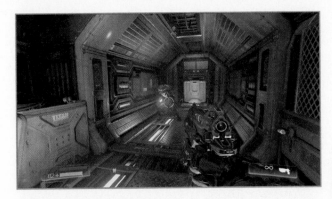

Before opening the gate, climb the crates again and return to the Security Station. Interact with the access control computer to override the area lockdown. This unlocks the gates and hatch that were previously locked. Move toward the Gore Nest location and enter the hatch on the right side of the hallway. Inside, take out The Possessed and Imps before collecting the Praetor Token from the **Elite Guard**. Before exiting the area, find another open hatch down another corridor. Climb inside to find a **Plasma Rifle**.

MODIFICATIONS: Heat Blast, Stun Bomb

The Plasma Rifle has a very high rate of fire and leverages plasma projectiles to pick apart enemies.

Jump across the hatch opening and climb inside the vent shaft. Kick out the cover to reach the Gore Nest room. Take the elevator up to where you found the Yellow Keycard and enter the gate on the right to reach the room above the locker room. Head left, crouch, and enter the shaft in the corner. Follow it until you drop inside a maintenance room. Collect another Praetor Token from the **Elite Guard** that leans against a forklift.

REALIGN THE RESOURCE OPS SATELLITE

Next, enter the yellow access gate and enter the security room ahead. A corpse still holds a **Heavy Assault Rifle**. Grab it from his cold hands. Collect the armor, use the Health Station, and then access the Airlock Control on the wall to open the exit. Proceed inside and use another Airlock Control to go outdoors.

MODIFICATIONS: Tactical Scope, Micro Missiles

With high velocity rounds, the Heavy Assault Rifle is ideal for hitting fast-moving targets.

Watch out for the Possessed Soldiers who immediately attack. Quickly take them down as you move outside. Follow the path to the right, taking out the demons and collecting the items that litter the sides. Look out for the **Berserk Powerup** on a metal walkway on the right. Your weapon is removed and you gain the ability to take out any enemy with one punch. Quickly move between the enemies since you don't have much time before it wears out. Keep an eye out for a new enemy, the Possessed Security, as the ability to punch through its shield is a huge time saver.

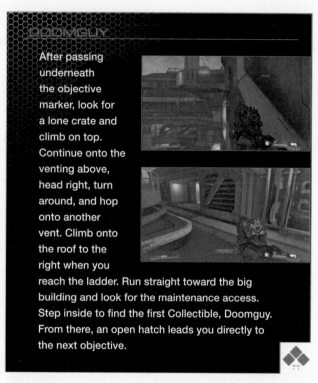

DOOMGUY

After passing underneath the objective marker, look for a lone crate and climb on top. Continue onto the venting above, head right, turn around, and hop onto another vent. Climb onto the roof to the right when you reach the ladder. Run straight toward the big building and look for the maintenance access. Step inside to find the first Collectible, Doomguy. From there, an open hatch leads you directly to the next objective.

POWERUPS

In many of the big arenas, where you must take on a large horde of demons, a powerup is provided to tip the battle in your favor. These items give you a boost in a specific area for a short time, such as 4x damage, a speed boost, or super strength. Collecting your first powerup unlocks the Powerup Effectiveness upgrades for your Praetor Suit. Purchase these upgrades to make the powerups even more powerful. Many fights introduce low-level foes first before bringing out the big guys. Try to save the powerup until these tougher enemies spawn in.

If you get low on health, search the perimeter for health and armor. Once the threat has been taken care of, look for an elevator on the main building. Step inside and ride it up a floor. This leads to a terminal. Interact with the body that leans against the desk to access the computer and realign the satellite dish.

GO TO THE VEGA TERMINAL

Ride the elevator back down, move under the terminal that was just used, and hop down to the new walkway. Climb onto the platform ahead, and then jump up two ledges on the right. Follow the red walkway, continuing straight ahead until you can't go any further. Hop down to the left and approach the VEGA Server Station. Demons burst out with guns blazing, so quickly return fire as you move to one side or the other. Kill the monsters as you move inside.

Activate the airlock by using the console and continue inside. Defeat the Imps and The Possessed as you follow the corridor ahead. Grab the **Data Log** atop a desk on the left, then enter the office on the right. Use the Access Control computer to override the lockdown. Watch out as a Possessed Soldier dives over the terminal.

More demons occupy the next corridor, so remain attentive. Turn left and enter the small opening on the left wall. Climb onto the ledge and enter the control room ahead, taking out the monsters that get in your way. An Elite Guard rests against the equipment on the far side of the room. Grab the Praetor Token, open the munitions crate, and pick up the armor before returning to the previous hallway.

PROCEED TO THE FOUNDRY AIRLOCK

Push further into the building as more demons attempt to stop you. Fight your way through until you reach a semi-circular room. Once you're ready to complete the mission, enter the door ahead, collect the **Argent Cell** that rises from the floor, and wait for an alarm to sound. Exit the room, turn left, and enter the airlock. Use the console to exit the facility.

BRONZEGUY

Before entering the VEGA terminal room, climb the pile of crates to the left and enter the maintenance shaft above. Follow the chute to find the second Collectible, Bronzeguy.

ARGENT CELLS

In most of the missions, a cache or two of Argent Cells can be found, hidden away in the UAC facilities or Hell. By collecting these cells, you are allowed to route the extra power to one of three subsystems of your Praetor Suit: Health, Armor, or Ammo—permanently increasing the maximum capacity of that subsystem. These are extremely valuable and should be sought out whenever available.

FOUNDRY

MAIN OBJECTIVE	Stop the Meltdown
NEW WEAPONS/EQUIPMENT	Rocket Launcher
NEW MONSTERS	Hell Razer, Hell Knight

CHALLENGES

CHALLENGE	DESCRIPTION
Three Possessed, One Barrel	Kill 3 of The Possessed with one Explosive Barrel.
Curb Stomp	Perform 3 "Death from Above" Glory Kills on Possessed Soldiers (attack from above).
Quite the Collector	Find 2 Collectibles.

COLLECTIBLES

COLLECTIBLE	UNLOCKS
Vaultguy	Possessed Engineer Model
Prototypeguy	Plasma Rifle Model

CLASSIC MAP DOOM - Nuclear Plant

LEGEND

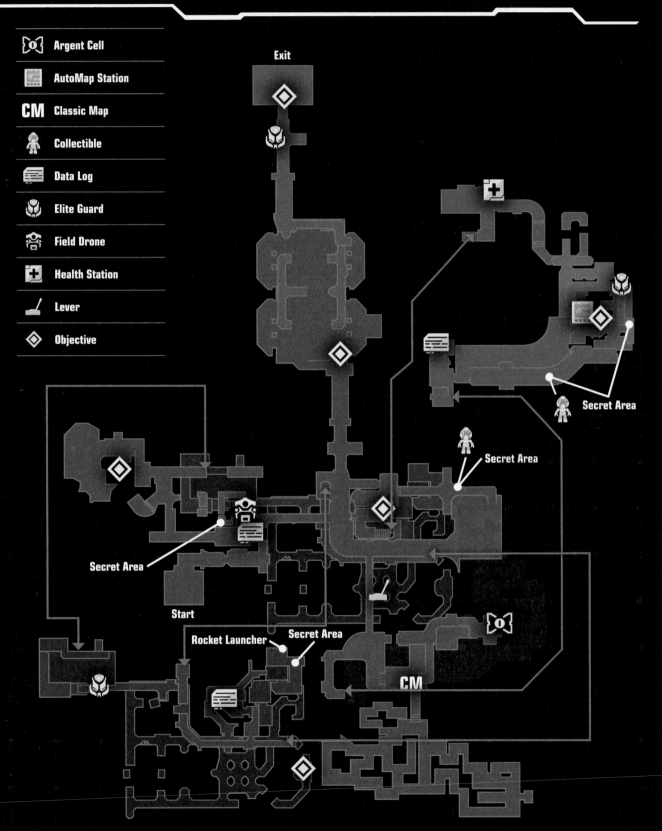

- Argent Cell
- AutoMap Station
- CM Classic Map
- Collectible
- Data Log
- Elite Guard
- Field Drone
- Health Station
- Lever
- Objective

Exit

Secret Area

Secret Area

Secret Area

Start

Rocket Launcher

Secret Area

CM

DESTROY THE GORE NESTS

Follow the corridor until you reach the main room of the Foundry. Four Gore Nests need to be taken care of before you can proceed. Check our map to see all four locations. These do not need to be done in the order given here, just as long as you eliminate all four. Turn left, jump the gap, and enter the left door. Interact with the Field Drone in the corner to gain another weapon modification. Both the HAR and Plasma Rifle have great mods to select from, though the best option for you depends on your play style. Choose wisely.

COMBAT RATING

Starting with the third mission, combat rewards you with Weapon Upgrade Points. Find and kill as many demons as possible during a mission to maximize your Combat Rating. Gray icons appear in the upper-right corner of the HUD. As you defeat demons, these light up. Once they are all lit up, you have maximized the rating.

Follow the hall to the right and eliminate the demon threat inside the next room. Step up to the security desk on the left and interact with the console on the right wall to replay an echo recording. This shows a monster carrying away a corpse that is vital to your completion of the mission. Follow it into the area ahead.

GORE NEST #1

Pick up the Data Log on the desk in the opposite corner before exiting the opposite door. A Possessed Engineer charges your way, surrounded by a number of The Possessed. It's possible to score the first challenge immediately by targeting the red barrel at the intersection ahead.

Hop down to the far walkway and enter the doorway on the right to find the first Elite Guard in the Foundry. Return to the previous room and use the platforms around the perimeter to climb to the upper level. Just spin around and spot the green light on the next ledge.

Climb into the venting on the right, just after reaching the upper floor, to find armor. Exit the shaft and make your way to the doorway opposite from where you dropped down. Interact with the Elite Guard corpse to acquire the Tech Arm. Return to the security desk and use the hand to gain access to the first Gore Nest.

GORE NEST #2

Return to the main room of the Foundry and take down the demons that attack on the walkway ahead. Turn right before the blue access door and follow the path around to the left until you reach another group of demons, including Possessed Security. Wipe them out and then collect the Yellow Keycard off the corpse, found next to a crate further around to the left. Watch out as more monsters find your location.

Enter the new opening, just around the corner from the security desk. Destroy the Gore Nest in the middle of the room and kill the demons that are attracted to your position. Watch out for a new monster known as a Hell Razer. These guys fire a "powerful beam of unrefined Hell energy" that can do serious damage if contact is made. When you see them aiming their weapon, there's still time to avoid the attack. Quickly take them down or be ready to jump over the beam.

After collecting the Yellow Keycard, turn around and hop over the left railing onto a rock platform. Search under the walkway to find the first Collectible, Vaultguy.

Return to the main room. Turn right and follow the bridge left to the far side of the Foundry. Turn left and fight your way to the far wall to find an Argent Cell next to an inaccessible door. Return to the bridge, climb the nearby steps, and enter the yellow access door. Continue up more stairs and collect the Data Log on the desk ahead. Enter the open door to find more demons and take them out.

CLASSIC MAP:
DOOM - NUCLEAR PLANT

Stop as you cross the bridge overlooking the fourth Gore Nest and hop over the left railing onto the platform to find the lever. Pull it before returning to the bridge. Continue to the far side and look on the left wall for the new opening that leads to another DOOM Classic Map. This portion of Nuclear Plant is fairly big with plenty of enemies and items.

After collecting the Data Log and clearing out the demons in the next room, look inside the middle of three boxes on the conveyor belt. Inside is the second Collectible, Prototypeguy.

Follow the conveyor belt to another open door. Before entering, climb the stack of crates on the right and jump into the maintenance shaft to find another Elite Guard. Return to the door and move inside to find the second Gore Nest, surrounded by monsters. Eliminate the initial threat before destroying the nest. then kill another wave of demons that spawns in. Proceed upstairs to eliminate any remaining foes. On the top floor, remain on the walkway as you circle around to a dead end to find the AutoMap Station. Backtrack to the corner door and enter the next room to find the Blue Keycard on another human corpse.

GORE NEST #3

Stay on the walkway, hopping across a couple of gaps, then move through the blue access door. More demons attack as you proceed into the next room, where the third Gore Nest is found. Again, destroy the nest and eliminate the monsters that spawn around the room. Note that a Health Station hangs from the wall on the top floor, near your entrance.

GORE NEST #4

Return to the main room and spot another Gore Nest on the lower level, between the second and third nests.

Looking down at the Gore Nest, look for an opening to the left on the second floor. Enter the room, drop down one level, and follow the left hall to find another Data Log. Eliminating more demons along the way, head back up the steps and look into the room on the left.

Jump into an opening on the left wall and immediately turn right. Drop into the room to the right and then look up to find an access to the upper floor. Jump up to grab the ledge and follow the corridor to find a **Rocket Launcher** sitting on a desk. Drop back into the previous room and take the other path until you find yourself near the Gore Nest. At this point, several monsters infest the area. Wipe them out before hopping down to the nest and destroying it. Kill the demons that spawn into the big room.

NEW WEAPON
ROCKET LAUNCHER

MODIFICATIONS: Remote Detonation, Lock-on Burst

With a large blast radius and high damage, the Rocket Launcher is useful against all but the fastest enemies.

ACTIVATE THE COOLING TURBINE

Return to the level where you started and proceed through the now accessible exit, near the two blue access doors. Follow the path straight until you reach the Cooling Turbine terminal. Use it to activate the equipment. At this point, more demons attack. Stay on the move as you take them down. It's a big area with plenty of equipment to put between you and your foes.

INVESTIGATE THE SIGNAL

With the demonic threat taken care of, the exit opens on the far side of the room. Hop onto the right walkway, climb the steps to the upper level, and follow it to the door. Inside the next corridor, the third and final Elite Guard leans against a pile of crates.

Continue into the next room and use the console to open the shutters. Kill the Imps that spawn nearby, and move into the control room. Continue toward the objective and interact with the Airlock Control to exit the Foundry.

ARGENT FACILITY

MAIN OBJECTIVE	Shut Down the Argent Tower
NEW WEAPONS/EQUIPMENT	Super Shotgun
NEW MONSTERS	Summoner

CHALLENGES

CHALLENGE	DESCRIPTION
Walk the Path	Interact with a Rune Trial Stone.
Bird's Eye View	Acquire the AutoMap for the Argent Facility.
To Be Knighted	Perform 2 "Death from Above" Glory Kills on Hell Knights.

RUNE TRIALS

TRIAL NAME	OBJECTIVE
Rune Trial: Vacuum	Use the Combat Shotgun to eliminate 15 Imps before the timer expires.
Rune Trial: Dazed and Confused	Armed with the Pistol, destroy 30 barrels before the timer expires.

COLLECTIBLES

COLLECTIBLE	UNLOCKS
UACguy	Hell Knight Model
Stealthguy	Rocket Launcher Model

CLASSIC MAP DOOM - Toxin Refinery

LEGEND

- **Argent Cell**
- **AutoMap Station**
- **CM** Classic Map
- **Collectible**
- **Data Log**
- **Elite Guard**
- **Field Drone**
- **Health Station**
- **Lever**
- **Objective**
- **Powerup**
- **Rune Trial**

Secret Area
Super Shotgun

Secret Area

Exit

Secret Area

Start

CM

CHALLENGE 1: Walk the Path

Interact with a Rune Trial Stone. Simply complete one of the two Rune Trials during Argent Facility to complete this challenge.

CHALLENGE 2: Bird's Eye View

Acquire the AutoMap for the Argent Facility. Find the AutoMap Station during this mission. It's marked on our map and is mentioned in the walkthrough.

CHALLENGE 3: To Be Knighted

Perform 2 "Death from Above" Glory Kills on Hell Knights. The Hell Knight is a new enemy, first seen in the Foundry. They are big and tough, requiring several shots to take them down. Look for opportunities to attack from above even if it requires climbing onto a stack of boxes.

DISABLE THE ARGENT FILTERS

Move into the next room, up the stairs, and use the Airlock Control to open the exit. Step outside and drop off the left side of the bridge. Jump down to the lower level of the tower ahead and then over to the rock facing on the left. Climb to the top of the cliff and then hop onto the upper level of the tower. Turn left and jump down to the walkway. Follow the trail to your first Rune Trial.

RUNE TRIALS

Beginning with this mission, Trial Stones are found around the environment. Interacting with one provides a short test, such as killing enemies with a specific weapon or collecting a certain number of items—all within a time limit. Completing each trial earns a Rune that can be equipped in the Dossier. These provide valuable bonuses that can tip a battle in your favor. Each one can also be upgraded by completing a challenge.

RUNE TRIAL: Vacuum

OBJECTIVE: Use the Combat Shotgun to eliminate 15 Imps before the timer expires.

Count	15
Weapon	Shotgun
Time	10 Seconds
Bonus	+2 seconds per kill (+4 seconds per Glory Kill)
Reward	Vacuum – Increases the range that you can absorb dropped items.
Rune Upgrade	Absorb 300 dropped items. Further increases range for absorbing dropped items.

After jumping down from the tower, follow the trail right to find the first Trial Stone. Interact with it to attempt a challenge. Your goal is to kill 15 Imps with the Shotgun before the timer reaches zero. As you get kills, seconds are added to the timer, with an extra bonus for Glory Kills. Take advantage of this, as time is extremely valuable in these trials. The arena is relatively small for this one, so getting to each Imp is fast enough. They spawn in a couple at a time, so quickly spin around to find the next target. You can take these weak demons out with one close shot, but it's possible to weaken them from a medium range and then perform a Glory Kill as soon as you're close enough.

DISABLE THE ARGENT FILTERS

Climb the nearby steps, turn left, and hop onto the platform ahead to find a **Data Log**. If you did not get the Rocket Launcher in the Foundry, search behind the crates to find a dead body still holding a Rocket Launcher.

CLASSIC MAP:
DOOM - TOXIN REFINERY

After collecting the Data Log, pull the lever that hides behind a couple of barrels to the left. Proceed into the next facility and collect the Rocket Launcher. Enter the opening on the right to find the classic map, Toxin Refinery.

Continue through the far exit and use your newly found weapon to wreak havoc on the demons ahead, as they are nicely grouped together—perfect for the dangerous Rocket Launcher. With the monsters taken care of, move out onto the surface of Mars. Three Argent Filters must be disabled to shut down the Argent Tower. They do not necessarily have to be done in the following order, as long as all three are taken down.

FIGHTING THE POSSESSED SECURITY

The Rocket Launcher works well against the Possessed Security. Fire an explosive behind the foe or at a nearby wall to stagger it. You can then finish off the exposed demon with another weapon.

Move down the path and climb over the debris. Just ahead, a Field Drone is visible as it moves into position to the left. Turn left and climb into a small cave along the left wall to find the first **Elite Guard**. Return outside and move toward the Gore Nest in the open area on the left. You know how to handle the Gore Nests by now. Clear out the demons, interact with the nest, and kill the newly spawned monsters.

DEMON IN-FIGHTING

Quite often during the campaign, demons fight amongst themselves. This is usually observed as you approach from a distance. Get too close and they change their focus to you. Allow them to weaken each other up to thin out the horde of monsters.

From the nest's location, continue to the right and drop off the cliff to the right. Hop down to the right and enter the hangar. Proceed through the doorway on the left and interact with the **Field Drone** in the far corner. Return up the rock ledges, but instead of climbing all the way up, follow a path ahead and down to the right. Continue along the walkway to find another **Elite Guard**. Return to the Gore Nest's location to continue your mission.

ARGENT FILTER #1

Enter the nearby Cargo Station and wipe out the demon presence inside. Grab the **Data Log** off the crate next to an inaccessible door. Turn around, move through the far door, and interact with the Argent Filter Station to disable the first filter. Exit the building, turn left, and enter the garage ahead through a door on the right side. Search in the far corner to find an **Argent Cell**. Return outside and use the three containers to reach the upper platform.

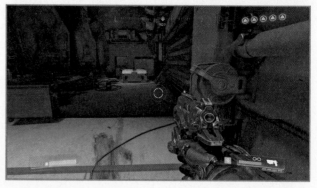

ARGENT FILTER #2

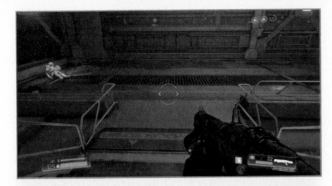

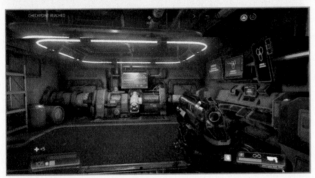

There's another Gore Nest just ahead. Take care of it just like the previous nests. Look toward Zone A and spot the Union Aerospace tank. Jump onto the walkway on the right, follow it toward the building ahead to find another **Elite Guard**, and then return to where you just destroyed a nest. Step inside the building on the right and follow the path around to the left. Eliminate the demons that inhabit the area before stepping into the room labeled 01.22.E on the far wall. Destroy the second Argent Filter inside and return to the hallway. Cut through the garage to return outside.

RUNE TRIAL: Dazed and Confused

OBJECTIVE: Armed with the Pistol, destroy 30 barrels before the timer expires.

Count	30
Weapon	Pistol
Time	6 Seconds
Bonus	+2 seconds per barrel destroyed
Reward	Dazed and Confused - Increases how long demons remain in a staggered state.
Rune Upgrade	Perform 25 Death from Above Glory Kills. Demon staggers last even longer.

After destroying the second Argent Filter and before hopping over the railing, enter the garage to the right and head over to the bays against the right wall. Climb onto the platform at bay 2 and interact with the stone to begin the Rune Trial. Thirty barrels are scattered

all around the map. Quickly detonate them with your Pistol. Since the Pistol has infinite ammo, feel free to quickly fire a few shots at distant barrels to be sure get your target. The arena is relatively small, but it is still a large distance to cover to get all 30 within the time allotted.

ARGENT FILTER #3

The third Argent Filter is inside the Cooling Tower to the left. There are three ways in; one on the lower level ahead, another is accessible from the upper walkway on the right, and the third is located to the left on the far side of the building. We use this last option to collect a few items along the way. Move through the area where the last Gore Nest was and climb onto the lone box near the forklifts. Continue up to the ledge above and enter the door.

Eliminate the demons inside and then climb the steps to the upper level. Search a desk to the right to find a **Data Log**. Once combat is complete in the area, a second **Field Drone** approaches this location, so keep a look out. Next, take the steps down to the bottom floor and exit via the back door. Follow the walkway around to the right, eliminating the demons that get in the way.

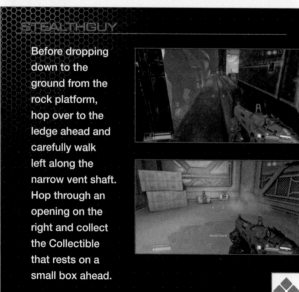

Before dropping down to the ground from the rock platform, hop over to the ledge ahead and carefully walk left along the narrow vent shaft. Hop through an opening on the right and collect the Collectible that rests on a small box ahead.

Drop down to the metal walkway below, hop the gap to the left, and continue right to the entrance. Before entering, though, cut through the opening in the left railing and follow the dirt path until you run into a few demons. Wipe them out and collect the **Super Shotgun** from the dead body.

NEW WEAPON
SUPER SHOTGUN

MODIFICATIONS: N/A (you are upgrading the base functionality of the weapon)

A devastating close range weapon, the Super Shotgun presents plenty of risk and reward.

Return to the Cooling Tower door and proceed inside. There's a Gore Nest in the middle of the building. Kill off the demon infestation, interact with the nest, and eliminate another wave of monsters. On the far side of the room, on the lower level, pry open the jammed door and enter the room to find the **AutoMap Station**.

Next, find the unlocked door on the second level, near the entrance you used. Inside, grab the **Data Log** off the desk and then interact with the Argent Filter Station to disable the final filter. Another wave of demons spawns into the previous room, including a new enemy, the Summoner. Clear the room of monsters and exit back outside.

Return to the upper floor of the garage, where you accessed the second Argent Filter. Run past the garage bays, enter the far door, and continue out the exit. The last Gore Nest of the mission is on the platform ahead. Take care of the initial demonic threat, destroy the nest, and then kill off the monsters that appear. This fight becomes a whole lot simpler by collecting the **Berserk Powerup** near the Building A entrance ahead.

Enter Building A and search behind the boxes on the left to find the final **Elite Guard**. Turn around and proceed the other way. Use the Airlock Control and go into the next room. Interact with the Argent Processor to disable it and unlock the left door. Press the Airlock Control to exit the facility.

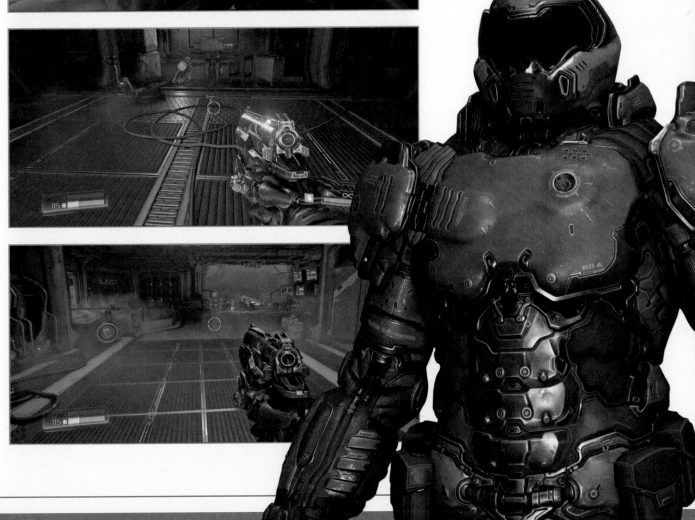

ARGENT ENERGY TOWER

MAIN OBJECTIVE	Kill Olivia Pierce
NEW WEAPONS/EQUIPMENT	Jump Boots, Gauss Cannon, Hologram
NEW MONSTERS	Revenant, Mancubus

CHALLENGES

CHALLENGE	DESCRIPTION
Chiropractor	Perform 4 Neck or Jaw Breaker Glory Kills on the Imp (attack from behind).
Searching High and Low	Find 3 Secrets.
Overkiller	Kill 15 demons using Quad Damage.

RUNE TRIALS

TRIAL NAME	OBJECTIVE
Rune Trial: Ammo Boost	Use the Super Shotgun to eliminate 30 Unwilling before the timer expires.
Rune Trial: Equipment Power	Armed with the Combat Shotgun eliminate 10 Unwilling with explosive barrel damage before the timer expires.

COLLECTIBLES

COLLECTIBLE	UNLOCKS
Orangeguy	UAC Pistol Model
Purpleguy	Summoner Model

CLASSIC MAP   DOOM - Halls of the Damned

LEGEND

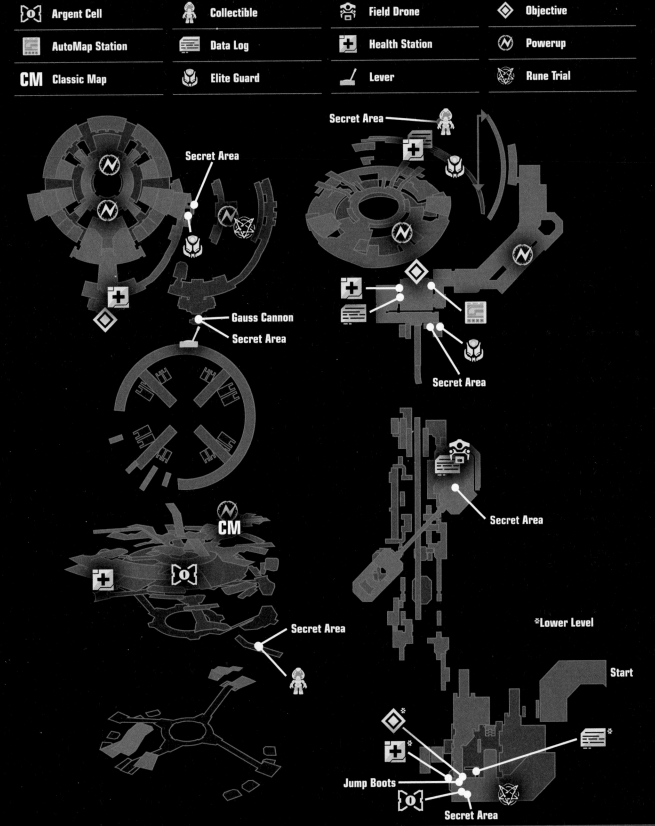

Argent Cell	Collectible	Field Drone	Objective
AutoMap Station	Data Log	Health Station	Powerup
CM Classic Map	Elite Guard	Lever	Rune Trial

Secret Area

Secret Area

Gauss Cannon
Secret Area

Secret Area

CM

Secret Area

Secret Area

*Lower Level

Start

Jump Boots

Secret Area

OBTAIN THRUST BOOTS

Jump down from the starting platform and enter the loading dock below. Demons infest the interior, so be ready for a fight. Look out for a new monster, Revenant, as it fires rockets from its Multiple Launch Rocket Battery. With the ability to take to the air, it can be tough to draw a bead on this enemy. Use a high rate-of-fire gun, such as the HAR or Plasma Rifle, to bring it down. Once the monsters have been dealt with, enter the locker room, located on the lower level in the far corner. Grab the **Jump Boots** from the shelf and the **Data Log** next to the vending machines. Exit the room and try out your new equipment, taking some time to get used to them. This mission does a good job of fully testing the ability.

NEW EQUIPMENT
DELTA V JUMP-BOOTS

The Jump Boots are extremely valuable as you proceed through the campaign, especially when ascending the tower later in this mission. There's no need to equip the item; simply press the Jump button in mid-air to perform a double jump. With good timing, you can jump impressive heights and distances.

PLATFORMING

With the ability to perform a double jump, the platforms in this mission seem to get a little higher or further away. Quite often accessible ledges have thin lights on the side. Use this to easily spot your next jump.

RUNE TRIAL: Ammo Boost

OBJECTIVE: Use the Super Shotgun to eliminate 30 Unwilling before the timer expires.

Count	30
Weapon	Super Shotgun
Time	6 Seconds
Bonus	+2 seconds per kill (+4 seconds per Glory Kill)
Reward	Ammo Boost – Increases the value of ammo received from demons and items.
Rune Upgrade	Pick up 500 Ammo Items. BFG ammo has a chance to drop from demons.

After collecting the Jump Boots, return to the loading dock entrance, turn around, and jump up to the next level. Turn left and drop into the room on the left to find a Trial Stone. The goal is to simply kill 30 Unwilling

before the timer runs out. Avoid getting surrounded as you quickly plow through the demons.

CROSS THE BRIDGE

From the entrance to the loading docks, jump up to the right ledge, then up to a higher level on the right, and then drop onto Loading Dock 06 below. Turn left and use the narrow ledges on the right to reach a small platform atop a pipe. Move to the back of the room and drop down to a maintenance access on your left. Just ahead, grab the **Argent Cell** before returning to the loading dock.

The bridge consists of parallel pipes with numerous platforms built on top. Following these ledges toward the tower gets you there, but a few times along the way, you must jump to the other side. Look around for the next accessible platform as you make your way across. Eventually, you reach an impasse as the pipeline has been severed. You must access the upper level of the bridge to reach your destination.

Head outside, climb onto the crates ahead, and get ready for some platforming fun. Jump over to the pipeline and make your way to the right. A series of long jumps is required to make it across. To make things worse, Imps launch projectiles your way. A well placed, charged shot from the Pistol takes each one out. The Tactical Scope modification on the HAR helps if you're having trouble hitting them.

Make your way to the left side and find the ledges and stairs that lead to up to a small building above. Be cautious as you climb inside—demons inhabit the interior. Take them out, wary of a Possessed Engineer that hides at the top of the steps. The monsters get steadily tougher as you cross a short walkway into a control room. Before entering the second area, pick off as many as you can from outside.

Once the threat has been dispersed, climb the steps and collect the **Data Log** on the left and the **Field Drone** ahead. Exit back out to the walkway and drop down to the pathway below. Head toward the tower, double jump across the gap, and approach the building. Before climbing onto the platform, look down to the right to spot an **Elite Guard**. Drop down, collect the Praetor Token, and return to the tower by utilizing the equipment and ledges behind you.

As you continue down this corridor, the monsters tend to get tougher. Pick them off from afar when possible, but stay on the move so that you don't succumb to their attacks. Use the weaker enemies, such as The Possessed, to collect health pickups when running low. There's a Quad Damage powerup on a platform in the middle of this area. Grab it when you can to make quick work of the enemies. With the area safe from demons, enter the maintenance door at the far end.

SCALE THE TOWER

After spotting Olivia inside, follow the footpath left and pull the door open. The elevator is inaccessible, so you must scale the tower; good thing you found the Jump Boots. Before continuing, grab the **Data Log** and Super Shotgun, still with its previous handler, on the left side of the room. Then access the **AutoMap Station** just to the right of the elevator. Pry open the Core door and move inside to find a horde of demons.

Cargo containers move through this area on multiple levels. Getting hit by them causes damage and can potentially pin you to a wall. Hop the rail and go right, staying between the containers. Jump to the ledge on the right when possible. Hop down to the ground, head right, and climb onto the left platform. An immediate left finds the next **Elite Guard**. Turn around and collect a **Data Log** on a small desk ahead. A Health Station is also available.

Once the demons have been taken care of, it's time to start scaling the tower. Three functioning elevators are available to get you started, each noted with an objective marker. Climb onto one and press the button to ride it up.

ORANGEGUY

After collecting the Data Log, turn toward the cargo containers and look up. There's a Collectible a couple levels above, but it takes a little effort to obtain. Drop down, go left to the far end, and climb onto the stationary container. Wait for the cargo above to pass and then jump to the narrow ledge. Walk up the beam, turn    around, and jump over to a smaller ledge. Wait for the next container to pass, then jump into the left hole and follow it through. Hop down to the left ledge to grab the Collectible, Orangeguy.

SCALING THE TOWER

Proceed carefully as you scale the tower; it's a long way up, requiring many precarious jumps. A wayward leap can drop you all the way back down to level 1. Watch out for moving machinery and be sure you can make each jump, especially as you reach the upper platforms. Fortunately, a second floor divides the climb in two.

Jump over to the yellow moving platform and ride it up to the small green platforms. Hop across them to a perpendicular walkway. Follow it up to the central area.

Continue down the pathway, enter the room on the left, and then drop into the hatch. Lift the next door to reach the interior of the tower. A Mancubus appears ahead. These guys are big and strong, requiring a whole lot of firepower to defeat. As you fight the foul creature, more demons pop into the arena, including a second Mancubus. If you have 5 fuel available, use the Chainsaw to quickly eliminate one of these guys. A Quad Damage powerup is available on the far side of the room, near the second Mancubus. Grab it early to help in the endeavor. As usual, keep moving and look for pickups scattered around the room.

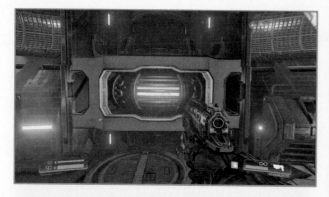

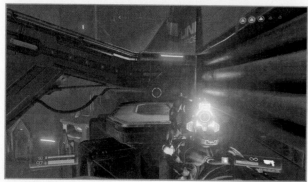

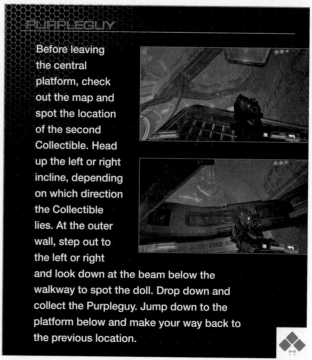

Before leaving the central platform, check out the map and spot the location of the second Collectible. Head up the left or right incline, depending on which direction the Collectible lies. At the outer wall, step out to the left or right and look down at the beam below the walkway to spot the doll. Drop down and collect the Purpleguy. Jump down to the platform below and make your way back to the previous location.

Follow the path left or right up another incline that returns to the outer wall. Jump up a couple of ledges, walk out toward the center, and make a long double jump to reach the central platform.

Move up the left or right incline and return to the outer wall. Jump either way to the next platform and follow the walkway back to the central area.

Climb onto the ledge on either side and turn back to the outside. Your goal is to climb into the hole above, but watch out for the moving machinery that juts out toward the center. Wait for it to retract and immediately jump over to it. From there, quickly climb into the opening and step out to the flooring before it moves again.

Inside, interact with the Argent Drone Station against the window. Search the far end of the room to find an **Argent Cell** and use the Health Station before exiting the room.

SCALE THE TOWER
PART 2

Quickly dispose of the demons that occupy the next floor. Jump pads scattered throughout this area provide a boost up to the next level. Use them to collect assets hidden on upper platforms, including an Invulnerability powerup. Use the map to find its exact location.

With the demons taken care of, use the jump pads to reach the platforms above and spot the 4-C designation on the outside wall. Jump onto the platform to the right of the drone and enter the control room.

CLASSIC MAP:
DOOM - HALLS OF THE DAMNED

After activating the argent drones, exit the control room and head to 4-A on the opposite side of the tower. Wait for the Drone to exit its dock and hop on. Ride it all the way up and jump forward to find the lever. Pull it to open the Classic Map directly below. With the drone away from its dock, enter the room to find ammo, health, and armor.

Hop onto one of the two argent drones and ride it all the way up before jumping over to a small platform against the wall. Hop across more platforms to the left or right, watching out for the moving floor above. Once it has stopped, climb onto it.

When it comes to a stop, moving parts jut out from the floor—making a connection to the center platform. As soon as it makes an appearance, take the opportunity to reach the center, being sure to hop off to the left or right before it retracts.

Travel around the middle until you spot a reachable ledge on the outside wall before walking out the nearby path. Jump up to the platform, climb onto the crate ahead, and continue up to the walkway. Quickly move out of the circle portion. A mechanism above you moves up and down. At the bottom, it fires electricity and damages anyone within this circle. Watch your step as you move around the perimeter of the room, being mindful of not only the electrical danger but also the Imps that harass you along the way.

At the other end of the pathway, jump across two more platforms onto the moving mechanism as it comes to a stop. Let it take you up to the top, then turn around and hop over to a jammed door. Pry it open and step inside.

Wipe out the demons inside the next room, using the pillars to break line of sight with the enemies. Once the area is clear, exit through the far door, ready to jump back as a Hell Knight immediately attacks. Proceed up the steps and wipe out more demons as you move through the narrow corridor.

OBJECTIVE: Armed with the Combat Shotgun, eliminate 10 Unwilling with explosive barrel damage before the timer expires.

Count	10
Weapon	Shotgun
Time	12 Seconds
Bonus	+3 seconds per kill with explosive barrels
Reward	Equipment Power – Increases effectiveness of Equipment items.
Rune Upgrade	Use 30 Equipment Items. Further increases effectiveness of Equipment items.

After clearing out the demon presence in the narrow corridor, proceed to the far end and turn left. Climb through the window above the 6-1 notation and continue left across the platform

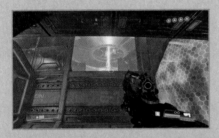

to reach the Trial Stone. The objective here is to take out 10 Unwilling by detonating the explosive barrels. Always stay a safe distance from the Unwilling. They can easily take you out; plus, you lose the trial if you are caught in a blast. The key is getting multiple hits with the explosions; the bonus received for each kill is a huge help. Quickly take out the explosives, staying on the move to avoid running into one of the monsters. Often, a detonation only weakens nearby demons, so be sure to get it with the next barrel.

At the end of the corridor, wait for the cargo container to pass by and jump into the windows ahead. Turn around and continue to the upper level. Go right and slip through an opening on the left. Climb onto the ledge to the left or right, turn around, and hop over to the platform to find another **Elite Guard**. Continue to the loading dock and run up the stairs to the left.

In the next room, move passed the elevator and grab the **Hologram** on the table against the far wall. Top off at the Health Station and then approach the elevator shaft. Look down to spot a ledge well below. Hop down and use the double jump to access it. Grab the **Gauss Cannon** and then use the console to open the doors behind you. Return to the upper floor and then jump across the elevator shaft to another small ledge. Turn around, equip the Pistol, and shoot the four flickering lights on the bottom of the elevator car to cause it to fall out of the way.

NEW EQUIPMENT
HOLOGRAM

By deploying a Hologram, the enemies' attention is directed to the fake Doom Marine while you gain the opportunity to get a better angle on a target. Use this to your advantage to escape hairy situations and get behind or above a tough demon.

NEW WEAPON
GAUSS CANNON

MODIFICATIONS: Precision Bolt, Siege Mode

While it has high damage potential, the concentrated beam of the Gauss Cannon demands accuracy from the user.

Double jump up to the next floor, move to the door ahead, and pull it open. Unfortunately, you are too late to stop Olivia, as she successfully escapes. A horde of demons has been left behind and they are eager to stop you from joining her. It isn't necessary to defeat all of the monsters. After the Facility Voice announces a category 4 dimensional event, you are transported to Hell. Though, if you have not maximized your Combat Rating or you have not achieved the Overkiller challenge, it's worth your time to kill as many enemies as possible. Grab the Quad Damage powerup to improve your odds of survival.

KADINGIR SANCTUM

MAIN OBJECTIVE	Get Back to Mars
NEW WEAPONS/EQUIPMENT	Chaingun
NEW MONSTERS	Cacodemon, Lost Soul, Baron of Hell

CHALLENGES

CHALLENGE	DESCRIPTION
Dead Man Stalking	Earn 4 Praetor Tokens.
Momentum Swing	Kill 10 demons while using powerups.
Sweep the Leg	Perform 4 "Leg Sweep" Glory Kills on the Hell Razer (attack right leg).

RUNE TRIALS

TRIAL NAME	OBJECTIVE
Rune Trial: Savagery	Kill Imps with the Super Shotgun to allow movement for 4 seconds. Imps may be killed or spared at your discretion. Reach the Altar before the timer expires.
Rune Trial: Seek and Destroy	Use the Heavy Assault Rifle to weaken and perform Death from Above Glory Kills on 3 Hell Knights before the timer expires.

COLLECTIBLES

COLLECTIBLE	UNLOCKS
Astroguy	Revenant Model
Redguy	Mancubus Model

CLASSIC MAP DOOM - Slough of Despair

Argent Cell		Collectible		Field Drone		Objective	
AutoMap Station		Data Log		Health Station		Powerup	
CM Classic Map		Elite Guard		Lever		Rune Trial	

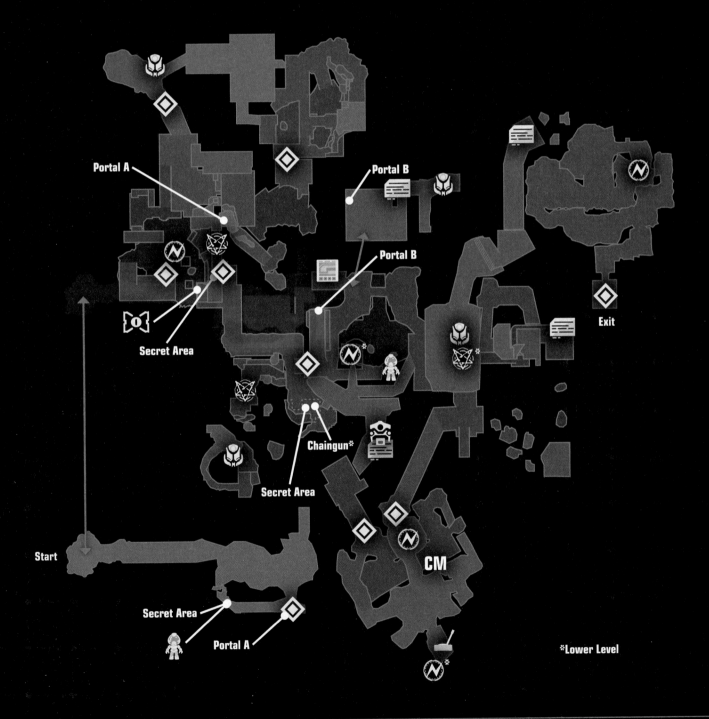

CHALLENGE 1: Dead Man Stalking

Earn 4 Praetor Tokens. Find all four Elite Guards in this mission to earn this one. Refer to our map and walkthrough for their locations.

CHALLENGE 2: Momentum Swing

Kill 10 demons while using powerups. Keep an eye out for powerups that often appear in the bigger battles. Pick it up early in the fight and aggressively go after the monsters.

CHALLENGE 3: Sweep the Leg

Perform 4 "Leg Sweep" Glory Kills on the Hell Razer (attack right leg). Give yourself more time to perform a Glory Kill by equipping the Dazed and Confused Rune. You must be precise when attacking the right leg.

FIND THE EXIT PORTAL MARKED BY THE UAC

You have been transported to Hell against your will and now must find a way back to Mars to stop the demons from absorbing your world. Follow the trail ahead, use the Skull Switch, and move through the tunnel. An echo recording shows the members of UAC planting a marker. Your goal is to find their exit portal.

Move to the overlook ahead and pick off the Unwilling that roam the surface below. Jump down to the ground and collect the Gauss Cannon that rests on the cases, if you did not find the one hidden in the tower. More demons spawn in to the right, while more wait at the top of the steps. Take care of them as you proceed up to the next area. Be sure to try out the new, powerful Gauss Cannon. At the top of the steps, hop up the rock platforms on the left to find a secret area.

Drop down another level, continuing to clear out any remaining demons. Look over the cliff to the left to spot a couple of Mancubi. Use the Gauss Cannon to weaken them up before following the path behind you down to their location. Pull out the Chainsaw and take one out if your fuel supplies allow. Clear out the remaining demons, using the entire area to avoid being surrounded and break line of sight. The full spectrum of monsters is represented in this fight. Take out the weaker enemies and use Glory Kills to gain extra health pickups.

After eliminating the demons, drop to the ground and find a Skull Switch hidden inside a rock pillar. Step inside and interact with it to lower a gate straight ahead. Step inside the small cave and collect the Yellow Skull. Then return up the stairs and use the skull on the yellow access door.

RUNE TRIAL: Savagery

OBJECTIVE: Kill Imps with the Super Shotgun to allow movement for 4 seconds. Imps may be killed or spared at your discretion. Reach the Altar before the timer expires.

Objective	Reach the Altar
Weapon	Super Shotgun
Time	5 Seconds
Bonus	+4 seconds movement time per kill
Reward	Savagery – Perform Glory Kills faster.
Rune Upgrade	Perform 25 unique Glory Kills while Savagery is equipped. Further increases the speed of Glory Kills.

After collecting the Yellow Skull, look for the stone archway on the ground floor and jump onto the roof. Turn around, double jump up to a small platform and continue up to the ledge ahead. Follow the corridor to the first Trial Stone. Your objective is to reach the Altar, but you can only move after killing an Imp. Each kill nets you four seconds of movement time, so make it count by running throughout. To reach the Altar, you must double jump from the cliff to one of the narrow ledges and then traverse the two ledges until you reach your destination. You must make a few tricky jumps between the ledges, taking out the Imps as you land. Make up as much ground as possible between the demons or it's a tough target with the shotgun.

Approach the **Artifact** ahead and interact with it. Turn around and find the **Elite Guard** on the ground at the intersection. Move up and out of the cave and pick off the Unwilling in the distance. As you continue forward, more demons attack, so dispose of them as they approach. Pull out the HAR and mow down the Summoner when it arrives. Continue to eliminate the Hell Knights and others in the upcoming arena.

DISTRACTION WITH A HOLOGRAM

Don't forget about your new piece of equipment, the Hologram. When in trouble, throw one down and move away from the action. This allows you to set up for a better shot.

Once the area is safe, collect any remaining ammo, health, and armor, then proceed out the opening at the objective marker. In the next area, floating platforms rise into position, giving you access to the cliff on the far side. Note that the stairs to the right lead back to an already visited area. Double jump over to the closest platform and continue up the highest one. From there, hop over to the cliff and use the Skull Switch to open the gate ahead.

Drop down, enter the new opening, and clear out the demons inside. Once you're ready to leave the area, step into the green portal to be transported into a cave elsewhere on the map. To the left is the Blue Skull. Grab it and exit through the new opening. This puts you in a familiar location just down from the yellow access door.

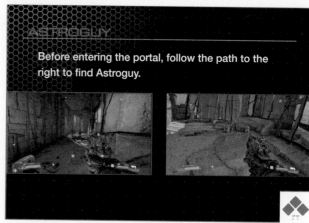

ASTROGUY

Before entering the portal, follow the path to the right to find Astroguy.

Descend the slope and then head to the right and down the stairs, fighting off the demons that have repopulated the area. As you approach the blue door area, a pair of Cacodemons shows up. Their projectiles can do serious damage, but they are easily avoided by ducking behind cover. They can be tough to finish off since they are often just out of reach of a Glory Kill. Pull out the Rocket Launcher and blow them out of the air. Eliminate the rest of the demons, including a Mancubus and another Cacodemon, then use the Blue Skull on the blue door.

Follow the path around to the right to find an **Argent Cell**, then return to the main hallway and continue right. Cautiously exit the tunnel as more demons approach your location. Be careful the Mancubus doesn't pin you inside. This is a great opportunity for a Chainsaw kill as there's a fuel tank near the Argent Cell. It can also be saved for the upcoming fight.

MODIFICATIONS: Gatling Rotator, Mobile Turret

Designed for sustained volleys, the Chaingun deals major damage at a very high rate of fire.

Move around to the left until the monsters spawn in, then hop down to the right. Grab the Invulnerability and quickly go after the foes. Once it has worn off, escape the action and go after the Chaingun. Be careful as demons may follow you inside the cave. A new monster, the Lost Soul, is presented in this fight. This kamikaze demon flies directly into its target, detonating on impact. The attack is deadly, so dodge to the side when you see one approaching. Stay on the move and finish off the remaining foes.

Just outside the cave, survey the area where the next big battle takes place. An Invulnerability powerup rests on the ground to your right. Inside a cave to the left, a **Chaingun** rests on a tripod, ripe for the picking. This powerful weapon has a high rate of fire, but it does take a little time to get going. The problem is getting down to the powerup quickly enough before being completely surrounded.

Before heading for the exit, jump onto the central platform and continue down to the ledge ahead. Climb up the left side and follow the trail through the tunnel. Once outside, search the right side to find an **Elite Guard**. Turn around and spot the series of floating platforms that leads to the far side. Jump across them to find a Skull Switch. Interact with it to open the door below. Drop down and move through the opening.

More demons occupy the large open area ahead. Pick off as many as you can from above before moving into the action. Stay on the move and use the different levels to break the enemies' lines of sight. A Haste powerup hides inside a corner cave on the lower level. Eventually, a Mancubus emerges from behind the skull door, just across the short bridge. Once the demons have been taken care of, enter that room and activate the **AutoMap** at the pedestal ahead. Turn around, cross the bridge, and climb up the steps ahead. Turn right and continue up the big staircase to exit the area. There's a portal that also takes you out of the area, but it is not necessary to collect everything.

RUNE TRIAL: Seek and Destroy

OBJECTIVE: Use the Heavy Assault Rifle to weaken and perform Death from Above Glory Kills on 3 Hell Knights before the timer expires.

Count	3
Weapon	Heavy Assault Rifle
Time	30 Seconds
Bonus	+20 seconds per Glory Kill
Reward	Seek and Destroy – Launch into a Glory Kill from much further away.
Rune Upgrade	Glory Kill 75 demons. Increases the distance that Seek and Destroy can be initiated.

Look for the tall staircase that leads out of the area. Before ascending it, turn left to find the second Trial Stone. The goal in this Rune Trial is to perform Death from Above Glory Kills on three Hell Knights before the timer expires. You are equipped with the

Heavy Assault Rifle, so use it to weaken the big guy. Only one spawns in at a time, so no worries about being ganged up on, though weaker enemies do present a small danger. Look for the Hell Knight to spawn in and immediately start firing at the foe. Once it begins to flash, perform a Glory Kill from above. If you're on the same level as the enemy, double jump into the air and perform the move.

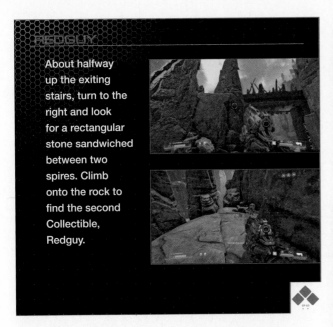

At the top of the steps, head straight and look right to find a green jump pad. Hop down next to it, cut through the tunnel, and search to the right to find an **Elite Guard**. Next, turn around and enter the structure. Grab the **Data Log** ahead and search further inside for an **Artifact**.

A portal on the other side of the room leads to the one mentioned earlier, so no need to follow it.

In the next area, follow the path to the right until you find a Baron of Hell fighting several weaker demons. You can let this play out or join the battle. This new monster is a giant that presents a grave danger to the Doom Marine. Stay clear as it charges your way, dodging to the side to avoid its mighty jump attack. It also has a strong projectile attack. Move to the side when it prepares a toss. Pelt the beast with your most powerful weaponry to take it down. More demons spawn into the area, including two more Barons of Hell. Collect the Quad Damage powerup in front of the big door and finish off the remaining foes. This is a good time to pull out the Chainsaw and eliminate one of the behemoths.

Return to the top of the stairs and continue straight ahead. A **Data Log** rests atop a case in the far corner next to a **Field Drone**. Descend the nearby steps and then up more to the left. Another echo recording shows the UAC moving through a gate, so follow right behind.

After defeating the Barons of Hell, look for the small cave directly across from the exit. Inside, throw the lever to open the hidden Classic Map. Move over to the big door and drop off to the right. Make an immediate right to spot the opening down the hill. Move inside and make your way through the maze to find two skulls on the walls ahead. Interact with both to open the wall, revealing several goodies, including a Mega Health.

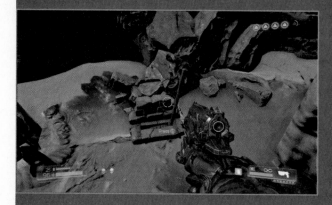 

Return to the big door as it opens for you. Descend the hill, killing the demons along the way. Jump out onto the floating platforms ahead, pull out the Gauss Cannon, and eliminate the lone Mancubus. Hop down to its location and kill the Cacodemons and Revenant to the left. Jump over to the steps and grab the **Data Log** on a small case. As you move up the trail to the left, more demons attack, including another Mancubus.

Continue up the path, hop up the right ledge, and climb the long staircase. Follow the trail to the right until you reach an **Artifact**. Climb up the rock face on the right and then jump over to the left to reach more demons. The final **Elite Guard** is on the left, so be sure to grab your Praetor Token.

Move toward the objective until you see the green lights left behind by the UAC. Step inside the ritual room ahead for another echo recording. Use the console on the far wall to activate the portal and end the mission.

Follow the objective through a building and grab the **Data Log** just outside the exit. Descend the platforms to the right until you run into more demons. This is a fairly big fight with multiple Barons of Hell. Wait for these large foes to show up and then grab the Quad Damage powerup that floats above a short pillar. Stay on the move as you take out the horde of monsters.

ARGENT FACILITY (DESTROYED)

MAIN OBJECTIVE	Go to the Lazarus Facility
NEW WEAPONS/EQUIPMENT	None
NEW MONSTERS	Pinky

CHALLENGES

CHALLENGE	DESCRIPTION
Skeet Shoot	Kill a Revenant while it is in mid-air.
Close Encounters	Kill 5 demons with the Chainsaw.
Knowledge is Power	Acquire 3 Data Logs.

RUNE TRIALS

TRIAL NAME	OBJECTIVE
Rune Trial: In-Flight Mobility	Collect all 15 Hell Relics and reach the Altar before the timer expires.
Rune Trial: Armored Offensive	Use the Combat Shotgun to eliminate all targets before the timer expires. Health levels are critical. Use armor to survive.

COLLECTIBLES

COLLECTIBLE	UNLOCKS
Rageguy	Cacodemon Model
Patriotguy	Baron of Hell Model

CLASSIC MAP   DOOM II - Underhalls

Secret Area

CM *

Start

Argent Cell		Field Drone	
AutoMap Station		Health Station	
CM Classic Map		Lever	
Collectible		Objective	
Data log		Powerup	
Elite Guard		Rune Trial	

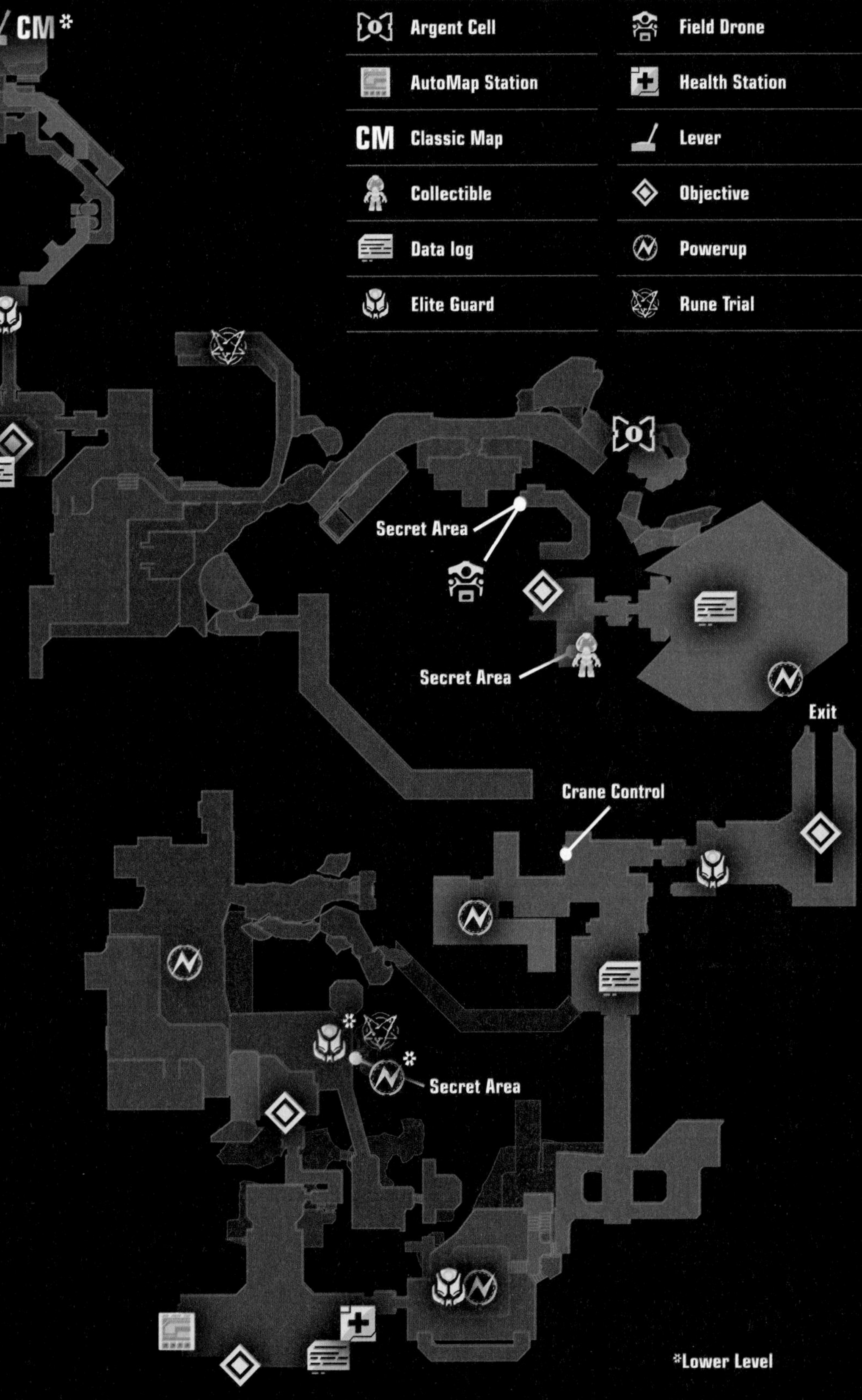

Secret Area

Secret Area

Exit

Crane Control

Secret Area

*Lower Level

CHALLENGE 1: Skeet Shoot

Kill a Revenant while it is in mid-air. With its thrusters, this demon occasionally takes to the air and launches rockets down on your location. Bombard one with weapon fire as it aims in the air until it falls to the ground.

CHALLENGE 2: Close Encounters

Kill 5 demons with the Chainsaw. The Chainsaw is extremely valuable in the big battles of DOOM, giving you an easy kill against any demon, assuming you have enough fuel. It's wise to save these kills for the tougher foes, but passing up fuel because you're maxed out is wasteful.

CHALLENGE 3: Knowledge is Power

Acquire 3 Data Logs. Find at least three of the Data Logs hidden around this mission to earn this challenge. Refer to our map and walkthrough for full details on their locations.

You return to Mars to the Argent Facility from the fourth mission, but the area appears different, as the demons have destroyed the place. This map is very similar to that mission, but the destruction has changed things up. Plus, your new Jump Boots open up new locations. Collect the **Data Log** off the crate, head upstairs, and exit the lab.

Follow the pathway to the right until a Cacodemon pops up ahead. Quickly take it down before continuing to the dead end. Climb up to the right and then jump to the conduit. Follow it toward the building and jump right to the upper platform.

CLASSIC MAP:
DOOM II - UNDERHALLS

After jumping right to the upper platform, search behind the cargo to find the lever. Activate it and return to the previous walkway. Turn around and hop down to level 1 to find the entrance to the Classic Map. Step inside to find health and a weapon.

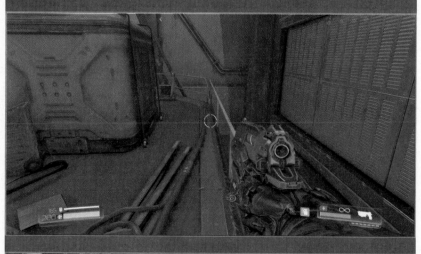

From the walkway, hop down to the level 1 platform and move into the cubbyhole on the left. The first Collectible is atop a small case ahead, surrounded by ammunition and armor.

Continue over to the walkway and follow it around to the left. With a running start, perform a long double jump to clear the gap and then drop down at the other end. Continue down to the left and enter the tunnel, where the first **Elite Guard** rests just behind you. With the Praetor Token collected, exit out the other side.

GO TO THE SECURITY STATION

Inside the control room, collect a **Data Log** in the far corner and then interact with the middle computer to learn of an artifact that could help in your search for answers. Olivia's Lazarus facility can be accessed from the Advanced Research Complex, so that's your next destination. A tram can be used to get there, but you need a clearance card to activate it. Proceed into the next room and activate the Airlock Control to return to the outdoors.

Be careful that a Revenant doesn't pin you down inside the airlock as you fight the big group of demons ahead. Move outside and clear them out. This is a great opportunity to score the first Challenge by knocking one of the Revenants out of the air. Once it's safe to move on, step up to the railing and look over the destruction ahead. You may recognize the location. You are currently above the garage where you disabled an Argent Filter. Most of the buildings accessed in the fourth mission are closed up now. The path to the left is still accessible, though, and it offers many helpful assets, as well as more demons to add to your Combat Rating.

A SECOND FIELD DRONE

If you did not access the second Field Drone in the fourth mission, you have another chance to get it. Once the demons have been eliminated in the area, use the crates to climb onto the balcony on the left to get your Modification.

A DEMONIC TAKEOVER

Demons have taken over most of the UAC facilities now, so always keep an eye out for monsters along the way. Stay on the move as you fight these hordes, remaining aware of your environment so that you do not get surrounded. As always, breaking line of sight from these foes is key to survival. Move around and through any structures and objects in the area to limit your damage. Take advantage of the wide array of weaponry to quickly eliminate a threat.

Hop over the railing to face another big group of monsters. A Berserk powerup floats above a crate in the middle of the arena, so grab it to tilt the odds in your favor. Clear them out and continue around to the left, toward the Security Station. There's no security lockdown in effect, so it's not necessary to defeat every last monster before proceeding, but every kill does count toward your Combat Rating.

RUNE TRIAL: In-Flight Mobility

OBJECTIVE: Collect all 15 Hell Relics and reach the Altar before the timer expires.

Count	15
Weapon	Super Shogtun
Time	16 Seconds
Bonus	+1 second per Hell Relic collected
Reward	In-Flight Mobility – Provides a significant increase in control over in-air movement after a double jump.
Rune Upgrade	Kill 30 demons while in mid-air. Applies air control to a single jump.

Climb up the crates toward the Security Station and turn left to spot the Trial Stone. Jump over and interact with it to begin the next challenge. Your objective is to collect 15 Hell Relics that are lined up along the two narrow ledges ahead and reach the Altar before

the timer hits zero. This is the same map used in the Savagery Rune Trial in the previous mission, so you may be familiar with the jumps required to reach your destination. This time your movement is not limited and there are no Imps to take out. Zigzag between the two sides as you collect the relics. You must be quick to reach the Altar with all 15, so stay on the move.

While on the butte that holds the first Trial Stone, step up to the far edge so that you're looking down at the pathway that runs alongside the big facility. There's an accessible pipe just below your location. Turn around and slip off the side. Quickly double jump into the pipe as soon as it appears. Collect the Mega Health, move further inside, and then grab the Praetor Token from the **Elite Guard**. Exit the pipe and double jump to the right to return to safe ground.

You can explore the surrounding area, which is full of pickups and monsters to defeat, but your next objective is up the stack of crates—leading toward the security station. Activate the Airlock Control, step inside, and use another console to gain access to the facility. Follow the hallway around and lift the unpowered door.

Immediately, a new monster called Pinky charges from the left. Pull out your assault rifle and try to get behind this demon to attack its un-armored back. A second joins the fight, making it a little tougher to dodge their assault. Keep track of them as you take them down. More demons find your location, so stay on the move as you battle them.

Once the lobby has been cleared of monsters, collect the **Data Log** off the bench to the left, top off at the Health Station, and use the **AutoMap Station** against the far wall. You are now ready to access the console next to the Security Station. This plays an echo recording depicting a Pinky carrying away a UAC member with a yellow access card that you need.

RETRIEVE THE YELLOW ACCESS KEY

Follow it out the exterior access, using the Airlock Control to reach the outdoors. Two Pinkies are joined by a number of demons in an attempt to keep you from the access key. Collect the Quad Damage powerup and go to town on them. There's a munitions crate in the far corner if needed. Once you're ready to proceed, use the jump pad to reach a platform above where an **Elite Guard** rests against some cargo.

Climb the steps as an echo recording shows that you're on the right track. Continue to fight off the enemy as you proceed through the next area, cross the bridge, and enter the building at the other end—being ready for the Mancubus and Pinkies that emerge from inside.

Collect the **Data Log** just inside and then follow the corridor to the left. There's a Field Drone above the crates on the left, but it moves into the next room to a more out-of-the-way location. Before going after it, you must clear out the demons and destroy the Gore Nest to the left. Finish off the new wave of monsters, which includes the tough Baron of Hell, before proceeding. A Mega Health offers some help as it floats above a stack of boxes on the upper level.

Once it's safe, return to the entrance and look into the facility. Approach the terminal just before the bridge and activate the Crane Control. This moves a cargo container from the left to a location just ahead. Double jump over to it

and continue up to a walkway on the right. Follow it around to find the **Field Drone**. Drop down and exit through the door on the right.

RUNE TRIAL: Armored Offensive

OBJECTIVE: Use the Combat Shotgun to eliminate all targets before the timer expires. Health levels are critical. Use armor to survive.

Count	8
Weapon	Shotgun
Time	1:10
Bonus	None
Reward	Armored Offensive – Glory Killing demons drop armor.
Rune Upgrade	Earn 3000 points of Armor. More armor drops per Glory Kill.

After exiting the facility, follow the path left and hop down to the right to reach another walkway. Follow this one right until you find the second Trial Stone. The goal here is to use the Shotgun to eliminate all eight demons before the timer reaches zero. You have 1:10 to get it done and there are no time bonuses. You start out against two Unwilling. As you proceed through the trial, two Imps, a Hell Knight, a Pinky, and two Possessed Soldiers spawn in. Your health is critical with no way to increase it, but there are piles of small armors throughout the map. Stay on the move, but you should spend almost the entire time firing shells at an enemy.

Once outside, move down the right path. A munitions crate is guarded by several weak demons on the left. Hit the engineer to take out the group. Continue across the rock ledges ahead and climb up to a landing pad. Turn around, double jump over to a butte, and drop off the far side to find an **Argent Cell**. Return to the previous area, eliminate the group of monsters, and destroy the Gore Nest. Finish off the new wave of enemies, taking advantage of the Haste powerup, located in the corner. This allows you to quickly break line of sight as you run around the ship.

Once it's safe to do so, collect the last **Data Log** on the ground next to the vehicle. Enter the facility and nab the Yellow Keycard from the corpse that is still in the clutches of the dead Pinky.

PATRIOTGUY

After grabbing the Yellow Keycard, stop at the top of the steps as you move toward the yellow gate. Jump up and climb into the maintenance access. The Collectible sits atop a case in the next room.

GO TO THE ADVANCED RESEARCH COMPLEX

Enter the yellow gate and drop down the shaft. Turn around and double jump into the venting above. Follow the path around to the left to find the final **Elite Guard**. Hop back down and re-enter the room where you destroyed the Gore Nest and found the Field Drone.

Head right and move through the yellow door, then pry open the next one to find the Tram Access. Take out the group of demons, step inside the tram, and interact with the Tram Control.

ADVANCED RESEARCH COMPLEX

MAIN OBJECTIVE	Go to the Lazarus Facility
NEW WEAPONS/EQUIPMENT	BFG
NEW MONSTERS	Cyber-Mancubus

CHALLENGES

CHALLENGE	DESCRIPTION
Bottle Opener	Perform 5 "Screw Top" Glory Kills on The Possessed (attack lower right leg or head from behind).
Double Take	Interact with 2 Rune Trial Stones.
Hide and Seek	Find 2 Collectibles.

RUNE TRIALS

TRIAL NAME	OBJECTIVE
Rune Trial: Blood Fueled	Armed with the Heavy Assault Rifle, eliminate all targets before the timer expires. Movement is only permitted for 3 seconds following any kill.
Rune Trial: Intimacy is Best	Use the Pistol to weaken and then Glory Kill 8 Imps before the timer expires.

COLLECTIBLES

COLLECTIBLE	UNLOCKS
Phobosguy	Super Shotgun Model
Pinkguy	Pinky Model

CLASSIC MAP DOOM - Phobos Lab

LEGEND

Argent Cell		Elite Guard	
AutoMap Station		Field Drone	
CM Classic Map		Health Station	
Collectible		Lever	
Data Log		Objective	
		Powerup	
		Rune Trial	

Exit

Secret Area

Secret Area

Secret Area

Secret Area

Secret Area

Secret Area

Secret Area

CM

Secret Area

*Lower Level

Start

MEET SAMUEL HAYDEN AT HIS OFFICE

You arrive inside the tram station at the office complex. Take the steps up to the second floor and take down the Mancubus who resides to the left. Enter the second restroom on the left, hop onto the sinks, and jump into the access door in the ceiling above. Follow the path until you drop into the break room.

Grab the Praetor Token from the **Elite Guard** and interact with the **AutoMap Station** before exiting the room. Take down The Possessed and step into the security office to find an **Argent Cell**. Activate the Access Control and fight your way through the newly opened door.

Move up to the lobby and clear out the remaining monsters. Approach the receptionist desk, pick up the **Data Log**, and interact with the Access Control to open the door to the left.

The facility has seen better days, but at least one worker still makes use of it. A Gore Nest resides on the lower floor. Kill off the initial demons before destroying the nest. Use the multiple floors to escape trouble as you take out the second wave. Collect the Berserk powerup that's tucked into a corner on the lower level to help in your efforts.

INFILTRATE THE WEAPONS DIVISION

Return to the hallway and run to the far end where a Health Station is available if required. Step into the elevator and activate the controls to ride it down. Move out and grab the **Data Log** on the floor. Follow the corridor around to find more demons. Take them down, search to the left for an **Elite Guard**, and then head the other way. Watch out for the Possessed Engineer and friends.

Collect any remaining pickups as you climb to the top floor. Use the Access Control to enter the Executive Wing. Follow Samuel into his office and grab any armor and ammo that you need. Approach his desk to find out what he knows about the artifact.

Cut through a storage room on your way to an airlock. Use the console to access the outdoors. There's a Gore Nest on a platform to the right. Pick off the engineers scattered around the area, interact with the nest, and then battle the demons that spawn in. This includes the new Cyber-Mancubus. A Haste powerup, located near the control room, offers some help. With the monsters out of the way, move up to the control room and turn off the security field at the Cargo Access Gate.

OBJECTIVE: Armed with the Heavy Assault Rifle, eliminate all targets before the timer expires. Movement is only permitted for 3 seconds following any kill.

Count	15
Weapon	Heavy Assault Rifle
Time	1:00
Bonus	None
Reward	Blood Fueled – Move faster for a short time after performing a Glory Kill.
Rune Upgrade	Kill 50 demons during the speed boost. Extends how long you can move faster after a Glory Kill.

Disable the security field and then, instead of exiting through the new opening, go through the airlock ahead to find the first Trial Stone. With the HAR equipped, kill the demons around the arena before the one-minute timer expires. There are no time bonuses and

you can only move for three seconds after each kill. When the movement icon appears on screen, you should quickly move toward ammo or the next enemy, though the Imps do tend to run at you. Occasionally, you may need to take one out from a distance, so always be looking for your next target.

TIME FOR A GAME

Inside the room with the Trial Stone, search the right corner to find an arcade game. Interact with the working machine to play Super Turbo Turkey Puncher 3. Simply punch the turkey until you get tired of doing so.

PHOBOSGUY

From the Argent Cell, turn around, jump over to the ledge on the left, and move right. Climb up the ledges to find a small cave. Hiding in the back is the first Marineguy.

Move through the gate, jump over to the platform ahead and continue over to the upper level on the left—fighting off the Lost Souls who spawn around the area. If you need armor, turn around and shimmy along the beam to the left. Jump right and climb to the top to collect a big armor. Return to the previous platform and look down to the left to spot a pipe running along the rock face. Jump down and follow the path to the right to find an **Argent Cell**. Turn around, wait for the pipe to open up ahead, and jump over to it. If you need some health, there's a Mega Health hidden above this pipe. It's accessible from the nearby rock formation. Watch out for the Cacodemon that spawns as soon as the item is picked up.

From the central rock formation, jump over to the ledge above the pipe entrance to collect the Mega Health. Hop across the rocks to the left over to the pipes and drop down to find the lever. Pull it to open a door near the previous Gore Nest. Make your way back to that area and continue to the far wall to find the Classic Map.

Follow the pipe until you drop into a small, square room. Move through the short corridor to an octagonal ventilation shaft and jump onto the right small ledge. Turn right, hop over to the arm, and then double jump into the hatch above. Climb through the window ahead.

Follow the corridor to the left, watching out for the Imp that occupies the area. Run all the way to ventilation shaft 2 and activate the switch on the window to turn the fan off. Drop into the shaft and then into the hatch. Find the **Field Drone** that hangs out in the nearby tunnel. Return to the upper corridor in the same manner that you used for shaft 1.

Reactivate the fan and ride the current up into the octagonal passageway. At the intersection, turn left to retrieve a big armor, straight to reach the first ventilation shaft, and right to continue toward your objective.

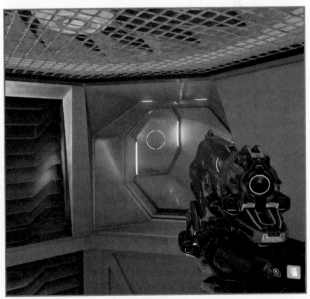

ACCESS THE LAZARUS ELEVATOR

In the next room, turn left and move through the door to find an **Elite Guard**. Top off your health at the Health Station and enter the BFG Labs. Demons infest all areas of this facility, so always be ready for a fight. There are two rooms to the right and two to the left, but your goal is to reach the BFG Prime Lab accessible on the opposite side.

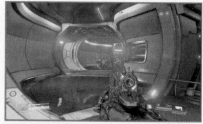

PINKGUY

Head right from the maintenance room and enter Prototype Lab 01 at the second door. Climb onto the equipment in the middle of the room and face right. Jump into the small shaft and follow the maintenance access until you find a Marineguy. Continuing through this access drops you into the Server Room.

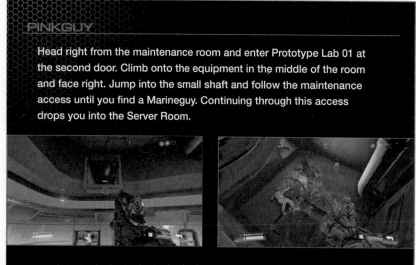

Return to the corridor and, once you're ready to move on, approach the BFG Prime Lab. Use the worker's eyes to fool the retinal scan and get inside. Here you find the ultimate weapon, the BFG, but security protocols lock it up tight.

Enter the Server Room to the right and collect the **Data Log** on the floor below. Return to the hall and move left past maintenance to the Security Room. Inside, grab the Corpse Upper Torso. Exit back to the hall and enter Prototype Lab 02 to the left. Collect another **Data Log** on the equipment on the far side.

Quickly climb on top of the BFG chamber and jump over to one of the four small platforms as they move into place against the wall. Lasers that appear below slice you up if you drop down while lasers from above deter you from jumping onto the chamber. With the upper lasers above you, use your Pistol to shoot out four of the red fuses to cause it to drop.

Jump over to what's left of the chamber and collect the **BFG**. At this point, the platform drops to the floor below. Lift open the door ahead and step into the next room where a horde of demons resides. Hit one of them with the Argent Energy from the BFG to wipe out the entire room. Interact with the Control Console to open the Lazarus Elevator access and continue forward.

NEW WEAPON
BFG

Powerful weapon that delivers streams of supercharged Argent plasma to multiple targets and is somewhat self-guiding. Like the Chainsaw, an assigned button/key gives you access to the BFG-9000. Ammunition for this powerful gun is extremely limited, so use it sparingly. It fires Argent Energy at your target and then splits off toward any nearby enemies. It kills anything in one shot and has the ability to eliminate several foes at once.

RUNE TRIAL: Intimacy is Best

OBJECTIVE: Use the Pistol to weaken and then Glory Kill 8 Imps before the timer expires.

Count	8
Weapon	Pistol
Time	20 Seconds
Bonus	+3 seconds per Glory Kill
Reward	Intimacy is Best – Demons become more Glory Kill friendly due to a high damage resistance when staggered.
Rune Upgrade	Stagger 100 demons. Demons stagger off of less damage.

After opening the Lazarus Elevator, turn right and enter Testing Chamber 1. Turn left and follow the narrow corridor to find the second Trial Stone. Using the Pistol, you must perform eight Glory Kills on the Imps before the timer reaches zero. A three-second bonus is given each time a Glory Kill is performed, but you still need to take the demons out quickly. Be careful not to kill the Imps. Rapidly fire a few shots into a demon as you move its way and once they begin flashing, press the Glory Kill button.

A group of demons waits at the other end of the hall. Quickly eliminate them before they pin you inside the corridor. Inside the next room, prepare for a big battle and destroy the Gore Nest. A Quad Damage powerup floats nearby and there's BFG ammo on the bottom and top floors. Use the BFG on big groups of enemies if possible, but remember you can only take one ammo with you, so not using the rest is wasteful. Two teleporters, blue and red, allow you to quickly move between the second and third floors. Use these tools to tip this fight in your favor. Use the different floors and walls to break line of sight as you pick off the monsters. With the enemies out of the way, step into the elevator and activate the Cargo Lift.

LAZARUS LABS

MAIN OBJECTIVE	Shut Down the Portal
NEW WEAPONS/EQUIPMENT	Siphon Grenade
NEW MONSTERS	Cyberdemon

CHALLENGES

CHALLENGE	DESCRIPTION
Variety is the Spice of Death II	Perform 5 different Glory Kills on Possessed Soldiers.
Thread the Needle	Kill 8 demons with a single shot.
Time Well Spent	Play a game of Demon Destruction.

COLLECTIBLES

COLLECTIBLE	UNLOCKS
Eliteguy	Olivia Pierce Model
Toxicguy	Samuel Hayden Model

RUNE TRIALS

TRIAL NAME	OBJECTIVE
Rune Trial: Rich Get Richer	Armed with the Rocket Launcher and using only the resources found in the area, eliminate all targets before the timer expires. Targets will not drop resources when destroyed.
Rune Trial: Saving Throw	Armed with the Gauss Cannon and using only the resources found in the area eliminate all targets before the timer expires. Health levels are critical and targets will not drop resources when destroyed.

CLASSIC MAP DOOM - Tower of Babel

LEGEND

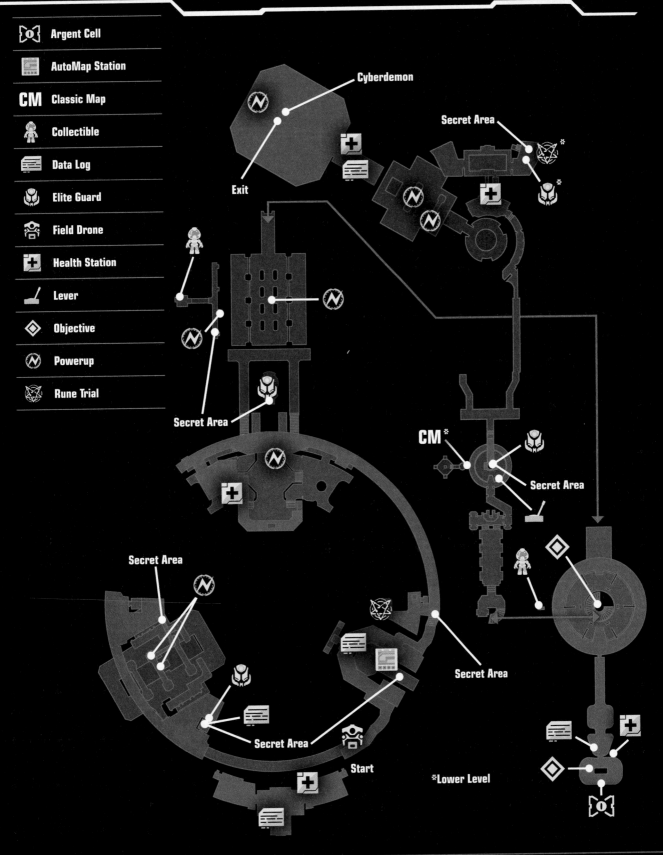 Argent Cell	
AutoMap Station	
CM Classic Map	
Collectible	
Data Log	
Elite Guard	
Field Drone	
Health Station	
Lever	
Objective	
Powerup	
Rune Trial	

Cyberdemon

Secret Area *

Exit

Secret Area

Secret Area

CM *

Secret Area

Secret Area

Secret Area

Secret Area

Start

*Lower Level

ACCESS THE HELIX STONE

Welcome to Lazarus Labs, where Olivia released the demons and activated the Lazarus Wave. Your goal is to find the Helix Stone in her private offices. This facility is overrun with monsters, so always be on alert. Exit the elevator, use the Health Station ahead to heal any injuries, and exit via the left door.

There's a **Data Log** on the counter to the left. Grab it while an echo recording plays. In the next room, collect the **Siphon Grenade** on the floor. Drop into the left shaft to join the demons below.

Eliminate the monsters in the room and then destroy the Gore Nest. Use the upper walkways and cargo containers to escape the next demon assault, staying on the move to avoid getting surrounded. The upper platforms are littered with small armors, so spend some time up there when damaged. More containers open up as the fight goes on, revealing some valuable items like the BFG ammo in the pit. There's a Haste powerup atop the container in the middle of the room.

NEW EQUIPMENT
SIPHON GRENADE

Your third and final equipment item, the Siphon Grenade slightly damages enemies within its radius while healing the player. It's great against groups of demons, especially if you're low on health.

Wipe out the monsters that come to investigate your arrival and then move down the corridor on the left. In the next room, grab supplies from the munitions crate and move around the white crates. Climb up the chute in the corner to find a Mega Health and drop into the next battle arena.

With the lockdown negated, exit via the unlocked door and climb the equipment at the other end to reach the Sector 5 door. Before exiting, turn around and hop into the maintenance access. Follow it to the end and pry off the vent cover to find a **Data Log** and **Elite Guard** inside an elevator.

Return to the previous door and proceed inside. Take the walkway through a second maintenance door to find a **Field Drone**. Double jump into the hatch above and kill the two Possessed Soldiers ahead. In the next room, jump into the hole in the right wall, move around to the left, and drop into the room below. Interact with the AutoMap Station against the right wall before crawling into the vent on the far side of the room. Climb onto the ledge to the left or right and then jump to the middle. Punch out the vent cover to end up in a control room, just past where you jumped into the wall.

Grab the **Data Log** off the desk and then continue left. Fight your way through the door on the left and up the steps. Take out more demons in the following long corridor and then enter the Research Division on the left. A Health Station offers an opportunity to heal before moving on to another big fight. Follow the passageway to a hole in the floor and drop down to the lower floor.

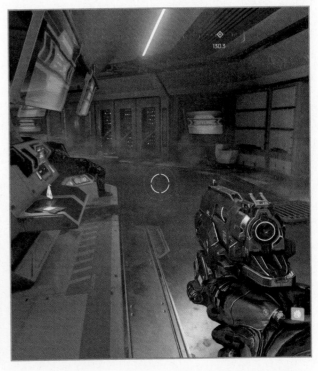

OBJECTIVE: Armed with the Rocket Launcher and using only the resources found in the area, eliminate all targets before the timer expires. Targets will not drop resources when destroyed.

Count	14
Weapon	Rocket Launcher
Time	1:30
Bonus	None
Reward	Rich Get Richer – Firing your standard weapons will not cost ammo when you have 100 Armor or more.
Rune Upgrade	Fill your Armor value to max 12 times. Activate Rich Get Richer at 75 Armor.

At the top of the steps, open the hatch in the floor to drop into a maintenance access. Move further inside and double jump up through the hole in the ceiling to find the Trial Stone. Equipped with a Rocket Launcher, take out 14 demons around the arena in

1:30. There are neither time bonuses nor any health pickups. There are a few ammo pickups in case you run out of rockets. You must stay on the move and always be aware of your surroundings. Take too many hits from the monsters and there is no way to recoup the losses. Quickly fire rockets at the enemies, finishing them off with Glory Kills when available. Splash damage also works to weaken the foes, so firing an explosive at their feet or a nearby wall is better than nothing.

A large assembly of monsters attempts to keep you from progressing toward your objective. The arena is made up of six rooms, providing some cover if things get too hairy. Portals located in the far left and right corners send you back into the middle room if you end up getting pinned down. A Quad Damage powerup in the middle room offers a little help. Use your full arsenal to kill the demons and then move to the back of the room. Climb up to the big cargo door and use the console on the left wall to gain access. Step inside to find an **Elite Guard**. Exit through one of the two doors at the base of the back stairs.

Follow the corridor until you find a munitions crate in the right corner and then pry open the door. Several demons occupy the next room, including Pinkies. Grab the Haste powerup in the middle of the room to assist in avoiding their charge attacks. More monsters spawn in as you defeat them, so stay on your toes. If you need a health boost, climb behind the second **Artifact** on the left to find a Mega Health.

ELITEGUY

Once the threat has been taken care of, move over to the artifacts along the left side of the room. Slip around one of them and crawl through the vent to reach a hidden hallway. Move toward the center and search down the perpendicular passage to find a Marineguy.

Return to the room and head left toward the exit. Activate the Lift Access to descend into the Lazarus Archives. Move through the lobby into the archives proper.

Exit via the other side and follow the corridor to a desk and an echo recording of Olivia. Swipe the **Data Log** from the desk and interact with the terminal to disable the security lock and reveal a hidden lab behind you. Move inside and collect the resources around the room, including BFG ammo and an **Argent Cell**.

TOXICGUY

Once inside the Lazarus Archives, climb onto the second level on the right. Find the red, transparent display and then turn toward the archives. One can be interacted with, so go ahead and use it to reveal an Collectible.

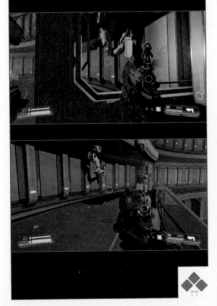

TIME WELL SPENT

Inside Olivia's hidden lab, access the computer on the left desk to play a game of Demon Destruction, a match 3 mini-game. This completes the third Mission Challenge.

Interact with the Helix Containment Field console to disable the protection for the Helix Stone. Return to the archives and access the console in the middle of the room.

Demons spawn into the archives, so begin taking them down. Pillars around the outside of the room do offer a little protection. Move around the outside as you pick the monsters off. Once the room is clear, descend the spiral staircase that has emerged in the middle of the room.

Fight off more demons as you continue through the dark depths of the Lazarus facility. Run through the door on the right and follow the passageway until you enter a circular room. Drop into the pit in the middle to find another **Elite Guard**.

Step over to the computer and interact with the Energy Refractor. Heal at the Health Station behind you before exiting the nearby doors, fighting your way into the next area. Step into the right room and climb into the vent shaft. Drop down to the lower floor and continue into the adjacent room to find the final **Elite Guard**. Watch out as demons may continue to attack.

CLASSIC MAP:
DOOM - TOWER OF BABEL

Before departing the chapel, search the nooks around the pit in the middle of the room. The lever will be next to some candles. Once activated, continue into the hatch room and drop into the pit to find the Classic Map entrance.

Climb onto the balcony and use the Maintenance Hatch Disposal terminal on the far side of the room. As the device comes down on the hatch, jump on top and ride it into a maintenance access.

Move forward and drop down to the lower level. Exit through the door where more demons wait for your arrival. Kill the monsters and then head right. Follow the corridor past more enemies until you find another echo recording playback.

OBJECTIVE: Armed with the Gauss Cannon and using only the resources found in the area, eliminate all targets before the timer expires. Health levels are critical and targets will not drop resources when destroyed.

Count	9
Weapon	Gauss Cannon
Time	35 Seconds
Bonus	+2 seconds per kill
Reward	Saving Throw – Get one chance to survive a death blow and recover health. This resets on death.
Rune Upgrade	Kill 10 demons while Saving Throw is active. Get an additional Saving Throw per life.

After dropping down the shaft and finding the Elite Guard, access the Trial Stone ahead to begin the final Rune Trial. Equipped with the powerful Gauss Cannon, kill the nine demons that spawn around the map before the 35-second timer reaches zero. Your health is

critical and there's no way to heal, so avoiding the enemy attacks is the key to success. Ammunition is scattered all around the area, so pick these up to keep your gun topped off. A variety of monsters show up in this challenge, including a Spectre. Each foe presents a danger, even the Imps, since one hit ends the trial. The Gauss Cannon requires precise accuracy to take these guys out. Stay on the move when not firing, but don't spend much time setting up your shot. Avoid getting surrounded when moving through the middle of the map.

Once you're ready to continue, push forward and slip into the narrow opening on the left. Drop into the circular room and proceed into the hall behind you. Walk into the portal to drop into the arena above.

Another group of demons is ready for you here. Grab the Quad Damage that floats above the container in the middle of the room to help in the struggle, though it may be best saved for later. Search the containers for ammunition and keep moving as you fight the monsters. Jump pads and two portals found inside the containers give you the ability to escape trouble and quickly move around the arena. Use your Jump Boots to traverse the multiple levels, breaking lines of sight when under fire. There's also a Haste powerup in one of the cargo crates. Don't forget about your special weapons, the Chainsaw and BFG, when things get really rough. A Cyber Mancubus and Mancubus show up at the end of the fight, so don't exhaust all of your best weaponry.

Collect any resources left over after the fight and then drop down to the circular room that's now accessible. Once the exit opens up, collect the **Data Log** and resources before activating the switch on the far door. Meet the Cyberdemon, the flagship creation of the Lazarus Project.

CYBERDEMON

The Cyberdemon is extremely formidable with its high-powered weaponry and quick attacks. Learn its moves and hit it with all of your best armaments to stand a chance of survival.

Rocket Launcher - When it pulls out its rocket launcher, it fires a series of rockets at a high rate of fire. Move from side to side to avoid the projectiles.

Melee - If you get close to the boss, it swipes or stomps. Quickly step back out of range.

Scythe - Watch out when he swipes from a distance, sending a scythe in your direction. Be ready to jump over the fire to avoid damage.

Charge - The Cyberdemon dips down a bit before charging, following it up with a ground pound. Look out for this motion and dodge to the side.

Missile Rain - When the behemoth throws its arms to the side and hunches over, it launches a massive missile attack that sends several explosive projectiles into the air. Circles appear on the floor showing their target locations. Move back until you can find a gap between them.

Energy Weapon - After taking about half damage, the boss pulls out a powerful energy weapon. As the Cyberdemon charges it up, a beam appears. Quickly move to the side to avoid taking damage. Note that the beam leads you until it changes color. This is accompanied by an audio cue. When this happens, immediately move in the opposite direction.

Pull out a high-damage weapon, such as the Gauss Cannon or Rocket Launcher, and hit it whenever possible. Occasionally resources are dropped, so grab them when you get the chance.

Hit it with the BFG to stagger it quickly following that up with your best weapons while each hit causes double damage. Health and ammo pickups drop from the beast as you attack, so collect them when possible to keep your supplies topped off. Equipping the Vacuum Rune allows you to grab the resources from a safe distance.

Stay on the move and keep a close eye on the boss, as its assaults can come pretty quickly. Saving Throw is an obvious Rune choice, while In-Flight Mobility is handy for dodging attacks. Continue to attack the beast until it falls to its knee. Perform a Glory Kill on its leg to finish it off.

At this point, you are transported to Hell as the boss gets back on its feet. Here it mixes things up a bit with a couple new attacks, more devastating than before

It has the ability to trap you in between two rows of rock shards. You know this move is incoming when it slams its fist into the ground. This keeps you from moving too much to each side, as it fires its rocket launcher or tosses scythes your way. Use short quick movements to each side to avoid the rockets. The scythe in Stage 2 always comes high/low/high. Press the Crouch button while jumping to drop much quicker. Note the further away you are when this move hits, the easier it is to dodge the attacks.

It still has its energy weapon, charge, flame wave, and missile attacks, so stay on alert. Use the BFG to stagger the boss, keeping an eye out for ammo to appear around the outside of the area. Continue to hit it with everything you've got until the Cyberdemon falls. Again perform a Glory Kill to finish it off—this time for good. Exit via the doorway and step into the portal to complete the mission.

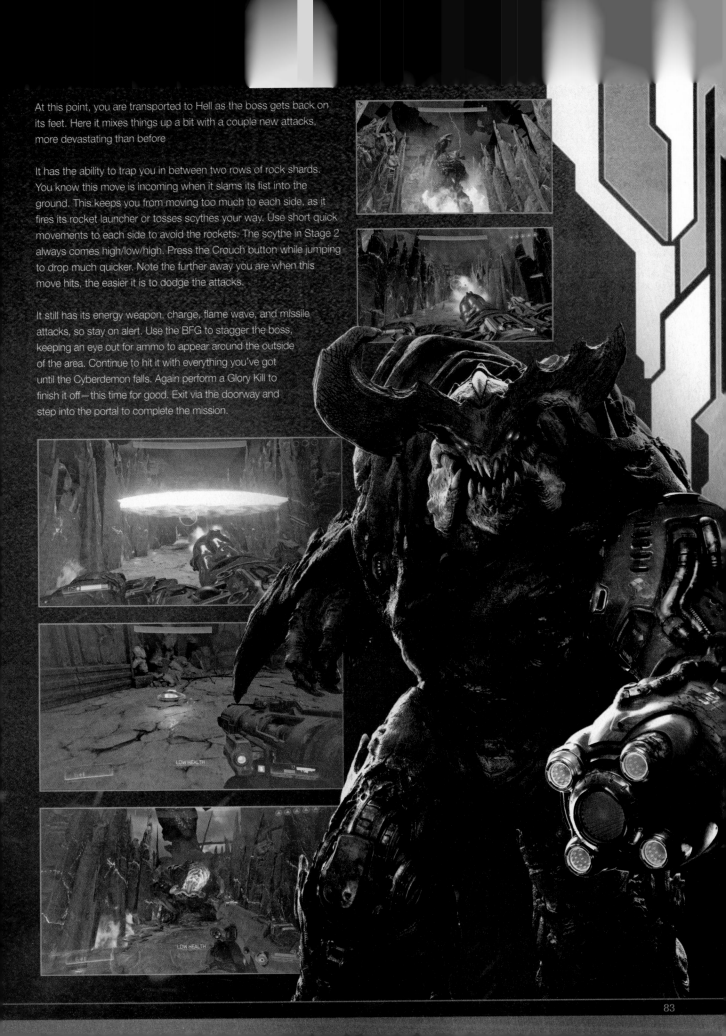

TITAN'S REALM

MAIN OBJECTIVE	Reclaim the Crucible
NEW WEAPONS/EQUIPMENT	None
NEW MONSTERS	Spectre

CHALLENGES

CHALLENGE	DESCRIPTION
Trick Shot	Kill a Lost Soul with another Lost Soul.
Atop the Mountain	Perform a "Death from Above" Glory Kill on a Baron of Hell (attack from above).
Dominator	Kill 20 demons while using powerups.

COLLECTIBLES

COLLECTIBLE	UNLOCKS
Keenguy	BFG-9000 Model
Silverguy	Cyberdemon Model

CLASSIC MAP   DOOM - Phobos Anomaly

Argent Cell	Collectible	Field Drone	Powerup
AutoMap Station	Data Log	Lever	Rune Trial
CM Classic Map	Elite Guard	Objective	

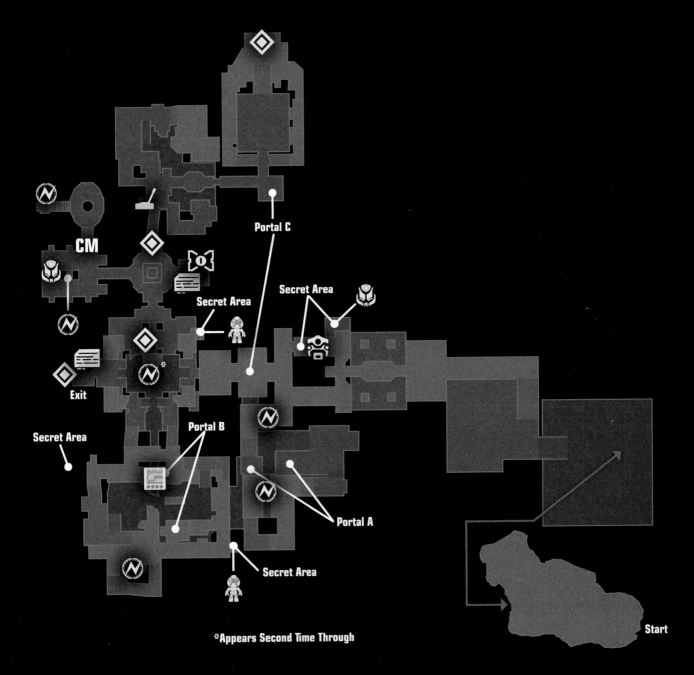

Portal C

CM

Secret Area

Secret Area

Secret Area

Exit

Secret Area

Portal B

Portal A

Secret Area

*Appears Second Time Through

Start

PASS THROUGH THE TITAN'S CORE

Investigating the Lazarus Labs, you have learned of another artifact, one that can remove the connection between Mars and Hell. The Crucible is the key to bringing peace to this planet. As you move toward the big skull ahead, an **Artifact** just to the right offers up more storyline. Drop through the "throat" to find your first resistance.

Cacodemons arrive first, so take care of them before ascending the staircase. Proceed up more steps to the right as you face more tough demons. Continue to fight as you enter Titan's Realm. Four Lost Souls occupy the bridge area ahead, giving you an opportunity to quickly accomplish the first Challenge.

Clear out the area and then hop over to the square platform on the left or right. Look under the bridge to spot a Skull Switch. Quickly use it and run into the small room in the far-right corner to find an **Elite Guard**. Avoid standing on the slime—it causes damage! Return to the bridge and proceed into the tunnel ahead.

Stay alert as more demons occupy the halls ahead. Take them out as you move into the right hall. With the first wave out of the way, two doors open, revealing valuable resources. Eliminate the second group of monsters to open a third, which holds a Skull Switch.

Activate the switch to open a gate in the other passage, releasing a Mancubus. Kill the brute to open another door inside the halls. Enter this new opening in the corner to reach the **Field Drone**.

Enter the next room where a monster battle ensues. A staircase around the outside takes you to an upper level, allowing you to escape danger when necessary. A Haste powerup floats above a gap on the upper level. Quickly take out as many demons as possible when under the influence of the powerup to work on the second Mission Challenge. Once the room is void of enemies, collect any leftover resources and enter the portal to transport deeper inside Titan's Realm.

Run into the big room on the right and dispose of the demons inside. Don't get trapped in the lower tunnels. Use the area's two levels to avoid becoming surrounded. A Quad Damage rests on a pedestal on the first floor. Use it to assist in the extermination and build your kill count for the second challenge. Eventually, two Barons of Hell spawn into the arena. Weaken them up in the open area of the lower level and then use the jump pad to quickly reach the floor above. Perform a Glory Kill from above to get the third Challenge. Equip the Dazed and Confused Rune to acquire more time to complete the move.

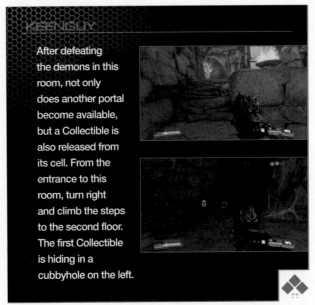
Enter the portal in the middle of the lower level to transport to a nearby passageway. Interact with the AutoMap Station on the left and then quickly exit the tunnel to the right before becoming an easy target of the Lost Souls. Fight off the numerous monsters that inhabit the room, using the pillars to break their line of sight. It's not necessary to take them all out, but it does add to your Combat Rating.

Jump pads are located in the corners closest to where you entered. These give you quick access to the upper floor. As soon as you land on the upper platform, hop over to the pillars and turn toward the big armor. Double jump to that ledge to open the gate.

Turn left from where you entered the room and use the jump pad to reach the upper level. Double jump to the ledge in front of you and collect the Collectible that stands on a pedestal in the corner.

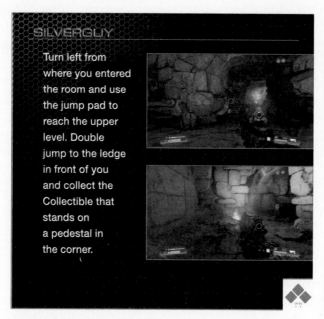

Grab the Yellow Skull that rests on a pedestal ahead. This causes the ceiling to lower, threatening to take you out. Step into the cubbyhole once available and wait for it to return to its original position.

Go right, drop down, and continue down into the left room, where slime eats away at your health. Avoid standing on top of it to reduce the damage. Run to the far side and collect the Praetor Token from the **Elite Guard** before activating the nearby Skull Switch. Quickly collect the Invulnerability powerup hiding in the middle of the room. Kill the Unwilling and Mancubi as you return to the first room. Pinkies join the fight here, so stay on the move as you eliminate the bad guys.

At this point, bars are removed in front of the yellow door and a small room to the right. Step inside to collect a **Data Log** and **Argent Cell** before placing the skull in the yellow door.

Once you're ready to move on, descend into the next room where a horde of fiends awaits your arrival. Kill the monsters and then climb onto the ledge to the right. A weight slams to the ground in front of the exit before rising back into the ceiling. After it impacts the floor, jump onto it and ride it up to find a Skull Switch. Activate it and then exit the room.

Defeat the demons in the room beyond the yellow gate and activate the Skull Switch in the ceiling. This reveals a lever near the entrance. Pull it and return to the poison room to find the Classic Map accessible on the right wall.

Collect the ammo as you follow the passageway into the next area. Grab the Blue Skull at the far end and then wait for a pair of Spectres to spawn at the entrance. These guys are very similar to Pinkies, but they are invisible and do not have armor. The demon can be spotted, but it has a transparent look to it, so it tends to blend into the environment. More monsters join the fight. Use the jump pads situated on each side of the room to escape trouble and kill every last fiend.

Monsters have returned to this familiar room, so take care of them. After disposing of some weaker foes, grab the Berserk powerup in the middle of the room and go to town on the bigger demons.

Place the Blue Skull in the blue door, collect the **Data Log** off the floor, and enter the portal to complete the mission.

Return to the ammunition room and step into the portal. Follow the corridor around to the left, interact with the **Artifact**, and then follow the tunnel behind you to find a Mega Health. Return to the previous passage and exit out the left gate.

THE NECROPOLIS

MAIN OBJECTIVE	Reclaim the Crucible
NEW WEAPONS/EQUIPMENT	None
NEW MONSTERS	Hell Guard

CHALLENGES

CHALLENGE	DESCRIPTION
A Pin Pops a Balloon	Kill a Mancubus with the Pistol.
Two Mouths to Feed	Kill 2 Cacodemons with one shot.
Wait For It	Kill 10 demons with Explosive Barrels.

COLLECTIBLES

COLLECTIBLE	UNLOCKS
Tealguy	Chainsaw Model
Hazmatguy	Gauss Cannon Model

CLASSIC MAP   DOOM - House of Pain

LEGEND

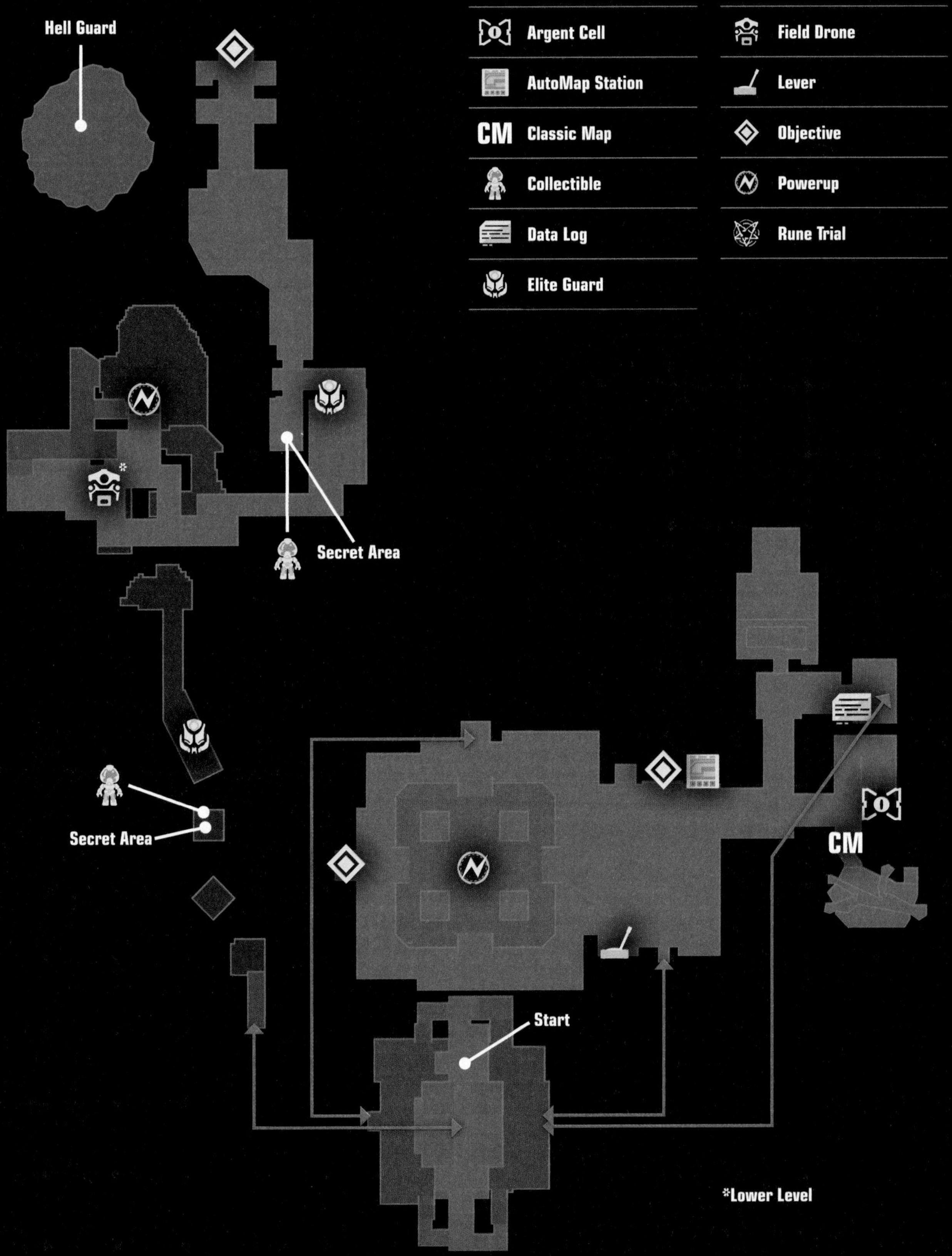

Hell Guard

🎗	**Argent Cell**		🤖	**Field Drone**
🗺	**AutoMap Station**		⌙	**Lever**
CM	**Classic Map**		◈	**Objective**
👤	**Collectible**		Ⓝ	**Powerup**
📄	**Data Log**		👹	**Rune Trial**
👾	**Elite Guard**			

Secret Area

Secret Area

CM

Start

*Lower Level

RECLAIM THE CRUCIBLE FROM ITS TOMB

The portal sends you to The Necropolis where the Crucible lies. Blue and yellow access gates are visible in the next room. To reach the tomb, you must navigate the Necropolis and find the two skulls. Drop off to the left and step through the portal.

Collect the **Data Log** and head down the steps. Right off the bat you have an opportunity to work on the third Challenge. There's an explosive barrel at the corner. Move back up the steps after the demons have spawned and allow a couple of Imps to get close to the explosive before hitting it with a shot from your Pistol. Turn left and climb more steps to find an **Artifact** and **Argent Cell**.

Eliminate the demons that spawn into the room, including a Mancubus and a few Lost Souls. Once they have been defeated, climb back up the stairs and approach the doorway. Step out of the way as a Spectre charges through the Unwilling and out the door. Kill the demons and then activate the Skull Switch at the back of the second room. Eliminate the two Hell Knights and Mancubus as you make your way out the exit at the bottom of the staircase.

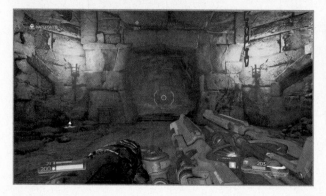

In the next room, several Unwilling make great targets for the explosive barrels positioned around the pillars and outer walls. Press the Skull Switch and wait for Cacodemons and others to appear around the room. Fire the BFG at one of the flying demons to complete the second Mission Challenge and then finish off the remaining foes.

Snatch the Yellow Skull off the pedestal, kill the two Spectres, and then activate the AutoMap Station in a cubbyhole just right of the pedestal. More demons pop in, so take care of them before entering the now-accessible portal.

CLASSIC MAP:
DOOM - HOUSE OF PAIN

After grabbing the Yellow Skull and defeating the ensuing attack, approach the exit portal and search the nook on the right to find the lever. Then return to the previous room where you found the Argent Cell to discover a new opening on the right wall. Step inside to unlock DOOM – House of Pain.

This returns you to the starting location. Climb up to the yellow door and place the Yellow Skull. Turn the crank found inside to drop the bars in front of the nearby portal. Step inside and transport to a new locale.

Mancubi appear on the platforms ahead, as other demons join in around the outside of the area. A variety of monsters continues to spawn in as you take them down. The pillars provide a little protection, but don't spend too much time in one location. When more Mancubi show up, grab the Quad Damage powerup that's unlocked in the center to improve your odds of survival. Stay on the move as you wipe out the opposition.

Grab the Blue Skull off the pedestal, re-enter the portal, and once again climb onto the central platform. Place the skull in the blue door to reveal another crank and turn it. Demons appear around the room. Take them out as more powerful monsters continue to spawn.

Once the two Barons of Hell have been disposed of, barriers drop and reveal a hole in the middle of the floor. Drop inside and interact with the **Artifact**. Just ahead, jump down to even lower depths. Destroy the Cacodemons in your path before hopping across the platforms.

TEALGUY

After shooting the two Cacodemons out of the air, jump across three platforms. Turn around to spot a Collectible on a lower level. Hop down to get it.

Jump into the cave, killing a Mancubus along the way. Collect a Praetor Token from the **Elite Guard**. Continue through the passageway, jump over to the steps on the left, and interact with the **Field Drone** up ahead.

Hop up to another set of stairs and follow the pathway around to the left to find a group of demons fighting amongst each other. You can let them weaken each other up or just jump into the battle. There's a Haste powerup on the ledge high above, and BFG ammo further up the steps, so take advantage of the firepower on a group of monsters.

Continue up the staircase and through the structure until a Baron of Hell jumps out from around the corner. Kill two Barons of Hell, two Mancubi, and three Spectres to lower the gate, allowing you to exit. Before you leave, though, search the Elite Guard against the wall for another Praetor Token. Descend the steps and stop at the landing as Cacodemons enter from the right.

HAZMATGUY

After exiting the structure, stop at the landing just outside and look up to the right at the Icon of Sin. Fire a rocket at the rune on its forehead to send the second Collectible to its resting location

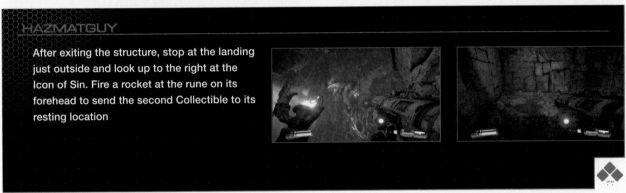

Defeat all of the monsters that spawn into the area and then move through the new opening below the Icon of Sin. Grab all of the resources that you can and then interact with the glyph ahead to transport to your next boss fight.

HELL GUARD

The Hell Guard is a heavily armored demon that carries two big melee weapons. An energy shield protects him for short periods while a multi-energy ball attack causes devastating damage if contact is made. Learn its telltales and how to avoid its assaults.

Shield - The demon has the ability to shield itself as it moves around the battlefield. If the yellow sphere surrounds the boss, don't waste your ammo; not even the BFG can penetrate it. It uses this to get in close to its target. This is an opportunity to charge the Gauss Cannon, releasing a powerful shot once the shield is down.

Weapon Attack - When in close, the Hell Guard slams or sweeps its club with devastating results. A Jump Slam is even more deadly as it gets momentum behind the move. Dodge away from the enemy when its club goes back.

Fire Attack - When the fiend waves its left weapon in the air, it spawns fireballs during its Weapon Throw. Run away if you see this coming to avoid taking damage. If you're already a safe distance away, fire a couple of rockets as it prepares the move.

Energy Ball - Watch for the boss to transfer its energy from the shield into energy spheres, throwing them straight ahead. This attack moves at a high speed, so start moving around the boss as soon as you see it coming. Shoot the Energy Ball, not the Hell Guard, to stun the demon during this attack.

Weapon Throw - The Hell Guard gains the ability to throw its weapons. Watch for it to wind up and move to the side.

Flame Carousel - If it puts up a shield and begins spinning, a powerful fire attack is incoming, so prepare. Six streams of fire spew out from the boss and spins as it does. Run with the pattern, then hop over the flames to avoid taking damage. As it becomes dizzy and hunches over, hit it with your best weapons. Fail to do so and it performs the same maneuver in the opposite direction.

Flame Spikes - Watch for it to rear back with its club and slam the ground three times in succession. Each hit sends a flame at its target. The fire moves along the ground very quickly. When you see this move coming, try to get behind the boss for a great opportunity to attack.

Cancel a Hell Guard's melee attack by blasting it with a powerful shot. If the boss is stunned, resources are dropped. Move in and grab them when the opportunity arises; equip the Vacuum Rune for an easier time with this. Continue to hit the boss whenever its shield is down, while dodging its many attacks. Eventually it falls to the ground. Move in and perform a Glory Kill to finish it off.

At this point two Hell Guards emerge from the ground. The duo moves around the battlefield very quickly, working in tandem to take their target down. The guard with the club is the melee, high pressure unit, while the staff fires from range and is more elusive.

Energy Ball – This attack is just like the previous demon's energy spheres, but with just one ball. Dodge to the side to avoid taking damage. Once again, shoot the Energy Ball, not the Hell Guard, to stun the demon during this attack.

Cyclone Spin – The demon spins around like a top, beating its target down with each revolution. Run away if you see this move coming. Like the boss before them, cause enough damage before the spin completes and the creature becomes stunned. Take advantage and hit it hard.

Charge Attack – Watch for the fiend to stick its weapon out in front and quickly move toward you. Step out of the way when you see its weapon out straight.

Flamethrower – They can shoot fire in a straight line across the battlefield. Cause enough damage before this attack starts to put the guard in a vulnerable state.

Jump Attack – This demon also has the ability to use its melee weapon in a devastating manner. Watch for it to jump in the air and then make sure you are nowhere near its landing zone.

Tag Team Attack – The Hell Guards team up to unleash their ultimate move: a punishing version of the Jump Attack that covers the entire arena and does massive damage. One demon uses its staff to hold the other aloft, while the suspended demon spins rapidly to build up energy. Once the hammer wielding demon is sufficiently energized, the partner slams its twin into the ground to create a massive shockwave. While this attack is extremely dangerous, it does require some buildup time. If you sufficiently damage the staff-wielding twin before it can charge its partner, the pair will tumble to the ground and be stunned. Let loose with everything you've got while they're immobilized!

If you have BFG ammo available, hit them with it and they may become stunned. Attempt to stay at a safe distance away from these guys as you fire your most powerful weapons at them. They move quickly as they switch up their attacks. They share an HP pool, so it doesn't matter which one you concentrate your fire on. Continue to give them everything you've got until one falls. Hit it with a Glory Kill and repeat with the other. Reclaim the Crucible once the fight is over to complete the mission.

VEGA CENTRAL PROCESSING

MAIN OBJECTIVE	Close the Well
NEW WEAPONS/EQUIPMENT	None
NEW MONSTERS	None

CHALLENGES

CHALLENGE	DESCRIPTION
Variety is the Spice of Death III	Perform 5 different Glory Kills on Imps.
Gore Piñata	Kill 3 demons with one Frag Grenade.
My Teeth are Sharper	Kill a Cacodemon with the Chainsaw.

COLLECTIBLES

COLLECTIBLE	UNLOCKS
Quakeguy	Hell Guard Model
Jungleguy	Cyber-Mancubus Model

CLASSIC MAP   DOOM - Command Control

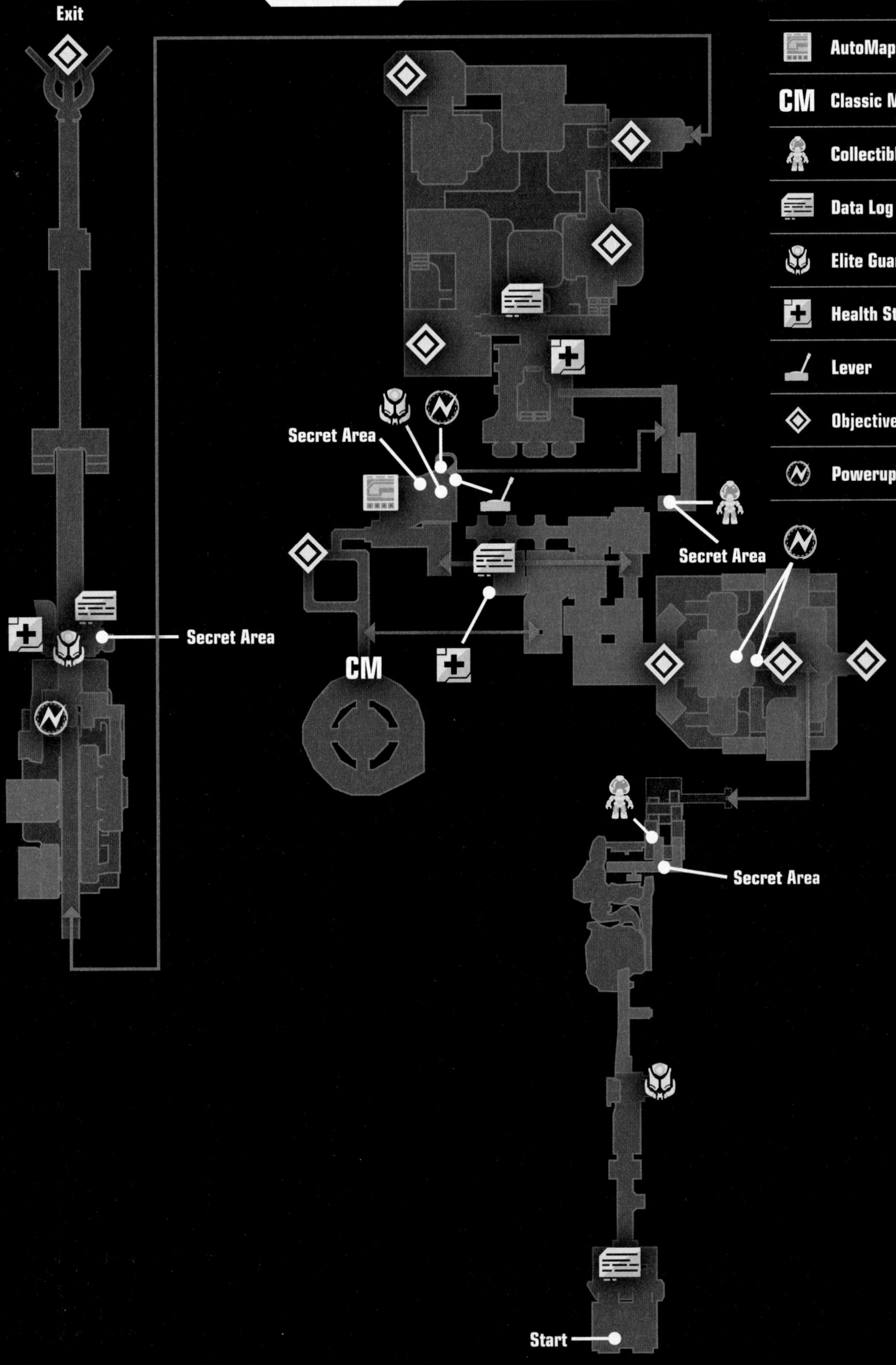

Exit

🗺️	AutoMap Station
CM	Classic Map
🧍	Collectible
📋	Data Log
🛡️	Elite Guard
➕	Health Station
⌐	Lever
◆	Objective
Ⓝ	Powerup

Secret Area

Secret Area

Secret Area

CM

Secret Area

Start

CHALLENGE 1: Variety is the Spice of Death III

Perform 5 different Glory Kills on Imps. This is the third time for the Glory Kill variety challenge, so you should be familiar with it. This time, you want to perform Glory Kill on five Imps from different angles. To get five unique animations, approach from the front, rear, side, above, and near a wall.

CHALLENGE 2: Gore Piñata

Kill 3 demons with one Frag Grenade. The first opportunity to get this challenge comes in your initial encounter. As three Imps gather on the walkway below the Collectible, drop the explosive between them. The demons may disperse too soon to get this one, but there are plenty more opportunities throughout this mission.

CHALLENGE 3: My Teeth are Sharper

Kill a Cacodemon with the Chainsaw. The flying demon is often out of reach, but there are plenty of opportunities to get these guys as they descend to your level. The second battle in the VEGA Security Station offers a chance as two spawn just ahead. Three fuel are required to make the kill.

GAIN ACCESS TO VEGA MAIN SECURITY TERMINAL

You have returned to Mars with the Crucible, but you must be sent back to Hell to close The Well. To do so, visit VEGA Central Processing. Move up into the control room and grab the **Data Log** from the console before cycling through the airlock behind you to access the outdoors.

Search around the right corner amongst the debris to find the first **Elite Guard**. Climb onto the corner platform and continue onto the pathway above. Instead of following the path downhill, hop over to the right wall and follow the pipes to a maintenance door. Grab the BFG ammo at the end of the shaft before taking the left path.

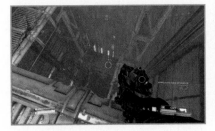

At the ledge, look down to spot Imps dancing between the walkways. This provides your first opportunity to take three out with one Frag Grenade and score the second Mission Challenge. Take out the closest guy and then look for more below. If you're quick enough, you can drop an explosive between the monsters as three group together.

Fight through the Imps as you drop to the bottom of the ventilation shaft. Follow the maintenance tunnel to a service hatch and descend into the VEGA Security Station.

TURN OFF SECURITY SWITCHES

Approach Network Station 1 just ahead and turn it off. This attracts a whole lot of demons to the room. A Berserk powerup floats high in the air in the center of the room, while an Invulnerability powerup is found just below, near the middle platform. Find BFG ammo behind the security terminal and below the platforms, giving a big boost to your efforts.

Fight your way through the fiends to the far side and find the second switch below the steps. Throw it to complete the objective and finish off any remaining monsters. Return to the upper floor where you dropped in and interact with the VEGA Security Station terminal to cancel the lockdown.

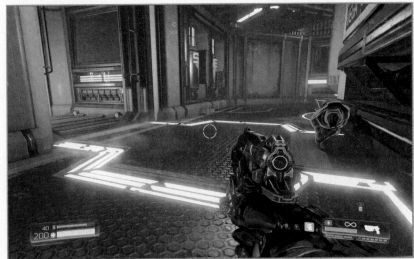

ACCESS COOLING ROOM

More demons spawn into the security station, including a couple of Cacodemons just in front of you. Equip the Chainsaw, wait for one to approach your location, and take it down—scoring the third challenge. Any resources not gathered during the first battle remain around the room, including the two powerups, so conserve during the first fight if possible. Eliminate the rest of the monsters before exiting the far door.

This facility is overrun with demons so always be alert, especially for the Pinkies and Mancubi. Back up and take each one out to avoid being overwhelmed. Go through the door to the right and make an immediate left. Search the far corner in the server area to find a **Data Log**. If you need BFG ammo, search the left elevator in the next corridor over.

Move around the crates in the adjacent area and drop into the hatch. Follow the pathway left, staying alert for Spectres who immediately charge your way. Continue until you find a corpse with the Blue Key card. Use it to enter the blue access door on the right.

Fight your way into Sector P Access on the left and access the **AutoMap Station** against the left wall. Step into the storage room behind you, take down the Revenant, and grab the Praetor Token off the **Elite Guard** before hopping into the center of the hole on the left. A Mega Health is collected as you drop onto a vent shaft in the middle.

CLASSIC MAP:
DOOM - COMMAND CONTROL

After you collect the Praetor Token but before you drop into the hole, search behind the crates to find the secret lever. Exit back to the hallway, turn right, and follow the pathway until you find the Classic Map, near the spot where you landed from the hatch above.

JUNGLEGUY

After dropping into the hole, go right to the end of the shaft and drop left to another level. Follow this path to the right to collect the Collectible. Climb back up the venting to return to the previous location.

Enter the vent shaft and follow it until you drop back inside the facility. The elevator ahead can take you back into the previous area if you missed anything. Otherwise, top off your health at the Health Station and exit out the opposite side to reach the Cooling Room.

DESTROY COOLING COILS

Pick up the **Data Log** from the balcony ahead. Four cooling coils must be destroyed to continue. Two are located on this level in the front and back-left corners. Another is found on the balcony to the right, while the last one is on the lower level in the back-right corner. Any weapon can be used to destroy the coil, but a charged shot from the Pistol does the trick.

Things are calm inside the Cooling Room until you destroy a cooling coil. At that point all hell breaks loose. There are a plethora of demons to fight off as you attempt to complete the objective. BFG ammo is found at a few locations around the area, including one behind a couple of crates on the far side of the room. There's also a Berserk powerup in a short tunnel, just outside another coil. Use the jump pads to escape trouble and traverse the multi-tiered facility. Kill every last monster and destroy the remaining three coils.

ACCESS VEGA'S CORE

Find the exit above a cooling coil located in the back-right corner of the room. Jump up to the small platform under the exit sign and interact with the Lift Access. Move through the corridor, wait for a tram to pull up below, and drop onto it.

It comes to a stop in a terminal, infected by demons. BFG ammo is available below and on a couple platforms above, while a Haste powerup rests on a platform high in the air on the left. The area below the tracks is electrified, so be careful you do not fall in. Powerful monsters make an appearance in this fight, including a pair of Barons of Hell. With the availability of BFG ammo, hit these guys right away. Take advantage of the many levels and structures to avoid enemy fire as you take the rest of the fiends down.

Once every last monster has been disposed of, run through the opening at the far end. Refill your health at the Health Station on the left and collect the **Data Log** on the right. Step onto the cargo lift, turn around, and look under the platform you just left. Hop off and double jump over to it to find the last **Elite Guard**. Hop on the elevator to the left and ride it all the way back up.

DESTROY VEGA'S NEURAL PROCESSORS

Follow the walkway through the doorway ahead. The path splits at the end. Follow it left and right to find the processors and destroy them.

OVERLOAD THE VEGA CORE

Climb the steps in the middle and interact with the Systems Operations Terminal to end the mission.

ARGENT D'NUR

MAIN OBJECTIVE	Close the Well
NEW WEAPONS/EQUIPMENT	None
NEW MONSTERS	Spider Mastermind

CHALLENGES

CHALLENGE	DESCRIPTION
Hold Still	Kill 2 Barons of Hell with one shot.
Uncharted Territory	Find all 3 "Skull Switch" secrets.
Big [REDACTED] Gun	Kill 25 demons with the BFG.

COLLECTIBLES

COLLECTIBLE	UNLOCKS
Cosmoguy	Chaingun Model
Goldguy	Spider Mastermind Model

CLASSIC MAP DOOM - Pandemonium

	AutoMap station
CM	Classic Map
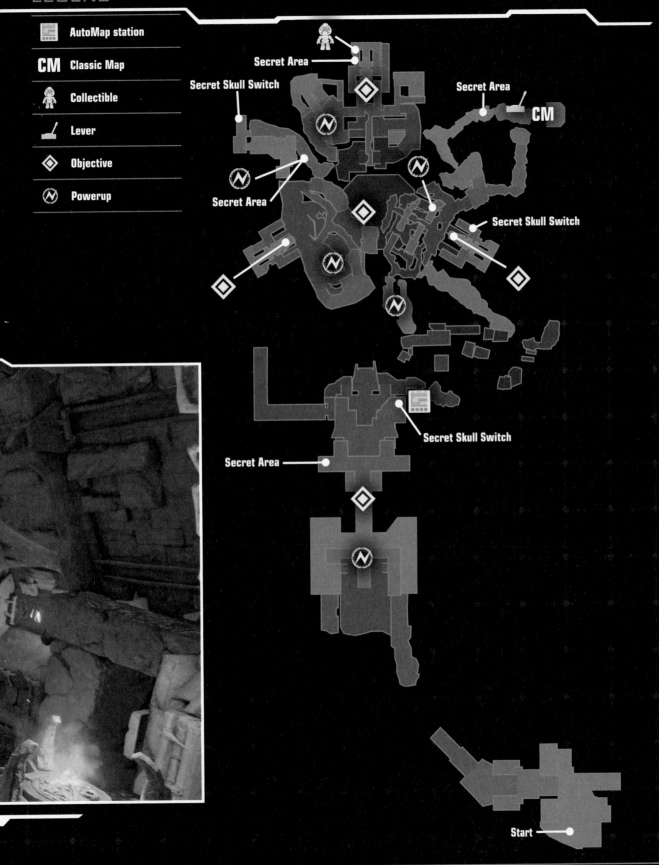	Collectible
	Lever
◇	Objective
Ⓝ	Powerup

Secret Area

Secret Skull Switch

Secret Area

CM

Secret Area

Secret Skull Switch

Secret Area

Secret Skull Switch

Secret Area

Secret Skull Switch

Start

105

ACCESS THE WELL CATHEDRAL

You are back in Hell in an attempt to finally sever the connection between the two worlds. Collect the resources and then head downhill to the left. Hop down to the area below when you reach the cliff edge.

Moving further ahead brings out the welcoming party led by a Cacodemon. You can stand back and fire shots at them for a little while, but you must eventually dive into the action. A blue portal on the left side of the arena leads to an upper level on the far side, while the red portal in the middle takes you to an upper level on the right side. Use them to quickly move between the floors and escape danger. There's a Berserk powerup in the middle of the battlefield. Use it after disposing of a few weaker enemies. Once the area is clear of monsters, pass through the doorway next to the blue portal.

LAY THE WRAITH'S SOULS TO REST

Three Wraith's Souls must be laid to rest, but demons guard all three. These groups of monsters are extremely intimidating. You must deal with them before tackling the Wraiths.

Take out the Unwilling as you drop to the middle level. Run over to the **Secret Skull Switch** in the far-right corner and activate it. This reveals a stepping stone to the left, which allows you to return to the upper floor. Collect the BFG ammo and fuel from the cubbyhole on the right. A passageway accessed on the left side of the bottom level leads to more resources, though this also spawns a Cacodemon and Hell Knight, so be prepared.

Exit the tunnel and follow the path out the far side. Before jumping across the ravine, take the route to the right to find the **AutoMap Station**. Then jump across and head right, taking out the Lost Souls before they attack. Zigzag your way down the ravine, killing the Cacodemons as you go. Climb the ledges on the right side and turn left toward your objective to find a rock formation blocking your way. Jump to the right of it and then double jump to the landing.

Take advantage of the high number of demons at these Wraith battles to work on the third Mission Challenge, pulling out your BFG when a big group presents itself. The fight can get hectic if you aren't careful. Stay on the run, quickly move between the different levels, and use the rocks to break line of sight.

WRAITH'S SOUL # 1

Stay on the trail and collect the Mega Health before reaching the first Wraith battle. The rock formations around the arena create plenty of platforms for you to hop across, using them to escape from danger or as vantage points. Short tunnels on the lower

Once the monsters have been disposed of, two gates open up, allowing access to the first Wraith. Collect any remaining resources and then move through the left opening. Ascend the steps until you reach the Wraith. Interact with it to lay its soul to rest. Drop off the right side to the landing and activate the **Secret Skull Switch**.

level offer a little cover when things get hairy. There's a Quad Damage powerup on a platform in the middle of the area, but it is best saved for later when the fight gets overwhelming. Red portals on each end of the battlefield allow you to move from one side to the other in a hurry.

Return to the battlefield and go right toward the objective. Instead of jumping up to the skull, enter the new opening on the right to find the second secret area. Collect the resources as you navigate the passage to the other side.

The Classic Map and lever are found inside the secret tunnel revealed by activating the second Skull Switch. Pull the lever found just after climbing the ledge to reveal the Classic Map at the end of the corridor to the right.

WRAITH'S SOUL #2

Turn right and observe the second Wraith battlefield. You can spend some time picking demons off, but watch out for the Imps' fireballs. This area is more structured than the previous with pillars and stone bridges providing a multi-level arena. A red portal on the ground level, below the gates, sends you to the main level at the far end of the space. There's a Berserk powerup on a butte just above the red portal. Save this for when the Mancubi appear to make quick work of them.

After eliminating the monsters, head up the stairs and lay the second Wraith's soul to rest. On the far side of the battlefield, a skull gives you an exit. Drop into the hole to drop into a passageway.

COSMOGUY

Once the demons have been removed from the area, climb the left stairs until you reach a hole in the steps. Duck inside to find the only hidden Collectible in this mission.

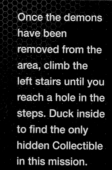

WRAITH'S SOUL #3

Follow the corridor up a short slope to find the final **Secret Skull Switch** in a small cubbyhole on the right. Go back down the passage toward your entry point and grab the resources inside a small room on the right. Continue along the path until you reach the third Wraith battle.

Be alert in the early stages of this fight as Imps launch fireballs, Hell Knights jump attack, and Pinkies charge at you. Things can get hectic, so be ready to flee to a higher location. Eventually, two Barons of Hell spawn into the area. Quickly switch to the BFG and take them out with one shot to earn the first Mission Challenge. It's possible for this to fail. Try to get them when they're close together. With the monsters taken care of, climb the steps to the final Wraith and lay its soul to rest.

Spend some time picking off the Hell Knights from above before dropping into the battlefield. A red portal near the point where you entered transports you to the middle of the area, next to the platform that holds a Quad Damage powerup.

FIND THE EXIT PORTAL

Collect any resources you can find around the area and then head for the objective marker. Drop down to find your final opponent, Spider Mastermind.

SPIDER MASTERMIND

Emerging from the ground, Spider Mastermind displays its prowess with four legs and a massive weapon below its head. It is well armored, with a couple of obvious weak spots at the top of its head.

Beam Salvo – When the spider flips over, it fires energy shots at a high rate of fire. Quickly move to the side and keep moving until the attack stops. It can fire this weapon from either side, changing up the angle of the energy shots.

Laser Beam Sweep – Watch for it to plant its two front claws into the ground. Three lasers shoot out each side while a seventh fires from its gun. It sweeps to one side and back, alternating low/high or high/low. Hop over the low beams. You can easily crouch beneath the high ones.

Side Step – The boss has the ability to move around the area quickly with a side step and hop. It can fire its energy gun as it does so.

Claw Swipe – Be careful when close to the behemoth, as it swipes its claw. Stay well clear of the boss to avoid getting hit.

Gas Cloud – About halfway through its health bar, the boss moves to the corner and launches a gas attack, which inflicts damage if you get caught up in it. When it bends over, quickly climb onto one of the pillars that appear around the battlefield and fire a high-power weapon at the boss. Be careful that you do not blow up your own platform.

Chain Beam – Once the electrified ground is removed, hop down to avoid spikes that shoot out from the top of the pillars. The demon sends a beam between the pillars that detonates the rock formations, so be careful. Destroy the first pillar before it charges to stun the boss.

Collapse - When Spider Mastermind's health gets to critical levels, it collapses to the ground. It retains the ability to shoot its energy gun and lasers, but with limited mobility.

Telekinesis Throw – Be ready to dodge out of the way as it raises a pillar above its head and throws it your way. Destroy the pillar before it's fully charged to stun the boss.

Pillars pop out of the ground, giving you a little cover as you fight the behemoth, though these are easily destroyed. Don't spend too much time behind one. Note that the pillars can contain health and ammo. If you're low on either, you can sacrifice some temporary cover to replenish.

Hitting the boss with the BFG causes it to collapse to the ground for a short time. Quickly pull out one of your more powerful weapons, such as the Gauss Cannon, and light the creature up. Resources spew out as you do so. Look for BFG Ammo as it spawns around the area.

Concentrate your weapon fire at the boss's brain until it finally falls in dramatic fashion. Move in and perform a Glory Kill to finish it off.

Note that you get bonus weapon upgrade points whenever you kill a boss (6 points) or destroy VEGA (5 points).

WEAPONRY

The weapons of DOOM range from classics like the Super Shotgun and Chaingun to the futuristic Gauss Cannon and Heavy Assault Rifle. Each has its purpose in your arsenal, but inevitably one or two do become favorites. You must learn to use them all, quickly switching between weapons in the heat of battle, based on your current target.

A handful of deployable equipment is found as you progress through the campaign. When used correctly, these charges help get you out of a jam or tip a fight in your favor. The Chainsaw and BFG 9000 allow for instant kills, but ammunition is limited, so use it wisely.

WEAPON SELECT

Tapping the Weapon Wheel button switches to your previous weapon, while holding the button brings up the Weapon Wheel. Push it in the direction of the weapon you wish to select and release the button. This takes some getting used to, but mastering this method can mean the difference between death and triumph. This applies only to the standard guns. The Chainsaw and BFG are selected with their own button.

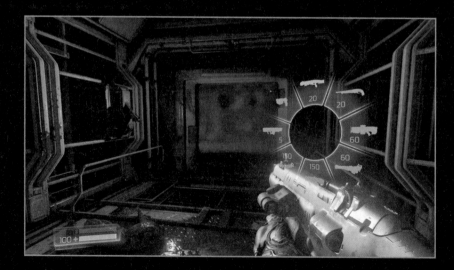

MODIFICATIONS

By finding Field Drones in the campaign, you can select up to two modifications to add to each weapon. Once these are selected from the bots, access the Arsenal tab of your Dossier to see the available weapons and mods, as well as progress toward the Mastery Challenges.

This is where you spend Weapon Upgrade Points to upgrade the mods. Earn points by collecting items, killing demons, and completing mission challenges. Once all upgrades are purchased for a mod, complete a challenge to earn Mastery for that mod.

Once a weapon is fully modded, select the desired mod, then press the Switch Weapon Mod button to quickly switch between them.

AMMO

If you stick to one or two weapons, ammunition can become rare. Learn the benefits of each weapon and ammo becomes more plentiful. Ammo is found around the environment and it's dropped from defeated enemies. Keep an eye out for the big munitions crates that top off all ammunition. Reroute an Argent Cell's power to Ammo to boost the capacity for each regular weapon. This can be increased four times.

✂ ARSENAL

Your standard weaponry selected from the Weapon Wheel.

CHAINGUN

LOCATIONS FOUND Kadingir Sanctum, Argent Facility (Destroyed)

Designed for sustained volleys, the Chaingun deals high damage at a very high rate of fire. It requires a little spin up time before it gets up to speed, so watch out, as you are vulnerable. Spin it up behind cover before moving out into the open.

MODIFICATIONS

GATLING ROTATOR

The Weapon Mod button can spin up the Chaingun barrels without firing. Keep the weapon ready to go with this modification. If you release the button, though, it takes time to spin it back up. Fully upgrade this mod to penetrate through your targets and hit those behind them.

DAMAGE

CHAINGUN	MAX DAMAGE	MIN DAMAGE
Standard	19	19
Gatling Rotator	19	19
Incendiary Rounds	24	24
Mobile Turret	22	22

AMMO CAPACITY (BULLETS)

BASE	UPGRADE 1	UPGRADE 2	UPGRADE 3	UPGRADE 4
90	120	150	180	210

The Delta-12 Chaingun (often referred to as "The D12" by operatives) is a high velocity heavy weapon capable of suppressing multiple targets at once. Recent changes to the firing mechanism have pushed the Delta-12 to the physical limits of a ballistic weapon. An Argent infused piston compresses gas within the firing crucible to over 220,000 PSI. When released, this launches a 15mm Tungsten Slug with a muzzle velocity of nearly 5,000 feet per second. The heat generated by this action is syphoned into a thermal gel compound that automatically recharges the 96-volt battery pack. This allows the weapon to sustain an almost endless firing cycle, as long as ammunition is present. The Delta-12 Chaingun weighs 45kg, making it a lethal but cumbersome armament.

UPGRADES*

UPGRADE	DESCRIPTION	COST (WEAPON UPGRADE PTS)
Improved Torque	Significantly increases the spin-up speed of the Gatling Rotator	3
Uranium Coating	Bullets penetrate through targets	6

*All upgrades can be purchased in any order.

MASTERY CHALLENGE

Get 5 kills in 5 seconds while using the Gatling Rotator.

REWARD: INCENDIARY ROUNDS

Bullets deal more damage when the Chaingun reaches its maximum rate of fire.

MOBILE TURRET

Hold the Weapon Mod button to transform the weapon barrels into a Mobile Turret. It stalls if it overheats.

UPGRADES

UPGRADE	DESCRIPTION	COST (WEAPON UPGRADE PTS)
Rapid Deployment	Drastically decrease the transformation time for the Mobile Turret	3
Uranium Coating	Bullets penetrate through targets	6

MASTERY CHALLENGE

Kill 4 or more demons during a single Mobile Turret deploy 5 times

REWARD: **ULTIMATE COOLING**

The Mobile Turret no longer stalls.

COMBAT SHOTGUN

LOCATIONS FOUND   The UAC

DAMAGE

SHOTGUN	MAX DAMAGE	MIN DAMAGE	SPLASH RADIUS
Standard	26	22	-
Charged Burst	26	22	-
Charged Burst – Power Shot	32.5	27.5	-
Explosive Shot Direct	100	100	-
Explosive Shot Splash	275	0	-
Explosive Shot - Cluster Strike	98	98	180

AMMO CAPACITY (SHELLS)

BASE	UPGRADE 1	UPGRADE 2	UPGRADE 3	UPGRADE 4
20	30	40	50	60

The UAC shotgun disperses a spread of high velocity buckshot for maximum impact against the enemy. Ideally suited for the operative who requires a speedy response for deadly close encounters, the wide coverage of this weapon loses impact at long range. The weapon is forged from a high quality Titanium Steel alloy to ensure maximum reliability, repeat rate, and yield strength.

Effective at medium and close range, the Shotgun is a versatile weapon for most encounters. This is the gun of choice throughout much of the campaign. It's most effective in close combat, but can also be used from a medium range.

MODIFICATIONS

CHARGED BURST

Hold the Weapon Mod button to charge up a three-round burst with a tighter spread. Successfully hitting all three shots from the Charged Burst increases the damage of the next burst. This effect does not stack. Charged Burst is also very effective at taking down Summoners.

UPGRADES

UPGRADE	DESCRIPTION	COST (WEAPON UPGRADE PTS)
Speedy Recovery	Reduces the recharge time between bursts	1
Rapid Fire	Increases the fire rate of the burst	3
Quick Load	Reduces the loading time for the Charged Burst	5

MASTERY CHALLENGE

Kill 5 Mancubi with the Charged Burst.

REWARD: **POWER SHOT**

Successfully hitting all three shots from the Charged Burst increases the damage of the next burst. This effect does not stack.

EXPLOSIVE SHOT

Hold the Weapon Mod button to charge up an arcing explosive round.

UPGRADES

UPGRADE	DESCRIPTION	COST (WEAPON UPGRADE PTS)
Speedy Recovery	Reduces the recharge time between explosive shots	1
Bigger Boom	Increases the size of the explosion	3
Instant Load	Removes the loading time for an explosive shot	5

MASTERY CHALLENGE

Get 20 direct hits on Imps.

REWARD: **CLUSTER STRIKE**

Getting a direct hit with an Explosive Shot spawns cluster bombs that deal additional damage.

GAUSS CANNON

DAMAGE

GAUSS CANNON	MAX DAMAGE	MIN DAMAGE	SPLASH RADIUS
Direct	650	650	-
Concuss	80	80	128
Precision Bolt	1200	300	-
Gauss Cannon Charged Sniper Mastery Splash	800	800	384
Siege Mode	1680	1680	-
Siege Mode Outer Beam	1680	1680	96

AMMO CAPACITY (CELLS)

BASE	UPGRADE 1	UPGRADE 2	UPGRADE 3	UPGRADE 4
150	200	250	300	350

The Gauss accelerator design has been used by the UAC as the basis for numerous industrial projects over the years—such as the Argent Tower itself, and the Ore Diggers found on Deimos and Phobos. With very few moving parts, the Gauss Cannon makes a reliable, powerful weapon. By accelerating steel flechettes through a magnetized chamber, extremely high velocities can be achieved. The weapon has near perfect accuracy thanks to the aerodynamic design of the projectiles. Ammunition is cheap and readily available, and is designed to maintain its composition when passing through organic material. The Gauss Cannon has a noticeable kick that must be compensated for by the operator.

While it has high damage potential, the concentrated beam of the Gauss Cannon demands accuracy. Get used to aiming this weapon. It can take out any standard enemy with just a few shots, but accuracy is key with this one. Note that 15 Cells are used in each shot, while Siege Mode requires 30 Cells.

A standard Gauss beam penetrates through fodder enemy classes. To minimize time stuck in place with Gauss Siege Mode, it can be deployed in mid-air and you maintain your momentum. A fully charged Gauss Sniper can take out a Hell Knight or Cacodemon if hit in the head or eye, respectively.

MODIFICATIONS

PRECISION BOLT

Use the Weapon Mod button to zoom in and charge a high damage shot.

UPGRADES

UPGRADE	DESCRIPTION	COST (WEAPON UPGRADE PTS)
Energy Efficient	Reduced time to max charge and reduced time between shots	3
Light Weight	Move at full speed when zoomed in	6

MASTERY CHALLENGE

Kill 5 Hell Knights with a Precision Bolt headshot.

REWARD: VOLATILE DISCHARGE

Demons killed by the Precision Bolt explode, dealing damage to nearby demons.

SIEGE MODE

Use the Weapon Mod button to charge up a powerful beam that penetrates targets. Movement is disabled while using Siege Mode.

UPGRADES

UPGRADE	DESCRIPTION	COST (WEAPON UPGRADE PTS)
Outer Beam	The beam now has a devastating area of effect around it	3
Reduced Charge Time	Beam charge time is reduced	6

MASTERY CHALLENGE

Kill 3 or more demons with a Siege Mode beam 10 times.

REWARD: MOBILE SIEGE

Allows movement while using Siege Mode.

HEAVY ASSAULT RIFLE (HAR)

LOCATIONS FOUND Resource Operations

DAMAGE

HAR	MAX DAMAGE	MIN DAMAGE
Standard	40	40
Micro Missiles Direct	10	10
Micro Missiles Splash	100	0
Tactical Scope	40	40
Devastator Rounds	70	70

AMMO CAPACITY (BULLETS)

BASE	UPGRADE 1	UPGRADE 2	UPGRADE 3	UPGRADE 4
90	120	150	180	210

Although recently superseded by the Plasma Rifle as the UAC's standard issue weapon, the Heavy Assault Rifle is still in widespread use due to its dependable mechanical firing mechanism, high accuracy at long range, and an abundant supply of ammunition. The weapon is effective at all engagement distances, and is best used against a solitary target, unless a micro missile modification is present. The standard issue ammunition is a .50 caliber FMJ round.

With high velocity rounds, the Heavy Assault Rifle is ideal for hitting fast-moving targets. Pull this one out when facing enemies such as the Spectre or Lost Souls.

MODIFICATIONS

MICRO MISSILES

Hold the Weapon Mod button to bring up a rack of Micro Missiles.

UPGRADE	DESCRIPTION	COST (WEAPON UPGRADE PTS)
Ammo Efficient	Reduces the ammo cost of Micro Missiles	1
Advanced Loader	Greatly improves reload time for Micro Missiles	3
Quick Launcher	Instantly activate the Micro Missile rack when it's ready to fire	5

MASTERY CHALLENGE

Stick 4 different demons in 5 seconds.

REWARD: BOTTOMLESS MISSILES

Micro Missiles can be fired indefinitely without requiring a reload.

TACTICAL SCOPE

Attaches a Tactical Scope that allows for zooming in on targets with the Weapon Mod button.

UPGRADE	DESCRIPTION	COST (WEAPON UPGRADE PTS)
Uranium Coating	Bullets fired while zoomed will penetrate through targets	1
Skull Cracker	Bullets fired while zoomed will deal additional headshot damage	3
Light Weight	Move faster when zoomed in with the Tactical Scope	5

MASTERY CHALLENGE

Get 50 headshot kills while using the Tactical Scope.

REWARD: DEVASTATOR ROUNDS

Ammunition fired while zoomed uses experimental, heavy damage rounds.

PISTOL

LOCATIONS FOUND The UAC

The Pistol is a sidearm with limitless ammo that's most effective against weaker targets. This UAC standard issue is ideal when high damage is unnecessary. Rapidly pull the trigger to maximize the weapon's usefulness. Great for staggering lower-level enemies without killing them.

MODIFICATIONS

CHARGED ENERGY SHOT
Hold the Weapon Mod button to power up a Charged Energy Round. Charged Pistol Shot can penetrate through fodder enemy class.

DAMAGE

PISTOL	MAX DAMAGE	MIN DAMAGE	CHARGE TIME (MS)	DISCHARGE TIME (MS)
Standard	20	20	-	-
Charged Shot	200	43	1500	750
Charged Shot – Increased Power	320	53	1000	350

AMMO Infinite

UPGRADES

UPGRADE	DESCRIPTION	COST (WEAPON UPGRADE PTS)
Charge Efficiency	Decreases the time it takes to power up a Charged Energy Shot	1
Quick Recovery	Decreases the recovery time for the Pistol after using a Charged Energy Shot	3
Light Weight	Move at full speed when using the Charged Energy Shot	5

Every UAC employee is provided a standard UAC EMG (Energy-Matter-Gel) Sidearm upon promotion to Tier 2 and above. This sidearm is reliable and effective at short range. A gravity gear dynamo in the stock charges a capacitor whenever the operator moves. When the weapon is fired, the capacitor compresses up to 4 megawatts of Argent Energy into a hardened plasma gel and launches the slug at high velocity. The gel slug has the same impact properties of conventional ammunition, making the weapon act and feel like a standard ballistic firearm.

The weapon is constructed of thermally diffusive metal alloys that allow it to discharge rapidly and repeatedly without overheating or compromising the accuracy. The capacitor in the EMG can also be upgraded to concentrate the energy into one large pulse for more stopping power.

MASTERY CHALLENGE
Get 15 headshot kills with the Charged Energy Shot.

REWARD: **INCREASED POWER**

Increases the maximum power of the Charged Energy Shot, resulting in higher damage potential.

PLASMA RIFLE

LOCATIONS FOUND Resource Operations, Foundry

DAMAGE

PLASMA RIFLE	MAX DAMAGE	MIN DAMAGE	SPLASH RADIUS
Direct	25	25	-
Splash	10	10	96
Heat Blast	350	5	-
Heat Blast Upgraded	600	10	-
Stun Bomb Direct	1	1	-
Stun Bomb Splash	1	1	256
Stun Bomb Splash Upgraded	1	1	320

AMMO CAPACITY (CELLS)

BASE	UPGRADE 1	UPGRADE 2	UPGRADE 3	UPGRADE 4
150	200	250	300	350

The Plasma Rifle became standard issue among military units with the advent of Argent powered electromagnetic accelerators. Based off the HIPGD design of the early 21st century, this weapon delivers a rapid salvo of plasmoids that inflict both impact and thermal damage to the target.

The Plasma Rifle has a very high rate of fire and leverages plasma projectiles to pick apart enemies. The Heat Blast gives the weapon higher damage, while Stun Bomb makes it more tactical. Hit a group with the Stun Bomb and then follow up with some rapid fire mayhem. Note that each shot uses 10 cells.

MODIFICATIONS

HEAT BLAST

Firing the Plasma Rifle builds up excess heat that can be released as a powerful blast by using the Weapon Mod button.

UPGRADES

UPGRADE	DESCRIPTION	COST (WEAPON UPGRADE PTS)
Super Heated Rounds	Shots from the Plasma Rifle now build heat much faster	1
Improved Venting	Significantly reduces the weapon's recovery from a Heat Blast	3
Expanded Threshold	Increases the amount of heat that can be contained, resulting in more potential damage	5

MASTERY CHALLENGE

Kill multiple demons with a single Heat Blast 20 times.

REWARD: **HEATED CORE**

Generate heat passively without needing to spend ammo.

STUN BOMB

Pressing the Weapon Mod button launches an electrified projectile that stuns demons within its detonation radius. It must recharge after firing. This knocks out a Possessed Security shield.

UPGRADES

UPGRADE	DESCRIPTION	COST (WEAPON UPGRADE PTS)
Quick Recharge	Stun Bomb recharges much faster.	1
Big Shock	Increases the size of the Stun Bomb detonation	3
Longer Stun	Demons hit by the Stun Bomb will stay stunned for a longer duration	5

MASTERY CHALLENGE

Kill 30 stunned demons.

REWARD: **CHAIN STUN**

Demons killed while stunned release a secondary stun detonation that affects nearby demons.

LOCATIONS FOUND Foundry, Argent Facility

DAMAGE

ROCKET LAUNCHER	MAX DAMAGE	MIN DAMAGE	SPLASH RADIUS
Direct	130	130	=
Splash	350	0	320
Remote Detonation Splash	350	0	340
Remote Detonation – Improved Warhead	350	0	408
Remote Detonation – Jagged Shrapnel	450	0	340/408
Lock-on Burst Direct	300 or 375 (based on demon)	300	-
Lock-on Splash	25	0	128

AMMO CAPACITY (ROCKETS)

BASE	UPGRADE 1	UPGRADE 2	UPGRADE 3	UPGRADE 4
15	20	25	30	35

This weapon has seen little design modification since its development in the late 21st century. It's standard issue to Heavy Weapons Specialists in all military forces due to its unparalleled direct impact and radius damage. The UAC improved the design slightly by adding an automated quick reload. The weapon casing has been retrofitted to accept UAC developed modifications.

With a large blast radius and high damage, the Rocket Launcher is useful against all but the fastest enemies. These rockets are easily avoided, but effective against the big, lumbering demons such as the Mancubi.

MODIFICATIONS

REMOTE DETONATION
Press the Weapon Mod button to detonate any rockets in flight. This can easily take out a pack of Lost Souls with a well-timed detonation.

UPGRADES

UPGRADE	DESCRIPTION	COST (WEAPON UPGRADE PTS)
Improved Warhead	Using Remote Detonation will generate a larger rocket explosion	3
Jagged Shrapnel	Demons that are hit by a Remote Detonation will be pierced with additional shrapnel and continue to take damage for a short time	6

MASTERY CHALLENGE
Kill 3 or more demons with a single detonation 15 times.

REWARD: **EXTERNAL PAYLOAD**

Explosives are now mounted around the rocket, allowing a Remote Detonation to occur without destroying the projectile.

LOCK-ON BURST
Press and hold the Weapon Mod button to lock onto a target. Once locked, firing quickly launches three rockets at the target. Lock-on Mod is very effective against the Summoner.

UPGRADES

UPGRADE	DESCRIPTION	COST (WEAPON UPGRADE PTS)
Quick Lock	Lock onto demons much faster	3
Faster Recovery	The time before another lock can be acquired is reduced	6

MASTERY CHALLENGE
Kill 5 Summoners using the Lock-on Burst.

REWARD: **MULTI-TARGETING**

Holding the Weapon Mod button to lock now supports up to three targets. Rockets are divided amongst established locks.

LOCATIONS FOUND Argent Facility, Argent Energy Tower

A devastating close range weapon, the Super Shotgun presents plenty of risk and reward. Super Shotgun spread makes it effective at killing multiple enemies with a single shot. This weapon does devastating damage up close, making it particularly effective against elusive foes like the Summoner.

MODIFICATIONS

IMPROVEMENTS

Improvements is not technically a mod. It simply improves the weapon.

UPGRADES

UPGRADE	DESCRIPTION	COST (WEAPON UPGRADE PTS)
Faster Reload	Decreases the time to reload the next shot	3
Uranium Coating	Shots penetrate through targets	6

MASTERY CHALLENGE

Kill multiple demons with a Super Shotgun blast 30 times.

REWARD: **DOUBLE TROUBLE**

Fire twice with the Super Shotgun before having to reload.

DAMAGE

SUPER SHOTGUN	MAX DAMAGE	MIN DAMAGE
Standard	60	40

AMMO CAPACITY (SHELLS)

BASE	UPGRADE 1	UPGRADE 2	UPGRADE 3	UPGRADE 4
20	30	40	50	60

While this weapon has been removed from the UAC's approved weapon arsenal, many veteran operators insist that there's no better alternative for close combat. It offers incomparable destructive power at extremely close range, but is completely ineffective at long range. The weapon is light and small, making it a favored secondary weapon that no self-respecting combat specialist would be seen without.

:X SPECIAL WEAPONS

Two classics from the old Doom series make a return in this campaign. The Chainsaw and BFG are instant-kill weapons, but their ammunition is limited. Use wisely during the big arena battles and always keep an eye out for fuel tanks and BFG ammo. Both are selected with a special key/button, making them easily accessible.

CHAINSAW

LOCATIONS FOUND Resource Operations

There have been reports of this item being seen at the Argent Facility, though there are no known uses for it. Security personnel have been made aware that this item has likely been smuggled onto Mars, and have been directed to confiscate it immediately. As there are no practical uses for it, it must be assumed that this item should be considered a black market enthusiast's weapon.

A powerful close-range weapon that one-shots weak enemies and finishes off the elite ones. Enemies shower ammunition upon death. Using the Chainsaw requires fuel—the bigger the demon, the more you need. Fuel tanks are found sparingly around the maps, so conserve when possible. With that said, it's a waste to not use it. Try not to leave a big battle with maximum fuel or you may regret not using it when you find your next fuel tank.

AMMO CAPACITY (FUEL)

BASE	UPGRADE 1	UPGRADE 2	UPGRADE 3	UPGRADE 4
3	4	5	6	7

FUEL COST

MONSTER	FUEL
Fodder (The Possessed, Imps…)	1
Heavies (Hell Knight, Pinky…)	3
Baron of Hell and Mancubi	5

LOCATIONS FOUND Advanced Research Complex

AMMO 3 (unaffected by upgrades)

The theoretical design for the BFG-9000 was first put forward by the R&D department in the Advanced Research Complex, and the concept was later given its own funding program. The BFG Division was formed to develop a working design. Several prototype weapons have since been made.

The prototypes never went into full production due to numerous testing accidents and the deadly radiation spikes produced. Previous versions of the weapon had slightly different energy patterns to the current generation. Some released solitary Argent spheres that unleashed a deadly wave upon impact, others formed an Argent laser that cut through anything in its path. The current prototype, the BFG-9000, creates Argent streams that seek out targets and boils them alive.

This is a powerful weapon that delivers streams of supercharged Argent plasma to multiple targets and is somewhat self-guiding. Just getting the shot near a target zaps it and any other nearby demons along the way. The most effective BFG shot is one that travels through the world for a long time. Try to thread it through a group rather than aiming at a single, nearby target.

:X EQUIPMENT

Three pieces of equipment are collected during the campaign: Frag Grenades, Holograms, and Siphon Grenades—each with its own benefits. Kill or weaken groups of enemies with the Frag, distract your opponents with a Hologram, and steal health from the demons with the Siphon Grenade. Don't forget about these items. They can be lifesavers when a battle gets tough.

Press the Next and Previous Equipment buttons to toggle between these items. The selected equipment is highlighted in the lower-right corner of the HUD.

Equipping the Equipment Power Rune increases the effectiveness of Equipment items. Damage, splash damage, splash radius, healing multiplier, and duration are all improved. Purchase Equipment System upgrades for your Praetor Suit to decrease the recharge duration and increase total number of charges.

FRAG GRENADE

The UAC

The design of this weapon is conventional in nature, though it has been refined to perform at the limit of its ballistic capabilities. The UAC Fragmentation Grenade uses a Comp-D explosive package encased in a steel alloy shell, and has an effective fatality radius of about 5 meters. Improvements on the antiquated M67 grenade include a more reliable chemical fuse mechanism, interior machining of the casing to provide more efficient projectile dispersion and a trigger switch safety clip to prevent unwanted activation. The newer Comp-D explosive also ensures the radial pressure wave has no "drop spots"—ensuring full damage potential within the fatality zone.

DAMAGE AND SPLASH RADIUS

	MAX DAMAGE	MIN DAMAGE	SPLASH RADIUS
Direct	20	20	-
Direct (Equipment Power I)	30	30	-
Direct (Equipment Power II)	40	40	-
Splash	420	0	400
Splash (Equipment Power I)	638	0	425
Splash (Equipment Power II)	800	0	450

The Frag Grenade is great against packs of demons, especially weaker ones such as The Possessed and Imps. Use it when in danger to give yourself time to get away. Equip the Equipment Power Rune to improve damage and radius. Tweaking the Equipment System of your suit allows you to carry more charges and use them more often.

HOLOGRAM

Argent Energy Tower

This ancient piece of tech is as effective today as it was when it was first invented in the early 21st century. The Holocaster discharges an invisible cloud of ionized Argon, which a camera then uses to project an image through. The refracted light creates a "holographic" effect above the device. The decoy image has a broad color spectrum, and can be quite convincing. The device was first theorized by popular culture media of the late 20th century.

Don't forget about your Hologram; it can be extremely effective in tight spots. Throw down a decoy and flee the area or setup at a better angle. Equip the Equipment Rune to extend the active time. Spending tokens on the Equipment System lessens the time between uses.

SIPHON GRENADE

Lazarus Labs

DAMAGE AND SPLASH RADIUS

	MAX DAMAGE	MIN DAMAGE	SPLASH RADIUS
Damage (w/ or w/o Equipment Power)	6	6	350

HEALING MULTIPLIER

	HEALING MULTIPLIER
Standard	.18
With Equipment Power I	.25
With Equipment Power II	.286

The Siphon Grenade was designed to work with the Doom Marine's Praetor suit—specifically to make use of the Argent receptors found in the gloves and chest plates.

The grenade has three stages. When primed, the grenade releases a positively charged particle field around itself and the operator's hand. Then, when the grenade is released and explodes, it releases a negatively charged particle field over a distance of a few meters. The negatively charged particles attract Argent plasma from any demon caught in the radius, tearing the plasma from their cells. Finally, the positively charged Praetor suit then attracts the negatively charged Argent cloud, and gathers the plasma. This siphons energy back into the suit, partially healing the Doom Marine.

The Siphon Grenade is handy when fighting big groups of demons. Toss it in the middle of the pack to create a red dome. The charge does not do much damage, but it does transfer part of that lost HP to the player's suit. Equip the Equipment Power Rune to increase the amount of health received. Your suit's Equipment System can be upgraded to carry more charges and make it available for use more often.

PRAETOR SUIT

In all but the final mission of DOOM, corpses of Elite Guards lay around the environment. Look for these red-armored soldiers and interact with them to collect a Praetor Token from each one. These are used to upgrade your Praetor Suit in one of five categories.

Accessing the Praetor Suit tab in your Dossier allows you to upgrade a variety of its capabilities. Here, you can spend the tokens and view requirements to unlock the remaining categories. Where you spend your points depends on your play style. In this chapter, we reveal how to unlock the upgrades, providing descriptions and cost for each. Note that these upgrades must be purchased in order.

The Praetor Suit can also be improved by finding Argent Cells. These white containers open up to reveal the cell. The energy from this item is then rerouted to increase your maximum Health, Armor, or Ammo. Refer to our Campaign Walkthrough for locations of these valuable caches.

⠳ UPGRADES

ENVIRONMENTAL RESISTANCE

UNLOCKED: Find the Praetor Suit.

 These upgrades improve resistance to environment and explosive damage. If you like those explosive barrels, but keep hurting yourself, then focus on this category first. Barrels O' Fun is especially good, allowing you to hit the explosives point blank while only damaging nearby enemies.

ICON	UPGRADE	DESCRIPTION	COST (TOKENS)
	Hazard Protection	Decrease explosive barrel and environment damage taken.	1
	Self Preservation	Decrease weapon self-damage.	2
	Barrels O' Fun	Immune to explosive barrel damage.	3

AREA-SCANNING TECHNOLOGY

UNLOCKED: Use an AutoMap Station to unlock these upgrades.

 These upgrades improve the capabilities of Navigation Systems. If finding the Exploration items is important to you, then Area-Scanning is the way to go. Max out this category and the items appear in the AutoMap automatically.

ICON	UPGRADE	DESCRIPTION	COST (TOKENS)
	Item Awareness	The AutoMap reveals Exploration items in a wider radius around your position.	1
	Secret Sense	The compass will pulse when near secret areas.	2
	Full View	Exploration items appear in the AutoMap automatically.	3

EQUIPMENT SYSTEM

UNLOCKED: Pick up an Equipment item to unlock these upgrades.

 These upgrades improve equipment capacity and recharge time. Frag Grenades, Siphon Grenades, and Holograms are useful tools when battling demons. They can wipe out groups of enemies, steal much needed health, and distract your foes. These upgrades make your equipment even more relevant, giving extra charges and less time between.

ICON	UPGRADE	DESCRIPTION	COST (TOKENS)
	Quick Charge	Decrease the recharge duration for equipment.	2
	Stock Up	Increase total number of equipment charges.	3
	Rapid Charge	Further decrease recharge duration of equipment.	4

POWERUP EFFECTIVENESS

UNLOCKED: Use a powerup.

 These upgrades improve the effects of powerups. A Berserk powerup in Resource Operations is your first opportunity to use these powerful pickups. As you progress through the campaign, they become more prevalent and necessary in the big battlefields. These upgrades make the items even more useful, which is required for some of the later fights

ICON	UPGRADE	DESCRIPTION	COST (TOKENS)
	Power Surge	When a powerup wears off, a damaging blast wave is released.	1
	Healing Power	Upon activating a powerup, health will be filled to maximum capacity.	2
	Power Extender	Increases the length of time that a powerup will remain active.	3

DEXTERITY

UNLOCKED: Acquire 4 Weapons.

 These upgrades affect the speed of certain actions. They are possibly the most valuable in the heat of battle. The ability to switch between weapons and their modifications is huge when facing a big mix of demons. Quick Hands allows for quicker escape as you climb to safety.

ICON	UPGRADE	DESCRIPTION	COST (TOKENS)
	Adept	Switch weapons faster.	2
	Quick Hands	Grab ledges faster.	3
	Hot Swap	Swap weapon mods faster.	4

BESTIARY

Welcome to the Bestiary. This section contains everything you need to know about the demons inhabiting the worlds of DOOM.

BARON OF HELL

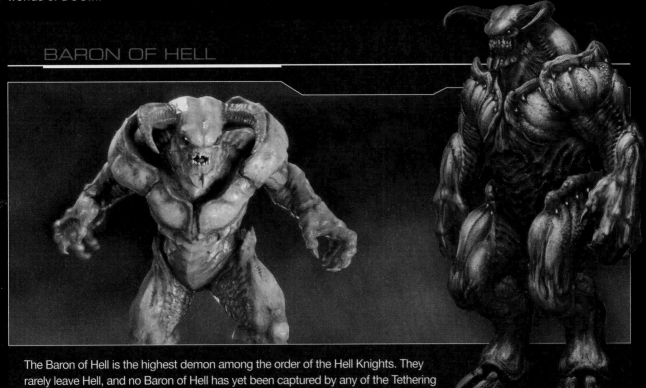

The Baron of Hell is the highest demon among the order of the Hell Knights. They rarely leave Hell, and no Baron of Hell has yet been captured by any of the Tethering Operations. Details regarding their behavior and physiology are therefore limited.

First Appearance	Kadingir Sanctum
Health	3500
Type	Melee
Strengths/ Weaknesses	Shots to the head cause the most damage. Use the plasma rifle's stun ability to stun the Baron, allowing you to keep your distance while still attacking.
Behavior	Barons of Hell chase after the player and try to claw them to death. These demons are so relentless they can even attack during traversals. In addition to robust close-quarters combat abilities, Barons of Hell can throw fireballs while closing the distance, or when a player gets out of reach.
Restrictions	N/A

ATTACK CHART

NAME	TYPE	LEVEL	DISTANCE	DAMAGE BONUS	NOTES
Swipe	Melee	Basic	Medium	N/A	Can chain together for 3-hit combos
Smash	Melee	Advanced	Medium	AoE, Displace	Can only use as a combo finisher
Ground Slam	Melee	Advanced	Long	AoE	Can use during traversals
Fireball	Range	Basic	Long	N/A	Splash damage

CACODEMON

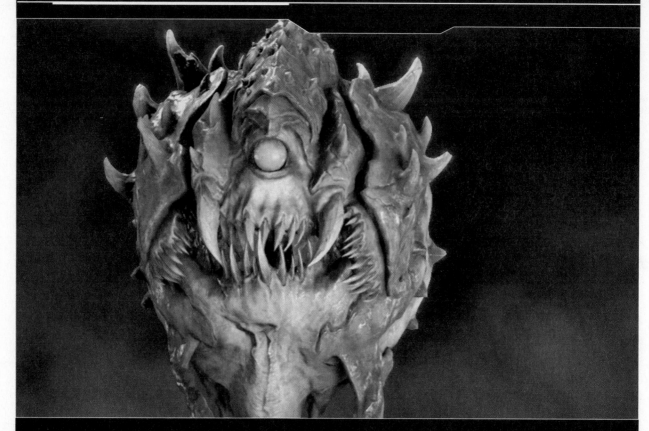

When a Cacodemon senses the presence of the living, it hunts them tenaciously until it gets close enough to gnaw on them with an impressive set of mandibles. To aid the hunt, the Cacodemon has a psychoactive narcotic bile that it spews at range. On contact, this bile inhibits the perception of the target and compromises movement. The effects wear off after a few moments, but this is often just enough time for the lumbering beast to get within bite range.

First Appearance	Kadingir Sanctum
Health	2000
Type	Aerial (rush)
Strengths/ Weaknesses	The Cacodemon's eye is not as sturdy as the rest of its body and takes additional damage when struck. Defeating a Cacodemon by destroying its eye causes it to freak out and fire uncontrollably at nearby allies until it expends all of its energy and collapses to the ground.
Behavior	Cacodemons chase after the player and try to eat them. While their ultimate goal is a melee finisher, these creatures have a potent ranged attack that impair their quarry and make it easier to chomp them.
Restrictions	N/A

ATTACK CHART

NAME	TYPE	LEVEL	DISTANCE	DAMAGE BONUS	NOTES
Bile	Range	Basic	Long	Blind	Splash damage, briefly obscures the player's vision
Chomp	Melee	Advanced	Short	N/A	Has audio cue when they get near players

CYBER-MANCUBUS

The Mancubus strain of demon has long been a subject of fascination among the Lazarus Project scientists. Eager to understand the biology of these creatures, a team of bio-geneticists was formed to research and manipulate the behavior and effect of them.

First Appearance	Advanced Research Complex
Health	3500
Type	Range
Strengths/ Weaknesses	Mancubi torsos are lightly armored and take reduced damage; however, their belly and face are completely exposed. Mancubi innards are volatile by nature and, by executing a Glory Kill, the AI explodes and rains whatever hazard they have stored inside on nearby allies. Targeting flesh deals the most damage. Armor shots deal only 70% damage.
Behavior	Mancubi fire from long range. If you get too close, they clear some room with a swat from their massive gun arm, or a close range AoE attack. This Mancubus type excels at long range with its signature Goo Pile attack.
Restrictions	Must be introduced after Mancubus

ATTACK CHART

NAME	TYPE	LEVEL	DISTANCE	DAMAGE BONUS	NOTES
Gooball	Range	Basic	Long	N/A	Splash damage
Goo Pile	Range	Advanced	Far	Hazard	Damage frequency increases over time
Swipe	Melee	Basic	Short	N/A	-
Shootdown	Melee	Basic	Medium	AoE, Displace	-

HELL KNIGHT

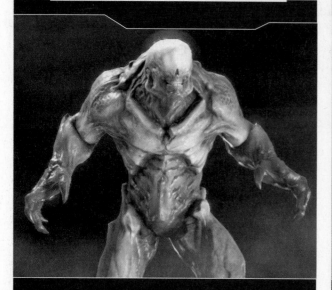

A towering brute bred for combat deep in the bowels of Hell. These diabolical creatures are the prized gladiators of the demon-horde. They relentlessly stomp toward their targets, smashing their massive fists into the ground to create shockwaves that stagger their opponents.

First Appearance	Foundry
Health	1800
Type	Melee
Strengths/ Weaknesses	A well placed shotgun blast to the head stuns the Hell Knight, allowing you to make short work of it when it's not trying to charge you.
Behavior	Hell Knights chase after their prey and try to claw them to death. They don't have any ranged attacks, but do perform aerial strikes that can quickly close the distance.
Restrictions	N/A

ATTACK CHART

NAME	TYPE	LEVEL	DISTANCE	DAMAGE BONUS
Swipe	Melee	Medium	Short	N/A
Ground Slam	Melee	Advanced	Medium	AoE
Smash	Melee	Advanced	Short	AoE

NOTES

Swipe	Can chain together for a multi-hit combo
Ground Slam	Can use during traversals

HELL RAZER

An astute tactical foe that engages enemies from a distance with a powerful beam of unrefined Hell energy. The beam emanates from an arm-like protrusion composed of cartilage and other osseous tissue. A charged shot obliterates anything that stands in its path.

First Appearance	Foundry
Health	600
Type	Range
Strengths/ Weaknesses	Long range weapons like the Assault Rifle can make short work of this medium range foe. When up close, keep an arm's length away to avoid getting hit by its backhand.
Behavior	Hell Razers fire from medium range. If you get too close, they perform a smack with their beam arm and then retreat back to medium range.
Restrictions	N/A

ATTACK CHART

NAME	TYPE	LEVEL	DISTANCE	DAMAGE BONUS
Beam Sweep	Range	Basic	Long	N/A
Charged Beam	Range	Advanced	Long	N/A
Backhand	Melee	Basic	Short	N/A

NOTES

Beam Sweep	Will cancel attack prematurely if another AI enters the path
Charged Beam	Triggers after tracking beam locks-on
Backhand	Can chain together for a multi-hit combo

IMP

These ferocious and agile demons are found all over Hell, and are often used on the front line in a concerted attack in either dimension. They revel in battle, feeding off their victims when the hunger takes them.

First Appearance	The UAC
Health	150
Type	Range
Strengths/ Weaknesses	The Imp has low health, so any weapon quickly kills it. Headshots with the Heavy Assault Rifle are great for taking Imps out from a distance.
Behavior	Imps chuck projectiles from medium range. If you get too close, they swipe at you with their claws and then retreat back to medium range. Imps can also climb obstacles and attack from a zhanging position.
Restrictions	N/A

ATTACK CHART

NAME	TYPE	LEVEL	DISTANCE	DAMAGE BONUS
Fireball	Range	Basic	Medium	N/A
Charged Fireball	Range	Advanced	Medium	N/A
Swipe	Melee	Basic	Short	N/A

NOTES

Swipe	Can chain together for a multi-hit combo

LOST SOUL

Demons found aimlessly within the temples of Hell as they search for a host to inhabit. When a potential victim is found, Lost Souls converge on the target and explode with a Hell blast.

First Appearance	Kadingir Sanctum
Health	75
Type	Aerial (kamikaze)
Strengths/ Weaknesses	Lost Souls immediately detonate when hit with explosive weapons. Slow rate of fire power weapons (like the Shotgun) displace them and trigger a delayed explosion, while high rate of fire low power weapons (like the Plasma Rifle) defuse them.
Behavior	Lost Souls coordinate rushes against a target and explode whenever they come into contact with you or solid geo. Lost Souls are immune to monster in-fighting. Only one Lost Soul charges you at any given time; two in Nightmare.
Restrictions	N/A

ATTACK CHART

NAME	TYPE	LEVEL	DISTANCE	DAMAGE BONUS
Explode	Melee	Basic	Long	AoE, Displace

NOTES

Explode	Only one Lost Soul can charge at a time; two in Nightmare

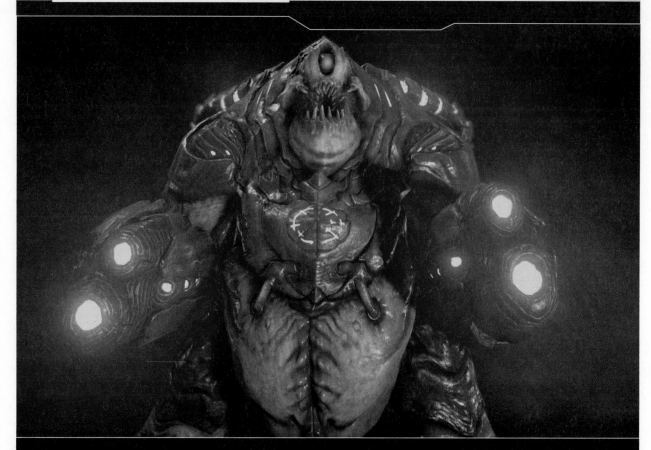

A lumbering behemoth demon with a foul odor that accompanies its grotesque presence. These vile creatures are decked in light armor when they reach maturity, but their grotesque frame soon outgrows it, exposing their stomach and face.

First Appearance	Argent Energy Tower
Health	2500
Type	Range
Strengths/ Weaknesses	Mancubi torsos are lightly armored and take reduced damage; however, their belly and face are completely exposed. Mancubi innards are volatile by nature and, by executing a Glory Kill, the AI explodes and rains whatever hazard they have stored inside on nearby allies. Targeting flesh deals the most damage. Armor shots deal only 70% damage.
Behavior	Mancubus (Flame) fires from long range. If you get too close, they clear some room with a swat from their massive gun arm. This Mancubus type excels at medium range with its signature Flamethrower attack.
Restrictions	N/A

ATTACK CHART

NAME	TYPE	LEVEL	DISTANCE	DAMAGE BONUS	NOTES
Fireball	Range	Basic	Long	N/A	Splash damage
Flamethrower	Range	Advanced	Medium	Hazard	Damage frequency increases over time
Swipe	Melee	Basic	Short	N/A	-
Shootdown	Melee	Basic	Medium	AoE, Displace	-

PINKY

These demonic animals are unnamed by those in Hell. They were colloquially named Pinkies due to their unusual skin pigmentation, when first discovered by the Lazarus Project. Their aggressive nature against the living is well documented.

First Appearance	Argent Facility (Destroyed)
Health	1000
Armor	2000
Type	Melee (charge)
Strengths/ Weaknesses	Pinkies are heavily armored in front and take reduced damage; however, their backs are completely exposed. You can also take advantage of Pinkies' natural aggression and get them to run off ledges to their death. All shots that do not hit the weak points deal only 10% damage.
Behavior	Pinkies chase after their prey and try to gore them. If you get too close, they clear space with a succession of bites. Pinkies don't have any ranged attacks, but can charge to cover a lot of ground quickly.
Restrictions	N/A

ATTACK CHART

NAME	TYPE	LEVEL	DISTANCE	DAMAGE BONUS
Bite	Melee	Basic	Short	N/A
Charge	Melee	Advanced	Long	Displace, Dizzy
Swipe	Melee	Basic	Short	N/A

NOTES

Charge	Only one Pinky can charge at a time; two in Nightmare. Damage scales depending on distance.

POSSESSED ENGINEER

Invariably created when an appropriate explosive material is readily available. Possessed Engineers exhibit self-destructive behavior, sacrificing themselves to provide food sources for other possessed humans.

First Appearance	Resource Operations
Health	150
Type	Melee (kamikaze)
Strengths/ Weaknesses	Possessed Engineers immediately detonate when hit with explosive weapons, while other weapons displace them and trigger a delayed explosion.
Behavior	Possessed Engineers chase after the player until they get within range to detonate. Once a Possessed Engineer has triggered its self-destruct sequence, there's no way to disable it—they've committed to the attack to the bitter end.
Restrictions	UAC maps only

ATTACK CHART

NAME	TYPE	LEVEL	DISTANCE	DAMAGE BONUS
Explode	Melee	Basic	Medium	AoE, Displace

NOTES

Explode	Triggers whenever you get within range or sequence times out

Possessed Security units exhibit the most complex battle strategies of all possessed humans, including mobile shield advances toward its victim and firing while in cover. They also drop their shields to adopt a more accurate firing stance.

First Appearance	Resource Operations
Health	500
Armor	1200
Type	Range (Rush)
Strengths/Weaknesses	A Possessed Security shield absorbs 100% of all damage types, but can be taken off-line by damage overload or the stun shot mod.
Behavior	Possessed Security fire at the player from short range. If you rush them, they smack you with their shield. These creatures never fight without their shield—if it's taken off-line, they stop and restart it.
Restrictions	UAC maps only, must be introduced after Possessed Soldier

ATTACK CHART

NAME	TYPE	LEVEL	DISTANCE	DAMAGE BONUS	NOTES
Burst Fire	Range	Basic	Short	N/A	-
Sustained Fire	Range	Advanced	Short	N/A	-
Shield Bash	Melee	Basic	Short	Dizzy	Briefly obscures the player's vision

If an individual has training in combat (as part of the UAC Military), the Lazarus Wave event transforms them into more than mere slaves. Some subjects continue to display tactical cognizance posthumously after being exposed to Lazarus Waves.

First Appearance	The UAC
Health	400
Type	Range
Strengths/Weaknesses	Aim for the head to deal extra damage.
Behavior	Possessed Soldiers fire from medium range. If you get too close, they smack you with the butt of their weapon and then retreat back to medium range.
Restrictions	UAC maps only

ATTACK CHART

NAME	TYPE	LEVEL	DISTANCE	DAMAGE BONUS	NOTES
Burst Fire	Range	Basic	Medium	N/A	-
Plasma Slug	Range	Advanced	Medium	N/A	Splash damage
Gun Butt	Melee	Basic	Short	N/A	Can chain together for a multi-hit combo

REVENANT

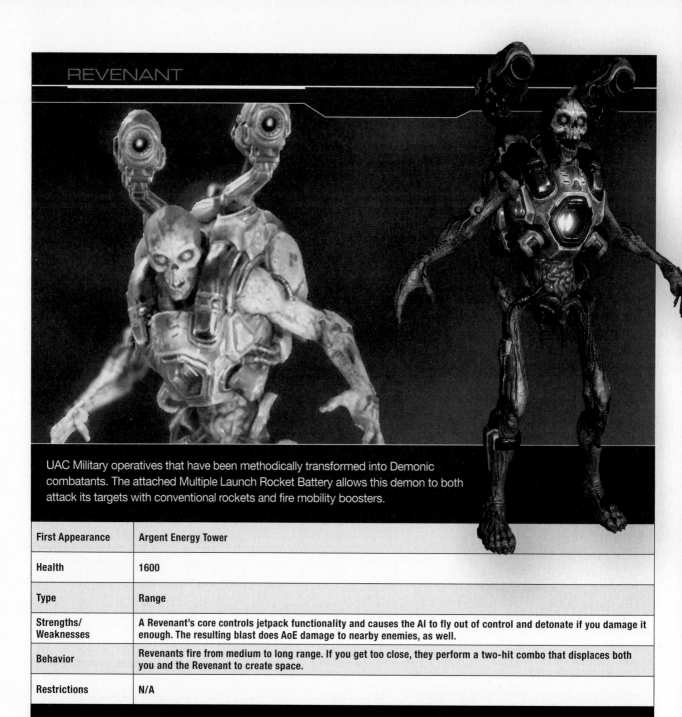

UAC Military operatives that have been methodically transformed into Demonic combatants. The attached Multiple Launch Rocket Battery allows this demon to both attack its targets with conventional rockets and fire mobility boosters.

First Appearance	Argent Energy Tower
Health	1600
Type	Range
Strengths/ Weaknesses	A Revenant's core controls jetpack functionality and causes the AI to fly out of control and detonate if you damage it enough. The resulting blast does AoE damage to nearby enemies, as well.
Behavior	Revenants fire from medium to long range. If you get too close, they perform a two-hit combo that displaces both you and the Revenant to create space.
Restrictions	N/A

ATTACK CHART

NAME	TYPE	LEVEL	DISTANCE	DAMAGE BONUS	NOTES
Burst Fire (ground)	Range	Basic	Medium	N/A	Splash damage
Burst Fire (aerial)	Range	Basic	Medium	N/A	Splash damage, can use while hopping in any direction
Missile Barrage	Range	Advanced	Long	N/A	Splash damage
Missile Lock-On	Range	Advanced	Long	N/A	Splash damage, triggers after tracking lasers lock-on
Swipe	Melee	Basic	Short	N/A	Can chain together for a multi-hit combo

SPECTRE

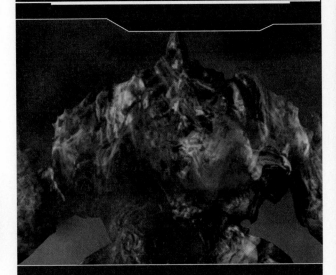

An unfortunate result of a misguided attempt to genetically modify a Pinky. Four beasts were captured; only one survived the vivisection and ended up with slight psionic abilities. The beast was accidentally released, thinking it had escaped its pen due to its new-found cloaking ability.

First Appearance	Titan's Realm
Health	2000
Type	Melee (charge)
Strengths/ Weaknesses	Unlike Pinkies, Spectres don't have any armor, but they do have a cloaking device and only a rough outline of them is visible. Take advantage of this creature's natural aggression by coaxing them into running off ledges to their death. Shoot them with a Stun Shot to disable their cloaking device.
Behavior	Spectres chase their victims and try to gore them. If you get too close, they clear space with a succession of bites. These beasts don't have any ranged attacks, but can charge to cover significant ground quickly.
Restrictions	Must be introduced after Pinky

ATTACK CHART

NAME	TYPE	LEVEL	DISTANCE	DAMAGE BONUS
Bite	Melee	Basic	Short	N/A
Charge	Melee	Advanced	Long	Displace, Dizzy
Swipe	Melee	Basic	Short	N/A

NOTES

Charge	Only one Spectre can charge at a time; two in Nightmare. Damage scales depending on distance.

SUMMONER

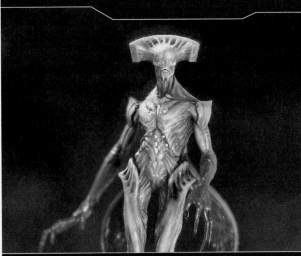

A cunning, primarily defensive summoning unit. The Summoner sustains the battle by opening a rift to Hell and calling forth reinforcements. When directly challenged in combat, the Summoner is capable of channeling Hell energy into a Lazarus Wave.

First Appearance	Argent Facility
Health	1400
Type	Range (Summoner)
Strengths/ Weaknesses	There's no limit to the number of AIs a Summoner can evoke, so it's best to eliminate them quickly to avoid being overrun. Use the chainsaw or rush them with a shotgun to take them down before they teleport.
Behavior	In offensive mode, Summoners stay at long range and relentlessly attack; in defensive mode, this creature prefers to summon other AI. If the player gets too close, they explode outward a bubble of energy and then teleport back to long range.
Restrictions	N/A

ATTACK CHART

NAME	TYPE	LEVEL	DISTANCE	DAMAGE BONUS
Waveblast (defense)	Range	Basic	Long	N/A
Waveblast (offensive)	Range	Advanced	Long	N/A
Energy Bubble	Melee	Basic	Medium	AoE, Displace

Created in a Lazarus Wave event. Those who survive absorb traces of Argent energy and enter a state of posthumous vigor. Despite necrosis of the internal organs, the victim continues to animate and exhibit dim awareness for weeks or even months after clinical death.

First Appearance	The UAC
Health	150
Type	Melee
Strengths/ Weaknesses	The Possessed can still keep fighting after limb loss.
Behavior	Possessed chase their victims and try to bludgeon them to death. They are great at surprising players, either by playing dead or dropping into encounters.
Restrictions	UAC maps only

ATTACK CHART

NAME	TYPE	LEVEL	DISTANCE	DAMAGE BONUS	NOTES
Swipe	Melee	Basic	Short	N/A	Can only use if an arm is still intact
Bite	Melee	Basic	Short	N/A	Can only use if both arms are gone
Lunge	Melee	Advanced	Medium	N/A	Can only use if an arm is still intact

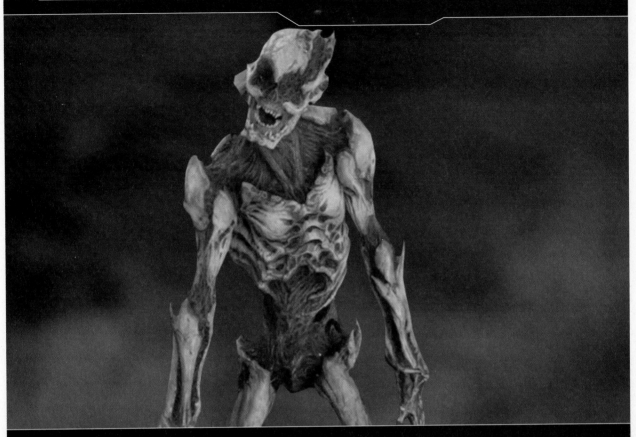

The Unwilling are fully transformed Hell Slaves that have been transported to Hell to serve as shrine worshippers, slave labor for higher level demons, or cannon fodder for battle within Hell.

First Appearance	Argent Energy Tower
Health	150
Type	Melee
Strengths/Weaknesses	Unwilling can still keep fighting after limb loss.
Behavior	Unwilling chase their victims and try to bludgeon them to death.
Restrictions	Hell maps only, unless summoned by a Summoner

ATTACK CHART

NAME	TYPE	LEVEL	DISTANCE	DAMAGE BONUS	NOTES
Swipe	Melee	Basic	Short	N/A	Can only use if an arm is still intact
Bite	Melee	Basic	Short	N/A	Can only use if both arms are gone
Lunge	Melee	Advanced	Medium	N/A	Can only use if an arm is still intact

RUNES

Starting with Mission 4, Argent Facility, two Trial Stones appear on the map. By interacting with one, you attempt a Rune Trial—a short test such as killing enemies with a specific weapon or collecting a certain number of items (all within a time limit). The trials end in Mission 9, Lazarus Labs.

Completing each trial earns a Rune that can be equipped in the Dossier. These Runes provide valuable bonuses that can tip a battle in your favor. Each one can also be upgraded by completing a Challenge.

You start with one slot, but after completing a certain number of trials, more can be equipped. Select the Rune tab in the Dossier to see how many slots are available and which Runes you've collected. You can also check your progress toward upgrading each Rune. Note that a Rune must be equipped to make any progress.

SLOTS

SLOT	HOW TO UNLOCK
1	Unlocked at first Rune Trial
2	Complete 4 Rune Trials
3	Complete 7 Rune Trials

:X THE RUNES

The following table lists the 12 Runes, along with upgrade information. The Rune Trials are also covered in this chapter in the order that they appear in the game.

RUNE	DESCRIPTION	UPGRADE REQUIREMENT	UPGRADE
Vacuum	Increases the range that you can absorb dropped items.	Absorb 300 dropped items.	Further increases range for absorbing dropped items.
Dazed and Confused	Increases how long demons remain in a stagger state.	Perform 25 Death from Above Glory Kills.	Demon staggers last even longer.
Ammo Boost	Increases the value of ammo received from demons and items.	Pick up 500 Ammo Items.	BFG ammo has a chance to drop from demons.
Equipment Power	Increases effectiveness of Equipment items.	Use 30 Equipment Items.	Further increases effectiveness of Equipment items.
Seek and Destroy	Launch into a Glory Kill from much further away.	Glory Kill 75 demons.	Increases the distance that Seek and Destroy can be initiated.
Savagery	Perform Glory Kills faster.	Perform 25 unique Glory Kills while Savagery is equipped.	Further increases the speed of Glory Kills.
In-Flight Mobility	Provides a significant increase in control over in-air movement after a double jump.	Kill 30 demons while in mid-air.	Applies air control to a single jump.
Armored Offensive	Glory Killing demons drops armor.	Earn 2500 points of Armor.	More armor drops per Glory Kill.
Blood Fueled	Move faster for a short time after performing a Glory Kill.	Kill 50 demons during the speed boost.	Extends how long you can move faster after a Glory Kill.
Intimacy is Best	Demons become more Glory Kill friendly due to a high damage resistance when staggered.	Stagger 100 demons.	Demons stagger off of less damage.
Rich Get Richer	Firing your standard weapons will not cost ammo when you have 100 Armor or more.	Fill your Armor value to max 12 times.	Activate Rich Get Richer at 75 Armor.
Saving Throw	Get one chance to survive a death blow and recover health. This resets on death.	Kill 10 demons while Saving Throw is active.	Get an additional Saving Throw per life.

:X THE TRIALS

ARGENT FACILITY

RUNE TRIAL: Vacuum

OBJECTIVE: Use the Combat Shotgun to eliminate 15 Imps before the timer expires.

Count	15
Weapon	Shotgun
Time	10 Seconds
Bonus	+2 seconds per kill (+4 seconds per Glory Kill)
Reward	Vacuum Rune

After jumping down from the tower at the start of the mission, follow the trail right to find the first Trial Stone. Interact with it to attempt the challenge.

Your goal is to kill 15 Imps with the Shotgun before the timer reaches zero. As you eliminate Imps, seconds are added to the timer, with an extra bonus for Glory Kills. Take advantage of this, as time is extremely valuable in these trials. The arena is relatively small for this trial, so getting to each Imp quickly is manageable. They spawn in a couple at a time, so quickly spin around to find the next target. You can take these weak demons out with one close shot, but it's possible to weaken them from medium range and then perform a Glory Kill as soon as you're close enough.

RUNE TRIAL: Dazed and Confused

OBJECTIVE: Armed with the Pistol, destroy 30 barrels before the timer expires.

Count	30
Weapon	Pistol
Time	6 Seconds
Bonus	+2 seconds per barrel destroyed
Reward	Dazed and Confused Rune

There are 30 barrels scattered all around the map. Quickly detonate them with your Pistol. Since this weapon has infinite ammo, feel free to quickly fire a few shots at distant barrels to be sure get your target. The arena is relatively small, but it's still a fair distance to cover to get all 30 within the time allotted.

After destroying the second Argent Filter and before hopping over the railing, enter the garage to the right and head over to the bays against the right

wall. Climb onto the platform at Bay 2 and interact with the stone to begin the Rune Trial.

ARGENT ENERGY TOWER

RUNE TRIAL: Ammo Boost

OBJECTIVE: Use the Super Shotgun to eliminate 30 Unwilling before the timer expires.

Count	30
Weapon	Super Shotgun
Time	6 Seconds
Bonus	+2 seconds per kill (+4 seconds per Glory Kill)
Reward	Ammo Boost Rune

After collecting the Jump Boots, return to the loading dock entrance, turn around, and jump up to the next level. Turn left and drop into the room on the left to find a Trial Stone.

The goal is to simply kill 30 Unwilling before the timer runs out, but with the slow reload of the Super Shotgun, the trial becomes a bit tougher. Avoid

getting surrounded as you quickly plow through the demons. Purchasing the Faster Reload upgrade for the Super Shotgun and equipping Runes that improve Glory Kills are a huge help in the trial.

RUNE TRIAL: Equipment Power

OBJECTIVE: Armed with the Combat Shotgun eliminate 10 Unwilling with explosive barrel damage before the timer expires.

Count	10
Weapon	Shotgun
Time	12 Seconds
Bonus	+3 seconds per kill with explosive barrels
Reward	Equipment Power Rune

After scaling to the top of the tower interior, you enter the outside rooms. Clear out the demon presence in the narrow corridor, move to the far end, and turn left. Climb

through the window above the 6-1 notation and continue left across the platform to reach the Trial Stone.

The objective here is to take out 10 Unwilling by detonating the explosive barrels. Always stay a safe distance from the Unwilling. They can easily take you out; you lose the

trial if you're caught in a blast. The key is getting multiple hits with the explosions, and the bonus received for each kill is a huge help. Quickly detonate the explosives, staying on the move to avoid running into one of the monsters. Often, a detonation only weakens nearby demons, so be sure to get it with the next barrel.

RUNE TRIAL: Savagery

OBJECTIVE: Kill Imps with the Super Shotgun to allow movement for four seconds. Imps may be killed or spared at your discretion. Reach the Altar before the timer expires.

Objective	Reach the Altar
Weapon	Super Shotgun
Time	5 Seconds
Bonus	+4 seconds movement time per kill
Reward	Savagery Rune

After collecting the Yellow Skull, look for the stone archway on the ground floor and jump onto the roof. Turn around, double jump up to a small platform, and continue up to the ledge ahead. Follow the corridor to the first Trial Stone.

Your objective is to reach the Altar, but you can only move after killing an Imp. Each kill nets you four seconds of movement time, so make it count by running throughout. To reach the Altar, you must double jump from the cliff to one of the narrow ledges and then traverse the two ledges until you reach your destination. You need to make a few tricky jumps between the ledges, taking out the Imps as you land. It's vital to make up as much ground as possible between the demons or else it's a tough target with the Shotgun.

RUNE TRIAL: Seek and Destroy

OBJECTIVE: Use the Heavy Assault Rifle to weaken and perform Death from Above Glory Kills on three Hell Knights before the timer expires.

Count	3
Weapon	Heavy Assault Rifle
Time	30 Seconds
Bonus	+20 seconds per Glory Kill
Reward	Seek and Destroy Rune

After defeating the demons in the AutoMap Station area, look for the tall staircase that leads out of the area. Before climbing it, turn left to find the second Trial Stone.

The goal in this Rune Trial is to perform Death from Above Glory Kills on three Hell Knights before the timer expires. You're equipped with the Heavy Assault Rifle, so use it to weaken the big guy. Only one spawns in at a time, so no need to worry about being surrounded. However, weaker enemies do present a small danger. Look for the Hell Knight to spawn in and immediately start firing at the foe. Once it begins to flash, perform a Glory Kill from above. If you're on the same level as it, double jump into the air and perform the move.

RUNE TRIAL: In-Flight Mobility

OBJECTIVE: Collect all 15 Hell Relics and reach the Altar before the timer expires.

Count	15
Weapon	Super Shotgun
Time	16 Seconds
Bonus	+1 second per Hell Relic collected
Reward	In-Flight Mobility Rune

Climb up the crates toward the Security Station and turn left to spot the Trial Stone. Jump over and interact with it to begin the next challenge.

Your objective is to collect 15 Hell Relics that are lined up along the two narrow ledges ahead and reach the Altar before the timer hits zero. This is the same map used in the Savagery Rune Trial during the previous mission, so you may be familiar with the jumps required to reach your destination. This time, your movement is not limited and there are no Imps to take out. Zigzag between the two sides as you collect the relics. You must be quick to reach the Altar with all 15, so stay on the move.

RUNE TRIAL: Armored Offensive

OBJECTIVE: Use the Combat Shotgun to eliminate all targets before the timer expires. Health levels are critical. Use armor to survive.

Count	8
Weapon	Shotgun
Time	1:10
Bonus	None
Reward	Armored Offensive Rune

After exiting the facility, follow the path left and hop down to the right to reach another walkway. Follow this one right until you find the second Trial Stone.

The goal here is to use the Shotgun to eliminate all eight demons before the timer reaches zero. You have 1:10 to get it done and there are no time bonuses. You start out against two Unwilling. As you proceed through the trial, two Imps, a Hell Knight, a Pinky, and two Possessed Soldiers spawn in. Your health is critical with no way to increase it, but there are piles of small armors scattered throughout the map. Stay on the move, but you should spend almost the entire time firing shells at an enemy.

RUNE TRIAL: Blood Fueled

OBJECTIVE: Armed with the Heavy Assault Rifle, eliminate all targets before the timer expires. Movement is permitted for only three seconds following any kill.

Count	15
Weapon	Heavy Assault Rifle
Time	1:00
Bonus	None
Reward	Blood Fueled Rune

Disable the security field. Then instead of exiting through the new opening, enter the airlock ahead to find the first Trial Stone.

With the HAR equipped, kill the demons around the arena before the one-minute timer expires. There are no time bonuses and you can move for only three seconds after each kill. When the movement icon appears on screen, quickly head for some ammo or the next enemy. Beware, though, the Imps do tend to run toward you. Occasionally, you may need to take one out from a distance, so always be looking for your next target.

RUNE TRIAL: Intimacy is Best

OBJECTIVE: Use the Pistol to weaken and then Glory Kill eight Imps before the timer expires.

Count	8
Weapon	Pistol
Time	20 Seconds
Bonus	+3 seconds per Glory Kill
Reward	Intimacy is Best Rune

After opening the Lazarus Elevator, turn right and enter Testing Chamber 1. Turn left and follow the narrow corridor to find the second Trial Stone.

Using the Pistol, you must perform eight Glory Kills on the Imps before the timer reaches zero. A three-second bonus is given each time a Glory Kill is performed, but you still need to take the demons out quickly. Be careful not to kill the Imps. Rapidly fire a few shots into a demon as you move its way. Once they begin flashing, press the Glory Kill button.

RUNE TRIAL: Rich Get Richer

OBJECTIVE: Armed with the Rocket Launcher and using only the resources found in the area, eliminate all targets before the timer expires. Targets do not drop resources when destroyed.

Count	14
Weapon	Rocket Launcher
Time	1:30
Bonus	None
Reward	Rich Get Richer Rune

At the top of the steps, open the hatch in the floor to drop into a maintenance access. Move further inside and double jump up through the hole in the ceiling to find the Trial Stone.

Equipped with a Rocket Launcher, take out 14 demons around the arena in 1:30. There are neither time bonuses nor any health pickups. There are a few ammo pickups in case you run out of rockets. You must stay on the move and always be aware of your surroundings. If you take too many hits from the monsters, there is no way to recoup the losses. Quickly fire rockets at the enemies, finishing them off with Glory Kills when available. Splash damage also works to weaken the foes, so firing an explosive at their feet or a nearby wall is better than nothing.

RUNE TRIAL: Saving Throw

OBJECTIVE: Armed with the Gauss Cannon and using only the resources found in the area, eliminate all targets before the timer expires. Health levels are critical and targets do not drop resources when destroyed.

Count	9
Weapon	Gauss Cannon
Time	35 Seconds
Bonus	+2 seconds per kill
Reward	Saving Throw Rune

After dropping down the shaft and finding the Elite Guard, access the Trial Stone ahead to begin the final Rune Trial.

Equipped with the powerful Gauss Cannon, kill the nine demons that spawn around the map before the 35-second timer reaches zero. Your health is critical and there is no way to heal, so avoiding the enemy attacks is key to success. Ammunition is scattered all around the area, so pick these up to keep your gun topped off. A variety of monsters show up in this challenge, including a Spectre. Each foe presents a danger, even the Imps, since one hit ends the trial. The Gauss Cannon requires precise accuracy to take these guys out. Stay on the move when not firing, but don't spend much time setting up your shot. Avoid getting surrounded when moving through the middle of the map.

CLASSIC MAPS

Each campaign mission hides a big secret—a map from the original DOOM or DOOM II. Once discovered in the game, the full map becomes playable. Select your campaign save slot and then click Classic Maps to see the available levels.

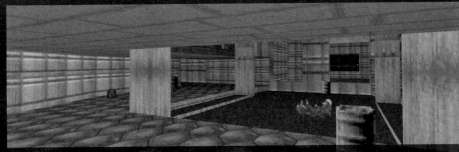

CAMPAIGN
CLASSIC MAPS

Doom - Hangar

Doom - Nuclear Plant

Doom - Toxin Refinery

Doom - Command Control

Doom - Phobos Lab

Doom - Phobos Anomaly

Doom - Halls of the Damned

Doom - Tower of Babel

Doom - Slough of Despair

Doom - Pandemonium

 SELECT   BACK

Doom - Hangar

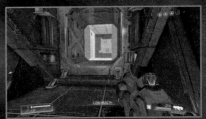

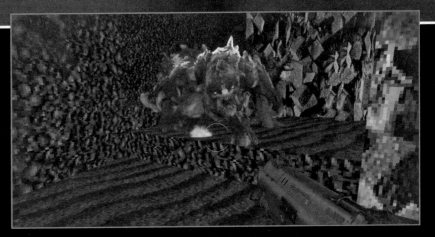

Look for a mechanical lever concealed in each mission. Often well hidden in the environment, accessing the lever may require completing an action before it is revealed. Once found, pull the lever to expose a new room containing a portion of the Classic Map. Enemies and resources are frequently found inside as the full level becomes available at the Classic Maps menu. Finding these secret areas contributes toward a Weapon Upgrade Point.

The maps are identical to the original games, but the enemies and your weapons come from the modern game. Your goal in every mission is to reach the exit, whether that's a switch or a symbol on the ground. This may involve finding a color key or two to open the corresponding color doors.

Instead of dropping their weapon, the monsters release resources similar to the main game. Perform Glory Kills on them to gain extra health. You do need to worry about the z-axis in this game; shooting straight ahead will not kill a demon above or below.

Use your double jump to reach ledges that are normally out of reach. You can also reduce the damage taken in toxic areas by double jumping your way through. Do not underestimate the barrels. If a group of enemies wanders near one, detonate it, but make sure you're at a safe distance.

MAP	MISSION FOUND	ORIGINAL MISSION NUMBER
Hangar	Resource Operations	E1M1
Nuclear Plant	Foundry	E1M2
Toxin Refinery	Argent Facility	E1M3
Command Control	VEGA Central Processing	E1M4
Phobos Lab	Advanced Research Complex	E1M5
Phobos Anomaly	Titan's Realm	E1M8
Halls of the Damned	Argent Energy Tower	E2M6
Tower of Babel	Lazarus Labs	E2M8
Slough of Despair	Kadingir Sanctum	E3M2
Pandemonium	Argent D'Nur	E3M3
House of Pain	The Necropolis	E3M4
Entryway	The UAC	DOOM II – Level 1
Underhalls	Argent Facility (Destroyed)	DOOM II – Level 2

Discover the locations of all 13 Classic Maps and how to unlock them.

:X DOOM - HANGAR

MISSION FOUND Resource Operations

ACCESS THE MAP

After dropping through the Maintenance Bay Door, move to the far corner of the room, climb onto the crates, and grab the armor. Follow the railing to the right and jump over to the left ledge. Climb up to find the lever. Pull it to open the door below. Drop down and enter the Classic Map room.

MAP STRATEGY

The first episode of DOOM, E1M1, acts as an introduction to the world and is fairly straightforward. Go left and grab the armor, then fight your way through the Possessed Soldiers and Imps until you reach the exit switch.

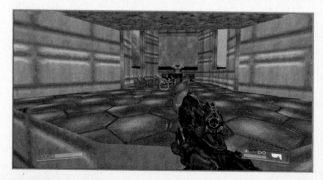

:X DOOM – NUCLEAR PLANT

MISSION FOUND Foundry

ACCESS THE MAP

Stop on the bridge that overlooks a Gore Nest and hop over the left railing onto the platform to find the lever. Pull it before returning to the bridge. Continue to the far side and find the Classic Map on the wall ahead to the left. This portion of Nuclear Plant is fairly big with plenty of enemies and items.

MAP STRATEGY

To exit this map, you must collect the red key found up the stairs before getting through the red door near the entrance. Activate a switch on the back of a pillar in the poison room. A second switch is found after defeating a group of demons. Follow the hallways to a staircase that leads down to the exit.

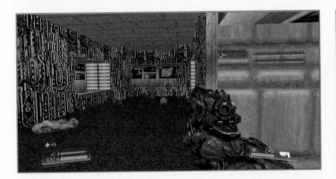

:X DOOM – TOXIN REFINERY

MISSION FOUND Argent Facility

ACCESS THE MAP

Near the start of the mission, after the first Trial Stone, search behind the barrels on the left platform to find a lever. Activate it, proceed into the next facility, and collect the Rocket Launcher. The Classic Map is accessed through the opening on the right.

Toxin Refinery requires a blue key to complete the level, while a yellow key provides access to a secret area. A switch near a second blue door is tucked into a corner, but it's visible through the window. Search in the middle of the computer room for the yellow key. This room has two secret passages. Return to the second step before the room and then quickly get on the left lift. When exiting that area, run for a second lift in the back. This gets you a Mega Health and Rocket Launcher. More secrets can be found from this second room by cutting through the toxin. After a short outdoor area, grab the blue key from its perch, but beware of an ambush. Return to the blue door and follow the path to the exit. There's another exit if you cross the raised path at the start of the map.

:X DOOM - COMMAND CONTROL

MISSION FOUND VEGA Central Processing

ACCESS THE MAP

Obtain the blue keycard and go through the blue keycard door. Take a left into the area labeled "Sector P Access" and go through the other blue keycard door next to the AutoMap Station. Look behind the crates the elite guard is propped up against to find the switch and interact with it. Return to area where the blue keycard was obtained and explore the halls. The entrance to the Classic Map area is at the end of the hall.

MAP STRATEGY

Two keys are required to finish this map, blue and yellow. Follow the left path to reach an octagonal room. Open one of the doors and take out the Imps before collecting the blue key. The blue door leads into a maze. Watch out for the Pinkies in the narrow corridors. It's tough to dodge their attacks. You can sometimes lure them back to an open area. Avoid their charge and shoot them in the back. The yellow key is just beyond the maze. Throw the switch next to the yellow door and proceed to the exit.

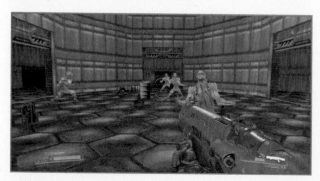
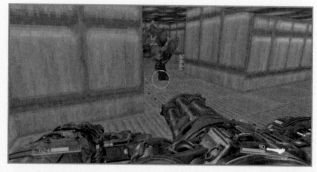

:X DOOM – PHOBOS LAB

MISSION FOUND Advanced Research Complex

ACCESS THE MAP

After disabling the force field, hop across the platforms ahead to reach the top of the left rock formation. Double jump to the ledge above the pipe exit to collect the Mega Health. Hop across the rocks to the left over to the pipes and drop down to find the lever. Pull it to open a door near the previous Gore Nest. Make your way back to that area to find the Classic Map in the far wall.

MAP STRATEGY

You need yellow and blue keys to complete this mission. There are lots of enemies in the first area, so be ready for a big fight. Take care of the Pinky and Possessed Soldiers to the right before stepping onto the balcony. This raises a bridge along the wall. Follow the new path to the yellow key. At the poison pool, turn around and access the secret area for a chainsaw. Throw the switch and return to the yellow door room. The blue key is found by following the path ahead. This new path leads to the exit.

:X DOOM – PHOBOS ANOMALY

MISSION FOUND Titan's Realm

ACCESS THE MAP

Defeat the demons in the room beyond the yellow gate and activate the Skull Switch in the ceiling. This reveals a lever near the entrance to the room. Pull it and return to the poison room to find the Classic Map accessible on the right wall.

MAP STRATEGY

At the start, hit one of the barrels to take out the Pinkies. Ride the elevator to find a pair of Barons of Hell. It's possible to take cover inside one of the small rooms. Otherwise, take out the other demons before focusing on the big guys. Activate the switch and follow the steps up to the exit.

:X DOOM - HALLS OF THE DAMNED

MISSION FOUND Argent Energy Tower

ACCESS THE MAP

After activating the Argent Drones, exit the control room and head to 4-A on the opposite side of the tower. Wait for the Drone to exit its dock and hop on. Ride it all the way up and jump forward to find the lever. Pull it to open the Classic Map directly below. With the Drone away from its dock, enter the room to find ammo, health, and armor.

MAP STRATEGY

Halls of the Damned requires three keys to complete: blue, red, and yellow. Start by collecting the blue key. Use the Berserk powerup near the outdoor switch and enter the new door on the left, next to the blue door. Fight your way to the left to find the first key. The other two keys can be picked up in either order. Fight your way through the darker tunnels and search the corners to find the red key. A few Pinkies inhabit this area, so try not to attract a crowd. Look for the gray, stone corridor and follow it into a star-shaped room. Enter the right door to find the last key. Watch out for Cacodemons. To exit, go through the blue door you passed earlier, followed by the red, and finally yellow.

:X DOOM – TOWER OF BABEL

MISSION FOUND Lazarus Labs

ACCESS THE MAP

In the room with the pit, descend the staircase and look in the nook to the right. The switch is next to some candles. Drop into the pit to find the Classic Map entrance.

MAP STRATEGY

Tower of Babel starts out in a small room with three doors and switches. Activating them reveals steps in front of each door. Enter each one and grab the resources and then proceed outside to face the Cyberdemon. Light it up with the Rocket Launcher as you strafe to avoid its own rockets. Watch out when close as it swipes with a scythe. Defeat the beast to complete the mission.

DOOM – SLOUGH OF DESPAIR

MISSION FOUND Kadingir Sanctum

ACCESS THE MAP

After defeating the Barons of Hell, look for the small cave directly across from the exit. Inside, throw the lever to open the hidden Classic Map. Move over to the big door and drop off to the right. Make an immediate right to spot the opening down the hill. Move inside and make your way through the maze to find two skulls on the walls ahead. Interact with both to open the wall, revealing several resources, including a Mega Health.

As you reveal the map, it forms a boney hand. From the start, head left until you reach the blue key at the end of the "pinky." Look for skull switches in the fingers and activate them. One such switch hides behind the blue door. This reveals the exit to the left.

:X DOOM - PANDEMONIUM

MISSION FOUND Argent D'Nur

ACCESS THE MAP

After activating the second Secret Skull Switch, just after interacting with the first Wraith, jump down and find the new opening to the right. Follow the tunnel to the back and climb up the ledge. Pull the lever found just ahead to reveal the Classic Map to the right.

MAP STRATEGY

Head up the stairs and then take the narrow steps on the right. Follow the path right until you reach a metallic room. There are numerous secret areas and resources to collect, including the BFG, if you veer off the main path. Otherwise, return to the start and go right. Enter the blue door and exit the map.

:X DOOM - HOUSE OF PAIN

MISSION FOUND The Necropolis

ACCESS THE MAP

After grabbing the Yellow Skull and defeating the ensuing attack, approach the exit portal and search the nook on the right to find the lever. Then return to the previous room, where you found the Argent Cell, to discover a new opening on the right wall. Step inside to unlock the map.

MAP STRATEGY

Three keys must be collected to exit House of Pain. The left and right paths lead to resources. Head up the middle until you reach two round pits. Give them a wide berth to avoid triggering them. Throw the left and middle switches to raise the platforms in the pits. Quickly grab the resources. The right switch opens the path to the right. The blue key is in the far corridor. Enter the nearby blue door and follow the path ahead until you reach two pillars with skull switches. Two switches on the right open two doors to the right, one of which holds the yellow key. Two on the left pillar open the left doors. Find the red key behind one and the red door behind the other. Continue to the exit.

:X DOOM II - ENTRYWAY

MISSION FOUND The UAC

ACCESS THE MAP

After finding the Elite Guard and dropping to the surface, move further down the path and descend another level. Look at the map and spot the Field Drone icon on an upper ledge. If you've already approached this Drone, it may have moved further ahead. Just below its original location, a crate blocks an entrance. Turn around and find an opening in the cage on the left. Enter and pull the lever found inside. This removes the blockage, revealing the first Classic Map.

MAP STRATEGY

As the first level of DOOM II, this map is relatively short and straightforward. You start with only the Pistol, so immediately turn around and collect the Chainsaw. Follow the hall all the way down and turn right. Continue through the big room to find the exit on the left.

:X DOOM II – UNDERHALLS

MISSION FOUND   Argent Facility (Destroyed)

ACCESS THE MAP

Look for the octagonal platform on the right near the start of the mission. Jump over to the upper platform and search behind the cargo to find the lever. Activate it and return to the previous walkway. Turn around and hop down to level 1 to find the entrance to the Classic Map.

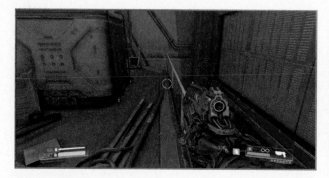

MAP STRATEGY

The second map of DOOM II is also fairly straightforward. From the start, go left to unlock the path, then follow the water to the right. Fight your way through Possessed Soldiers and Security until you reach a room with holes in two corners. Drop into the left one to find the blue key. Return to the water and enter the blue door across the corridor.

COLLECTIBLES

Look out for the Collectibles hidden throughout the environment in the DOOM campaign. There are two dolls per mission and each one unlocks a model at the Collectibles menu. Access this menu by selecting your campaign save slot.

The following list of collectibles is sorted by mission, in order of how they are found in game.

:X THE UAC

BLUEGUY

UNLOCKS Combat Shotgun Model

Just after collecting the blue access key, climb onto the crate. Jump over to the rock ledge and collect the first Collectible, Blueguy.

CLASSICGUY

UNLOCKS Imp Model

After clearing out the narrow valley, look for a tunnel on the left side. Follow it until you're back outside to find the second Collectible on the ledge.

:X RESOURCE OPERATIONS

DOOMGUY

UNLOCKS Doom Marine Model

On your way to the terminal in an attempt to realign the satellite dish, look for a lone crate and climb on top. Continue onto the venting above, then head right, turn around, and hop onto another vent. Climb onto the roof to the right when you reach the ladder. Run straight toward the big building and look for the maintenance access. Step inside to find the first Collectible, Doomguy. From there, an open hatch leads you directly to the next objective.

BRONZEGUY

UNLOCKS Heavy Assault Rifle Model

Before entering the VEGA terminal room, climb the pile of crates to the left and enter the maintenance shaft above. Follow the chute to find the second Collectible, Bronzeguy.

:X FOUNDRY

VAULTGUY

UNLOCKS Possessed Engineer Model

After collecting the Yellow Keycard, turn around and hop over the left railing onto a metal platform. Search under the walkway to find the first Collectible, Vaultguy.

PROTOTYPEGUY

UNLOCKS Plasma Rifle Model

Before you take care of the Gore Nest in the room past the conveyer belt, search inside the middle of three boxes on the belt. Inside is the second Collectible, Prototypeguy.

:X ARGENT FACILITY

UACGUY

UNLOCKS Hell Knight Model

Look for the stack of crates inside the Cargo Station after destroying the Argent Filter in the upper floor of the garage. Use them to reach a maintenance access area above the lights. Look left to find the Collectible, UACguy.

STEALTHGUY

UNLOCKS   Rocket Launcher Model

Exit via the back of the Cooling Tower and go left. Hop over the gap in the pathway and climb up the shaft to the left. Instead of jumping over the chasm, walk right along the narrow ledge. Hop through an opening on the right and collect the Collectible on a small box ahead.

:X ARGENT ENERGY TOWER

ORANGEGUY

UNLOCKS   UAC Pistol Model

After spotting Olivia at the elevator and defeating the demons in the next corridor, enter the maintenance access and collect the Data Log from the desk. Turn toward the cargo containers and look up. There's a Collectible a couple of levels up, but it takes a little effort to obtain. Drop down, go left to the far end, and climb onto the stationary container. Wait for the cargo above to pass and then jump to the narrow ledge. Walk up the beam, turn around, and jump over to a smaller ledge. Wait for the next container to pass and then jump into the left hole and follow it through. Hop down to the left ledge to grab the Collectible, Orangeguy.

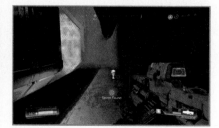

PURPLEGUY

UNLOCKS   Summoner Model

As you scale the tower, you move between platforms along the outer wall and center. At the second central platform, check out the map and spot the location of the second Collectible. Head up the left or right incline, depending on where the collectible is. At the outer wall, step out to the left or right and look down at the beam below the walkway to spot the doll.
Drop down and collect the Purpleguy. Jump down to the platform below and make your way back to the previous location.

:X KADINGIR SANCTUM

ASTROGUY

UNLOCKS Revenant Model

Activate the skull switch to open the yellow door ahead. There are rising rocks in the area beyond this door. Drop down and step inside to find a portal. Before entering it, follow the path to the right to find Astroguy.

REDGUY

UNLOCKS Mancubus Model

About halfway up the staircase next to the Seek and Destroy Rune Trial Stone, turn to the right and look for a rectangular stone sandwiched between two spires. Climb onto the rock to find the second Collectible, Redguy.

:X ARGENT FACILITY (DESTROYED)

RAGEGUY

UNLOCKS Cacodemon Model

From the walkway toward the beginning of the map and near a broken staircase, hop down to the level 1 platform and move into the cubbyhole on the left. The first Collectible is on a small case ahead, surrounded by ammunition and armor.

PATRIOTGUY

UNLOCKS   Baron of Hell Model

After grabbing the Yellow Keycard, stop at the top of the steps as you move toward the yellow gate. Jump up and climb into the maintenance access. The Collectible is on top of a case in the next room.

:X:ADVANCED RESEARCH COMPLEX

PHOBOSGUY

UNLOCKS   Super Shotgun Model

From the Argent Cell outside in the ravine, turn around, jump over to the ledge on the left, and move right. Climb up the ledges to find a small cave. The Collectible is in the back.

PINKGUY

UNLOCKS   Pinky Model

Head right from the maintenance room (where you used the fan to pass through the air scrubber area) and enter Prototype Lab 01 at the second door. Climb onto the equipment in the middle of the room and face right. Jump into the small shaft and follow the maintenance access until you find a Collectible. Continuing through this access drops you into the Server Room.

:X LAZARUS LABS

ELITEGUY

UNLOCKS Olivia Pierce Model

After finding the second Elite Guard, follow the steps into the next room. Once the monsters have been cleared out, move over to the artifacts along the left side of the room. Slip around one of them and crawl through the vent to reach a hidden hallway. Move toward the center and search down the perpendicular passage to find a Collectible.

TOXICGUY

UNLOCKS Samuel Hayden Model

Once inside the Lazarus Archives, climb onto the second level on the right. Find the red, transparent display and then turn toward the archives. You can interact with one, so go ahead and use it to reveal a Collectible.

:X TITAN'S REALM

KEENGUY

UNLOCKS BFG-9000 Model

Enter the building and enter the first portal. Move into the next room and defeat the demons inside. From the entrance to this room, turn right and climb the steps to the second floor. There's a Collectible in a cubbyhole on the left.

 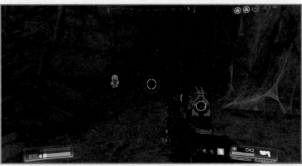

SILVERGUY

UNLOCKS Cyberdemon Model

Enter the second portal and walk into the room with the blue skull key door. Turn right and use the jump pad to reach the upper level. Double jump to the ledge to the right and collect the Collectible on a pedestal in the corner.

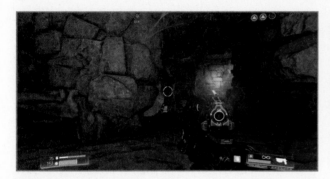 

:X THE NECROPOLIS

TEALGUY

UNLOCKS Chainsaw Model

Drop down after completing the area with the yellow and blue skull key switches. After shooting the two Cacodemons out of the air, jump across three platforms. Turn around to spot a Collectible on a lower level.

HAZMATGUY

UNLOCKS Gauss Cannon Model

Look up to the right at the Icon of Sin. Fire a rocket at the rune on its forehead to send the second Collectible to its resting position behind you.

:X VEGA CENTRAL PROCESSING

QUAKEGUY

UNLOCKS Hell Guard Model

Enter the building through the maintenance door at the start of the mission. The Collectible stands right in your way at the edge of the vent shaft.

JUNGLEGUY

UNLOCKS Cyber-Mancubus Model

Obtain the blue keycard and go through the blue keycard door. Take a left into the area labeled "Sector P Access" and go through the other blue keycard door next to the AutoMap Station. Drop down the hole to the left. Head right toward the end of the shaft and drop left to another level. Follow this path to the right and collect the Collectible. Climb back up the venting to return to the previous location.

:X ARGENT D'NUR

COSMOGUY

UNLOCKS Chaingun Model

Once the demons have been removed from the area at the second Wraith, climb the stairs on the left until you reach a hole in the steps. Duck inside to find the only hidden Collectible in the final mission.

GOLDGUY

UNLOCKS Spider Mastermind Model

You automatically receive the final collectible after defeating Spider Mastermind.

MULTIPLAYER
COMBAT PREP

Welcome to the Multiplayer portion of the guide. In this section, you'll learn how to take the skills you gained playing the Campaign and refine them for the highly competitive online arena. This chapter covers all of the fundamental aspects of *DOOM*'s robust multiplayer component and aims to provide you with the knowledge you'll need to begin your online career with confidence. The chapters that follow detail the weaponry, equipment, maps, and hundreds of challenges, medals, and commendations that you can earn during the course of play. There's a lot to learn, so dig in!

:X BASIC TRAINING

DOOM's multiplayer modes hearken back to a frenetic old-school style of gameplay in which the action is nonstop and far more intense than what you may have become accustomed to with other contemporary games. When it comes to playing multiplayer, you should understand several important things immediately:

Speed: This game is fast—incredibly so. There is no time to slow down, and definitely no safe place for you to camp. Don't even think about trying to play stealthy! Take off running (and jumping), preferably along a well-rehearsed route that leads you past several powerup spawns, and don't stop until the match is over.

Equality: A player's level and Echelon don't gain them abilities or perks that provide an unfair advantage. Once you've reached Level 17 and unlocked the last of the weapons (which doesn't take long), you can rest assured that your success and failure will be completely based on your skill with respect to those whom you play against. Everyone is given the same tools; it's how you use them that makes the difference. Those with a higher Echelon may have some customization options you don't have, but that's not why they may be better at the game. The only exception to this is Hack Modules, which are unlocked randomly through post-match rewards and by leveling up.

Patience: With the exception of the Demon Rune that drops on the first kill of Soul Harvest, the power weapons, powerups, and Demon Runes don't spawn until much later into the match. There is no need to rush the power weapon spawn point, as it won't appear until 1:45 has elapsed. It's also advisable to not rush a power weapon the moment it spawns unless you're certain that there are no enemies in the area.

Suicide: The map can be your friend, but it's a fickle relationship you share. Every one of the nine maps has hazards and places where you can fall to your death. Learn to use your thrusters for a Double Jump to escape plummeting to your demise. Also, avoid backpedaling unless you are certain that you're not about to walk off a cliff.

Pickups: Don't pass on an opportunity to collect any of the pickups scattered around the map. If it's yellow, green, or blue, pick it up because it's good for you! Health and armor pickups are key to staying alive because you are going to take damage—a lot of it! Similarly, Ammo Crates are critical to your survival, especially once you get better at staying alive. Just because you don't have to reload any of the weapons doesn't mean they don't run out of ammo. Keep them topped off!

Make no mistake: this is a difficult game to master, but proficiency comes with practice. Focus on learning the maps, understanding how the weapons work with their lone Weapon Modifiers (all weapons have a single multiplayer-specific modifier that you can use), and maintaining an unpredictable, constant motion. Evasiveness is every bit as important to your success as securing the BFG or the Demon Rune.

:X LOADOUTS

Players are automatically provided with three different loadouts at the start of play. As you level up, an additional five loadout slots become available. The three preset loadouts (Assault, Sniper, and Ambusher) cannot be customized, but the other five can. You can assign two standard weapons and a piece of equipment to each loadout. You can also select a different loadout between respawns or rounds. Be sure to customize your loadouts with different selections of weapons so that you can adjust to a given situation in the middle of a match.

When selecting weapons for a loadout, it's best to avoid doubling up on the same style of weapon. For example, it wouldn't be a good idea to select both the Combat Shotgun and the Super Shotgun for a single loadout. Similarly, you wouldn't want to rush into battle armed with both the Vortex Rifle and Static Rifle. It's far better to be equipped with weapons that can adapt to enemies at different ranges. Pairing either rifle with either shotgun is significantly more effective. Consider the following loadout suggestions, but feel free to experiment with your own, as well.

- Vortex Rifle, Super Shotgun, and Shield Wall
- Rocket Launcher, Burst Rifle, and Hologram
- Plasma Rifle, Combat Shotgun, and Frag Grenade
- Chaingun, Lightning Gun, and Siphon Grenade
- Heavy Assault Rifle, Vortex Rifle, and Tesla Rocket

:X HACK MODULES

In addition to selecting a loadout, players can also preselect four different Hack Modules (awarded in post-match rewards and by leveling up) that can aid in awareness, use of equipment and powerups, and survivability. Hack Modules have limited duration, but you can switch between different equipped Hack Modules each time you respawn, or between rounds. For strategic purposes, it's also possible to opt to respawn with no Hack Module equipped.

Hack Modules each come in three levels of quality: Bronze, Silver, and Gold. The Hack Module that you receive is entirely random, and it's not uncommon to earn a Gold-level Hack Module before obtaining the Silver or Bronze. Similarly, you can expect to be awarded duplicates from time to time. This actually comes in handy because it's possible to select multiple copies of the same Hack Modules.

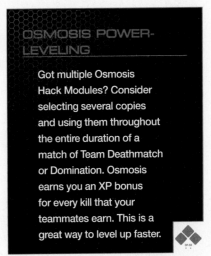

OSMOSIS POWER-LEVELING

Got multiple Osmosis Hack Modules? Consider selecting several copies and using them throughout the entire duration of a match of Team Deathmatch or Domination. Osmosis earns you an XP bonus for every kill that your teammates earn. This is a great way to level up faster.

Until you narrow down exactly which Hack Modules you want to use for a given gameplay mode or map, it's best to leave the "Auto-Fill" and "Auto-Select" features enabled on the Hack Module screen. The game will automatically assign four useful Hack Modules to your character at the start of a match. This is not only a great way to gain experience using a number of different Hack Modules, but it also ensures you can quickly return to the action between matches without having to manually swap out a lesser Hack Module for a newly acquired upgrade.

AWARENESS MODULES

These modules increase your ability to detect enemy positions, avoid damage, and collect pickups.

AWARENESS MODULE TACTICS

MODULE	COMMENT
Evasion	All-purpose module, particularly useful for Soul Harvest and Freeze Tag.
Alarm	Helpful for defending Control Points in Domination and Warpath, or for thawing teammates in Freeze Tag.
Magnet	Useful in Team Deathmatch and Soul Harvest. Never equip for Clan Arena.
Vital Signs	Use it to pinpoint weaker enemies in Clan Arena and Freeze Tag.
Speed Demon	Best used during Soul Harvest matches when a demon is nearly always present.
Supply Timer	Helpful module for when you really want to secure a power weapon or powerup.

 ### EVASION

Run faster when you take damage.

BRONZE	SILVER	GOLD
60 seconds	90 seconds	120 seconds

 ### ALARM

Alert you to nearby enemies.

BRONZE	SILVER	GOLD
60 seconds	90 seconds	120 seconds

 ### MAGNET

Increase pickup radius. 120-second duration.

BRONZE	SILVER	GOLD
2x pickup radius	3x pickup radius	4x pickup radius

 ### VITAL SIGNS

Show enemies' health.

BRONZE	SILVER	GOLD
60 seconds	90 seconds	120 seconds

 ### SPEED DEMON

Move faster near a demon. 120-second duration.

BRONZE	SILVER	GOLD
50-meter radius	75-meter radius	100-meter radius

 ### SUPPLY TIMER

Display respawn timers on pickups.

BRONZE	SILVER	GOLD
60 seconds	90 seconds	120 seconds

BOOST MODULES

These modules increase the effectiveness of your weaponry and equipment, decrease the damage you take, and increase the XP you earn.

BOOST MODULE TACTICS

MODULE	COMMENT
Blast Shield	Useful if you're equipping a Rocket Launcher, Plasma Rifle, or Frag Grenade.
Reinforce	Very helpful in Team Deathmatch, Domination, and other objective-based modes, especially when you're first learning.
Bounty	Great for power-leveling in Objective Based modes.
Infinite Ammo	Can be very useful in Freeze Tag or if you're using a Plasma Rifle and other high ROF weapons.
Osmosis	Excellent way to power-level when playing Team Deathmatch, Domination, and Soul Harvest.
Armor Plating	One of the most helpful modules for Objective Based modes.
Stockpile	Excellent all-around module that lets you use equipment with greater frequency.
Wingman	Useful in Team Deathmatch, or whenever you're playing with a group that coordinates and employs teamwork.

 ### BLAST SHIELD

Take less self-damage for 120 seconds.

BRONZE	SILVER	GOLD
50% reduction	75% reduction	100% reduction

 ### REINFORCE

Spawn with armor following a life without any kills. 60-second duration.

BRONZE	SILVER	GOLD
+50 armor	+75 armor	+100 armor

 ### BOUNTY

Gain bonus XP for each kill. 60-second duration.

BRONZE	SILVER	GOLD
+50 XP	+75 XP	+100 XP

 ### INFINITE AMMO

Unlimited ammo for loadout weapons.

BRONZE	SILVER	GOLD
60 seconds	90 seconds	120 seconds

 ### OSMOSIS

Gain bonus XP for each kill by a teammate. 60-second duration.

BRONZE	SILVER	GOLD
+20 XP	+30 XP	+40 XP

 ### ARMOR PLATING

Spawn with increased armor with each respawn. 120-second duration.

BRONZE	SILVER	GOLD
+5 armor	+8 armor	+10 armor

 ### STOCKPILE

Reduce equipment cooldown. 120-second duration.

BRONZE	SILVER	GOLD
25% reduction	40% reduction	50% reduction

 ### WINGMAN

Gain bonus XP when you collaborate on a kill. 120-second duration.

BRONZE	SILVER	GOLD
+50 XP	+75 XP	+100 XP

These modules make it possible to see through walls, and track enemies, allies, and power weapons.

WALLHACK MODULE TACTICS

MODULE	COMMENT
Counter-Intel	Allows you to see who can see you, provided they aren't tracking you from behind.
Demon Tracker	Very useful when playing Soul Harvest.
Manhunt	Helpful in Team Deathmatch and Soul Harvest matches, or when you're looking for bonus XP.
Power Seeker	Useful for when you don't know the powerup locations or are unsure of a map's layout.
Scout	Extremely useful in Team Deathmatch and Soul Harvest, especially late in matches.
Synchronization	Aids in coordinating with teammates during Objective Based modes, particularly if they aren't very communicative.
Blood Trail	A great way to pursue weakened foes in Team Deathmatch and Soul Harvest.
Retribution	Helpful in gaining revenge and earning medals.

 ### COUNTER-INTEL

Reveal enemies who are tracking your position.

BRONZE	SILVER	GOLD
60 seconds	90 seconds	120 seconds

 ### DEMON TRACKER

Reveal demons. 60-second duration.

BRONZE	SILVER	GOLD
In field of view	Anywhere on map	Also shows demon's remaining health.

 ### MANHUNT

Track the top enemy. 20-second duration.

BRONZE	SILVER	GOLD
100 XP	200 XP	300 XP

 ### POWER SEEKER

Track the nearest powerup or power weapon.

BRONZE	SILVER	GOLD
60 seconds	90 seconds	120 seconds

 ### SCOUT

Briefly reveal all enemies when you spawn.

BRONZE	SILVER	GOLD
60 seconds	90 seconds	120 seconds

 ### SYNCHRONIZATION

Show the location and health of allies. 120-second duration.

BRONZE	SILVER	GOLD
Location revealed	+Reveals health	+Highlights when they shoot

 ### BLOOD TRAIL

Track wounded enemies. 60-second duration.

BRONZE	SILVER	GOLD
2 seconds	3 seconds	4 seconds

 ### RETRIBUTION

Reveal the location of your killer. 30-second duration.

BRONZE	SILVER	GOLD
Location revealed	+Reveals health	+Highlights when they shoot

:X PICKUPS

Maps in DOOM multiplayer are littered with pickups ranging from health and armor to powerups that grant regeneration and invincibility and a Demon Rune that can turn you into a demon! Pickups appear in every mode except Clan Arena, and they spawn and respawn based on a timer. Collecting as many health, armor, and ammo pickups as you can while traveling the map will certainly increase your odds of surviving and achieving a higher kill ratio. Demon Runes, powerups, and power weapons are even more advantageous, but they are likely to be hotly contested. Proceed with caution whenever you go after one of these valuable pickups!

HEALTH

- Varies in size and grants **5**, **25**, and **50 health** based on the size of the pickup that you acquire.

- Respawns every **10 seconds**. Some health pickups are available immediately at the start of the match, while others spawn into the map after **15 seconds**.

MEGA-HEALTH

- Maximizes your health and armor. Players with maximum armor glow. Proceed with caution.

- Spawns **1:00** after the start of the match. Respawns after **1:00** from last pickup.

- Only one Mega-Health per map.

ARMOR

- Varies in size from small to large and grants **5**, **25**, and **50 armor** based on the size of the pickup that you acquire.

- Small, medium, and large armor pickups respawn every **15**, **30**, and **45** seconds, respectively. Some pickups are available immediately at the start of the match, while others spawn after **15 seconds**.

- Players drop small armor pickups upon their death.

- Player cannot exceed 50 armor unless they collect small armor pickups or acquire Mega-Health.

AMMO CRATE

- Grants approximately **50%** max ammo capacity per pickup.

- Both of the weapons equipped in the loadout gain ammo.

- Respawns every **10 seconds**. Available immediately at the start of the match.

HASTE

- Temporarily increases player movement speed and weapon fire rate.

- Effect lasts **30 seconds**.

- Respawns **1:45** after the powerup has been used. Available **1:45** after the match begins.

- Only one Haste powerup per map.

INVISIBILITY

- Grants a player the ability to become temporarily invisible to all other players.

- Effect lasts **40 seconds**.

- Respawns **1:45** after the powerup has been used. Available **1:45** after the match begins.

- Only one Invisibility powerup per map.

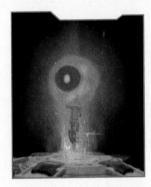

REGENERATION

- Temporarily grants a player a steady regeneration of health and armor.
- Effect lasts **40 seconds**.
- Respawns **1:45** after the powerup has been used. Available **1:45** after the match begins.
- Only one Regeneration powerup per map.

QUAD DAMAGE

- Temporarily triples a player's weapon damage for a short duration.
- Effect lasts **30 seconds**.
- Respawns **1:45** after the powerup has been used. Available **1:45** after the match begins.
- Only one Quad Damage powerup per map.

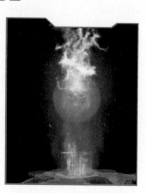

DEMON RUNE

- Spawns in various locations throughout the match (except Clan Arena and Soul Harvest) and temporarily transforms a player into a demon.
- Effect lasts **60 seconds** (or when the demon dies).
- Respawns every **1:35**. Available **1:35** after the start of the match.
- Only one Demon Rune per map.

POWER WEAPON

- Grants a player limited ammo and use of a BFG, Chainsaw, or Gauss Cannon. Switching weapons will drop the Power Weapon.
- Available **1:45** after the start of the match. Respawns every **1:45** after the ammo is used up or the weapon is removed from the map (Suicide).
- Only one Power Weapon per map.

:X: GAMEPLAY MODES

There are a total of six multiplayer modes, each of which pits two teams against one another. Teams can have as many as six players each. You can select gameplay modes individually, or you can choose an Objective Based or Round Based playlist. You can find map-specific tips for each mode in the Multiplayer Maps chapter of this guide.

ROUND BASED MODES

CLAN ARENA

Kill enemy players to win. Victory is awarded to the first team to win three rounds.

Clan Arena is a very fast-paced game that requires significant skill and teamwork. There is no margin for error, as each player is granted only one life. Clan Arena is played without pickups or demons, and without Hack Modules enabled. It is pure combat; you have just 100 Health, 100 Armor, two weapons, and a piece of equipment. Make it count!

FREEZE TAG

Freeze enemies and thaw your teammates. Victory is awarded to the first team to win three rounds.

Freeze Tag is a modified version of Clan Arena. Players still get only one life to live, but instead of being killed, they are frozen in place. Teammates can "thaw" their frozen allies by staying within the vicinity of the chilled victim for **3.5 seconds**. You can also knock them into hazards or off cliffs, which causes them to respawn thawed. All powerups, pickups, and Hack Modules are in play during Freeze Tag. What truly makes this mode unique is that you can slide frozen enemies across the map with weapon fire.

OBJECTIVE BASED MODES

DOMINATION

Control the zones to win. Victory is awarded to the first team to reach the score limit or have the higher score when the timer expires.

Capture any of the three Control Points by standing within the zone for **eight seconds** while keeping the opposition out of it. Captures take place faster if multiple teammates are in the same zone. A Control Point with members of both teams inside it is said to be "contested," and the Capture meter will not fill until one team is in sole possession of the zone. Teams are awarded a point for each Control Point in their possession every second. The announcer will keep you apprised of which zones are being contested and controlled, and by which team. Similarly, the color-coded indicators in the upper-left corner of the screen show the status of each Control Point. All powerups, pickups, and Hack Modules are in play during Domination.

SOUL HARVEST

Kill enemies and capture their Souls. Victory is awarded to the first team to reach the Soul count limit or have more Souls collected when time expires.

Soul Harvest is similar to Team Deathmatch, except each player drops a Soul upon death. The only way to accumulate points is to collect the Souls dropped by your opposition while trying to prevent them from collecting those that your teammates dropped. Humans drop **one Soul** when killed by another human, but they drop **two Souls** if a demon kills them. Demons drop **four Souls** when killed. The first player to die in Soul Harvest will drop a Demon Rune, and each subsequent slaying of a demon drops another Demon Rune that becomes active several seconds after death. Consequently, you can expect a demon to be on the loose at all times in Soul Harvest. Be on the lookout for Souls that are the color of your team, and collect them to deny your opponent a score.

TEAM DEATHMATCH

Kill enemy players to win. Victory is awarded to the first team to reach the kill limit or have more kills when the timer expires.

Out of all of the multiplayer modes, Team Deathmatch is the most straightforward. Two teams compete to be the first to accumulate the target number of kills. All powerups, power weapons, Demon Runes, and Hack Modules are in play. Teams are awarded one point for every enemy killed. Players respawn quickly, with a chance to change loadouts and Hack Modules between respawns. Teamwork is important, but there is room for improvisation, particularly if you're a skilled player. Stay on the move, gather the pickups along the way, and collect as many kills as you can. If neither team reaches the target score, the team with the most kills when time expires is the winner.

WARPATH

Control the moving zone to win. Victory is awarded to the first team to reach the score limit or have the higher score when the timer expires.

Warpath is similar to Domination, except both teams must fight over a single Control Point that follows a visible path that winds its way through the map. The Control Point takes **eight seconds** to capture (or less time with teammates), and the arrows along the path will indicate in which direction it is moving. Unique to this mode is that the Demon Rune will also spawn on the Warpath and migrate around the map with the path, as well, typically staying at the opposite side of the path from the Control Point. The direction of the Control Point is chosen randomly at the start of the match. The match is over when one team meets the target score (one point per second controlled) or when time expires.

:X BECOME THE DEMON

What really sets DOOM's multiplayer modes apart from other games is the ability to actually become one of four demons and use some inhuman, ungodly powers to eviscerate your opponents. All players begin with the Revenant unlocked, but the three other demon forms are unlocked through play. Don't worry: it won't take long. Select your demon at the start of each match, and then 1:35 into the match, be ready to grab the lone Demon Rune that appears. You're not indestructible as a demon, but you will become more powerful than your wildest dreams.

REVENANT

- Jetpack into the air and eviscerate opponents with a barrage of missiles.
- Unlocked at Level 1.

  HEALTH: 300 HP

  AMMO CAPACITY: Infinite

  DURATION: 60 seconds

The Revenant is one of the most versatile demons, as its ability to continuously hover in the air for up to four seconds means that there are few places it can't go in outdoor maps. Its twin missiles deliver overwhelming damage and are moderately accurate. However, thanks to their relatively slower flight speed, you may want to lead your enemies a bit when aiming at them. Anticipate their travel, and fire the rockets slightly in front of their position. It takes five seconds for the jetpack to completely replenish, so consider using it in small bursts.

When attacking an enemy Revenant, the first thing you need to do is target the power core that it wears. Doing so will disable the jetpack, which renders the Revenant grounded. The Revenant has a relatively slow firing rate. Pop in and out of cover with explosive firepower in between its rocket blasts.

BARON OF HELL

- Smash and tear apart opponents with massive demonic claws.

- Unlocked at Level 5.

  HEALTH: 750 HP

  AMMO CAPACITY: Melee only

  DURATION: 60 seconds

The Baron of Hell can run quite fast, but has very limited jumping ability. Avoid selecting the Baron on maps with lots of jumping to isolated pedestals and platforms (for example, Sacrilegious). The Baron of Hell is purely a melee fighter, with a main attack that consists of grabbing an enemy in its massive claws and ripping it limb from limb. The Baron's secondary attack is a vicious Ground Pound that shatters the surface with demonic force and causes an incendiary effect that burns directly in front of the Baron's position. Stay on the move at all times, and move erratically to avoid incoming fire as best as possible. Ground Pound any adversaries that are out of reach, and periodically spin around while melee attacking in case there are foes to your rear.

The Baron of Hell is perhaps the easiest of the demons to destroy, thanks to its very limited range of attack. Keep your distance and move to an elevated position where it would have difficulty reaching you. Unload on it with any projectile weapon that you have at your disposal. The 750 Health won't be diminished quickly, but you won't have to dodge any rockets while attacking it.

MANCUBUS

- Bombard enemies from a distance with volleys of rockets.

- Unlocked at Level 9.

  HEALTH: 800 HP

  AMMO CAPACITY: Infinite

  DURATION: 60 seconds

In many ways, the Mancubus is the complete opposite of the Revenant. This massive, slow demon can barely jump, let alone fly. And although it has twin Rocket Launchers on its arms, it can fire only one at a time, alternating from one arm to the other. Fortunately for the Mancubus, it has an overwhelming amount of health and is not defeated easily. Attack with its rockets wherever you see an enemy, but pay attention to the heat sensors in the middle of your screen—the more frequently you fire the rockets, the faster you run the risk of overheating. Use the Weapon Modifier button to "vent" the rockets. The Mancubus will place both rocket arms down on the ground and discharge the heat from the rockets across the floor. Consider this the Mancubus' melee attack, as fire spreads across the nearby floor, burning anyone in the vicinity.

Taking down a Mancubus requires teamwork. Its 800 Health is too much for one player to handle on their own. Attack it with Rocket Launchers, Plasma Rifles, Frag Grenades, and Hellshots while staying out of range of its vent attack and (preferably) in and out of cover from its rockets. Attacks that deal damage over time, such as the Hellshot's incendiary round and the Plasma Rifle's Plasma Pools, are useful. Of course, a slow-moving target like the Mancubus is also very easy to snipe with the Vortex Rifle and Static Rifle.

- ▶ Lurk in the shadows above, leaping down on unsuspecting enemies.

- ▶ Unlocked at Level 17.

  HEALTH: 275 HP

  AMMO CAPACITY: Melee only

  DURATION: 60 seconds

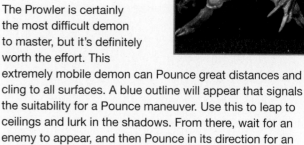

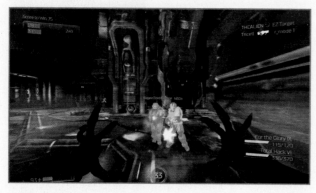

The Prowler is certainly the most difficult demon to master, but it's definitely worth the effort. This extremely mobile demon can Pounce great distances and cling to all surfaces. A blue outline will appear that signals the suitability for a Pounce maneuver. Use this to leap to ceilings and lurk in the shadows. From there, wait for an enemy to appear, and then Pounce in its direction for an instant Glory Kill. The Prowler need not be hanging from a wall or ceiling to successfully launch a Pounce attack, as you can Pounce at an adversary while standing. The Prowler can also perform a deadly melee attack on foes that are too close to Pounce onto. The Prowler is effective in nearly all situations, particularly in maps with corridors where he can Pounce back and forth, destroying opponents as they foolishly enter the room.

There's nowhere to hide when a Prowler is on the loose (they can see enemies through walls), so stick close to your teammates and hope that there truly is strength in numbers. The Prowler is shockingly fast when Pouncing, but it is the weakest of all of the demons and can be slain with a few coordinated attacks. Good luck!

:X XP, LEVELS, AND CUSTOMIZATION

At the conclusion of every match, you will receive two random Hack Modules. Then, you're shown a rundown of the XP that you earned through gameplay, earning of commendations, and via bonuses. All of this XP serves to increase your level. For every level that you increase, two additional random awards are bestowed upon you.

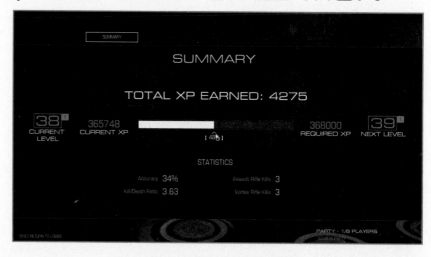

There are a total of 50 levels in 10 different Echelons (players technically begin in Echelon 0). You need 227,000 total XP to reach Level 50, and then, with a total of 232,000 XP, you will reach Echelon 1, Level 1. You need a total of 2,727,000 XP to reach the level cap at Echelon 10, Level 50. The Roman numeral in a small box next to your level number signifies which Echelon you are at. Echelons and levels are an indicator of a player's skill and the amount of time that person has spent playing DOOM. The system also awards those who diversify their techniques and master numerous weapons and play modes. Be sure to consult the lengthy series of tables in the "Challenges, Medals, and Commendations" chapter to see how you can earn enormous piles of bonus XP!

CUSTOMIZATION OPTIONS

Hack Modules are the only type of award that has an impact on gameplay, but there are hundreds of other awards to collect and help you stand out in a crowd of red-and-blue Doom Marines. Access the Customization screen in the Multiplayer Lobby to begin customizing your character's appearance and the appearance of the weaponry. Though this won't be clear during gameplay, your character's unique style will be proudly on display if you reach the podium and finish in the top three of scoring in any match.

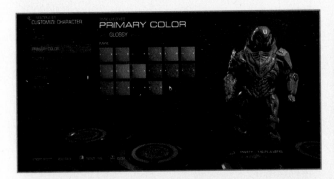

RANDOMIZE!

Feeling overwhelmed with the customization options? Back out to the customization categories screen (Armor, Paint, etc.), and hit the Randomize button for each option to roll the dice and let fate decide for you. This is a great way to quickly change up your character's appearance between matches.

Character Armor: There are 60 different varieties of Helmet, Torso, Left Arm, Right Arm, Legs, and Base Armor spread across five different styles (UAC, Demonic, Utilitarian, Templar, and Bounty Hunter). This makes for thousands of different possible combinations.

Colors: There are 96 different colors for both primary and secondary paint schemes, available in matte, glossy, and metallic styles.

Patterns: There are 62 different patterns that can be applied to your character, ranging from Abstract to Camo to Symbols. Each of the colors in these two-tone patterns can be assigned any of the 96 different colors you've unlocked.

Details: Finally, you can adjust the degree of cleanliness of the armor by adding dirt or scratches.

Weapon Customization: You can apply any of the unlocked colors and patterns to your weaponry, as well. It's possible to individually customize each of the 11 standard weapons in DOOM.

Taunts: There are 150 different Taunts that you can map to any of four Taunt buttons. Taunts are divided into the following categories: Dance, Celebration, Humor, and Mock. And the only thing funnier than a Taunt is watching a player get sniped mid-Taunt.

MULTIPLAYER ARSENAL

The difference between victory and defeat in multiplayer comes down to four things: skill, teamwork, knowledge of the maps, and mastery of the weapons. This chapter focuses on the latter. Here, you'll learn everything that you need to know about the 11 standard weapons, the three power weapons found in-map, and the seven pieces of equipment that you can select before heading into battle. Every weapon in the game has its advantages and its drawbacks; they all excel in certain situations and come up short in others. This chapter aims to help you make the best decisions possible when it comes to customizing your loadouts for a given map or scenario.

UNLOCKED AT LEVEL 3

PRIMARY: A selective-fire battle rifle equipped with a reciprocating barrel assembly and three-round burst mode.

MODIFIER: Aims down the sights and selects a semi-automatic mode using magnum ammunition.

BURST RIFLE: PRIMARY FIRE

DMG	ROF	SPLASH RADIUS	CRIT DMG	CRIT METHOD
10	3.03	-	15	Headshot

BURST RIFLE: WEAPON MOD

DMG	ROF	SPLASH RADIUS	CRIT DMG	CRIT METHOD
16	3.57	-	24	Headshot

The Burst Rifle fires a high-speed, three-round burst of bullets in a tight spread. Each bullet inflicts **10 DMG,** although it will be rare for fewer than two or three of the rounds to hit their mark. This means that each trigger press will inflict up to 30 DMG (45 if Critical Hits). Unfortunately, the Burst Rifle is not fully automatic, and there is a dangerous delay between bursts. Though a fine weapon for finishing off enemies, the Burst Rifle isn't suitable for taking on a healthy adversary at close or moderate range when alone. The Burst Rifle is best suited for assisting allies in finishing off distracted foes, preferably from a safe distance.

When used, the Weapon Modifier switches the Burst Rifle to a semi-automatic mode. The firing rate is much slower, but this aids in conserving ammo. Using the ironsights also assists with greater accuracy. The magnum ammunition used with the Weapon Modifier inflicts **16 DMG** per bullet (24 if Critical Hit). The Weapon Modifier is good to use if you get the drop on an enemy and want to snipe from long range, but the damage that you'll inflict is unlikely to finish off the opponent.

Consider using the Burst Rifle as a secondary weapon in Objective Based modes to finish off weaker enemies and to engage isolated foes with teammates by your side. Although the Weapon Modifier is nice to use for long-range targets, you are more likely to inflict greater damage while using the weapon's primary burst fire.

UNLOCKED AT LEVEL 1

PRIMARY: A large drum-fed rotary machine gun with a high rate of fire.

MODIFIER: Spins up the rotating barrel to maximum speed prior to firing. 1.4 seconds to fully spin up barrels. Movement speed reduced to 83% when spun up.

CHAINGUN: PRIMARY FIRE

DMG	ROF	SPLASH RADIUS	CRIT DMG	CRIT METHOD
6	10	-	9	Close Range

CHAINGUN: WEAPON MOD

DMG	ROF	SPLASH RADIUS	CRIT DMG	CRIT METHOD
-	-	-	-	-

The Chaingun is a powerful weapon that excels at short- to medium-range combat because of its very high rate of fire. Though each bullet inflicts only **6 DMG** (9 if Critical Hit), the Chaingun can chew through an enemy's armor and health in no time at all. Holding the trigger fires in fully automatic mode without the concern of overheating, although it does take a few moments for the rotating barrel to reach top speed. The Chaingun isn't the most accurate of weapons, with the bullet spread becoming wider at range.

The Chaingun is most effective when it's operating at top speed. Though the noise of the barrel rotating may alert enemies to your position, you can employ the Weapon Modifier to bring the barrel up to top speed without wasting any ammo. This is particularly useful when you're defending a position in Domination or attacking the enemy team in Round Based modes. Utilizing the Weapon Modifier does not inflict a movement penalty.

When it comes to using the Chaingun, practice makes perfect. Though there is certainly a "spray and pray" element to using it, there's also a sweet spot. The key is to stay close enough to your enemies to neutralize their Vortex Rifle or Burst Rifle, but far enough away to stay clear of Super Shotgun range. Aim for the torso, and try to keep the target entirely within the reticle. Most bullets will hit their mark, and some will even score Critical Hits. Resist the urge to aim for the head unless you're very close, as some of the bullets will likely miss the smaller target.

UNLOCKED AT LEVEL 1

PRIMARY: Fully automatic rifle that fires pulses of superheated plasma capable of dealing splash damage.

MODIFIER: Shoots a plasma orb that detonates, creating a small area of burning plasma. Plasma field deals full self-damage.

PLASMA RIFLE: PRIMARY FIRE

DMG	ROF	SPLASH RADIUS	CRIT DMG	CRIT METHOD
6	9.09	72	9	Consecutive Hits

PLASMA RIFLE: WEAPON MOD

DMG	ROF	SPLASH RADIUS	CRIT DMG	CRIT METHOD
85 / 4 secs	0.11	350	20	Direct Hit

The Plasma Rifle is one of the most versatile weapons in the multiplayer modes, thanks to its rapid rate of fire, above-average accuracy, and the addition of splash damage to its normal fire. A Plasma Rifle inflicts **6 DMG** per plasma pulse (9 if Critical Hit) and can be relied on for precision aiming. If you're head-to-head against an enemy using a Burst Rifle, the Plasma Rifle wins every time.

The Plasma Rifle's alternate firing method really sets the Plasma Rifle apart. Activate the Weapon Modifier to lob a plasma orb that not only inflicts **15 DMG** on contact (20 if Critical Hit), but also lights the ground aflame. Enemies standing upon the burning plasma will suffer an additional **10 DMG** repeatedly (nearly every half second) as long as they remain in the affected area. Though it does take **10 seconds** for another plasma orb to be ready, the gun is usable in primary mode during that time. The ground will continue to burn for **5 seconds**. The circular targeting reticle fills and flashes yellow as the plasma orb recharges. Similarly, the vertical meter visible on the Plasma Rifle indicates when the Weapon Modifier is ready to fire again.

Target an enemy with the plasma orb, then open fire with primary fire to finish him off. The Plasma Rifle is particularly useful in Domination and Warpath, where you can effectively foul an area of the capture point with the burning plasma. It's also worth firing the gun's alternate fire when you're low on health and about to die—this is a great way to collect deaths from beyond the grave. Fire the plasma orb at the ground where an enemy team is congregating, open fire with primary fire, and then fire another plasma orb as soon as it's available, especially if you have to retreat. Just be careful around the burning plasma because it can damage you, too!

UNLOCKED AT LEVEL 1

PRIMARY: Fires rockets that explode on impact, doing damage over a large area. Deals 80% self-damage.

MODIFIER: Immediately detonates all live rockets currently in flight.

ROCKET LAUNCHER: PRIMARY FIRE

DMG	ROF	SPLASH RADIUS	CRIT DMG	CRIT METHOD
40	1.14	164	55	Direct Hit

ROCKET LAUNCHER: WEAPON MOD

DMG	ROF	SPLASH RADIUS	CRIT DMG	CRIT METHOD
40	-	138	-	-

A direct hit from a single rocket is considered a Critical Hit and inflicts **55 DMG** to the targeted enemy while inflicting splash damage to those nearby. The Rocket Launcher is an excellent weapon for engaging multiple adversaries or for finishing off a weakened foe—you can inflict from **10 to 40 DMG** without actually hitting the enemy directly. The Rocket Launcher can fire only one rocket at a time; you cannot fire a second rocket until the one in flight has already detonated.

The Weapon Modifier for the Rocket Launcher detonates the rocket currently in flight. This is useful for several reasons. For starters, enemies don't often stand still while you fire the rockets at them. Use the Weapon Modifier to detonate the rocket you fire as it passes the foe moving out of the way, and you might just score some splash damage. Secondly, you can use the modifier to detonate rockets as fast as you fire them to effectively speed up the rate of fire. This is useful if you're firing at nearby opponents (but not too close!) and want to canvas an area in splash damage.

The Rocket Launcher is a potent weapon in Objective Based and Round Based modes, especially at the initial confrontation when both teams are at full strength. Try to flank around the battle and hit the other team from the side. It's best to aim low when using the Rocket Launcher so you can use the ground to your advantage and inflict splash damage. Fortunately, you can use the Weapon Modifier to detonate any errant shots without having to wait for them to fly across the map and into another surface. The Rocket Launcher is very effective at all ranges but is dangerous at very close range. Remember that the splash damage can also injure you unless you're equipped with the Blast Shield III Hack Module.

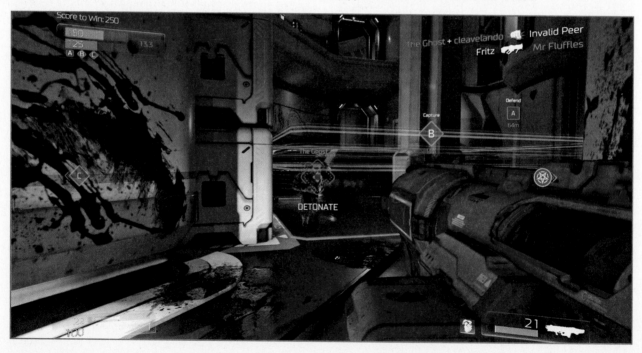

UNLOCKED AT LEVEL 1

PRIMARY: A break-action double-barrel shotgun that fires a wide spread of buckshot. Each shot consumes 2 ammo.

MODIFIER: Constricts the variable choke system retrofit into each barrel for a tighter spread pattern.

SUPER SHOTGUN: PRIMARY FIRE

DMG	ROF	SPLASH RADIUS	CRIT DMG	CRIT METHOD
80	0.68	-	-	High Damage

SUPER SHOTGUN: WEAPON MOD

DMG	ROF	SPLASH RADIUS	CRIT DMG	CRIT METHOD
-	-	-	-	-

The Weapon Modifier for the Super Shotgun tightens the spread of the buckshot. Enable the Weapon Modifier, and watch as the target reticle tightens partially. Shots fired with this enabled don't automatically inflict more damage, but more of the individual pieces of buckshot will likely hit their mark. It is those individual pieces of buckshot that inflict the damage: the more that hit the enemy, the greater damage you deal. A grazing shot will inflict as little as **7 DMG**. However, everything comes at a cost, and using the Weapon Modifier both narrows your field of vision and slows your movement speed.

The Super Shotgun can inflict heavy damage on close-range enemies. Since the spread of the buckshot widens with distance, shots fired at medium-range foes will deal only partial damage as a result of some of the buckshot missing the target. A close-range shot aimed at an adversary's body can inflict up to **80 DMG** on Critical Hits. Of course, the drawback to using the Super Shotgun is that it has a very slow rate of fire. Enemies glowing under the effects of full armor or who clearly have full health (visible with the Vital Signs Hack Module) should be kept at distance.

You should not view the Super Shotgun as a primary weapon. Under no circumstances should you run around the map with the Super Shotgun in hand, hoping to blast away enemies at close range. This is a recipe for disaster because any foe with full health (especially one armed with a Chaingun, Plasma Rifle, or Burst Rifle) can keep you at arm's length and rip you to shreds before you get your second shot off. Instead, engage from afar with a longer-range weapon, and close the gap on the enemy. Switch to the Super Shotgun to finish him off! The Super Shotgun is also effective when contesting Control Points in Domination and Warpath, especially if your teammates have already softened the opponents up with a Rocket Launcher or the plasma pools of a Plasma Rifle. A Frag Grenade also works well with the Super Shotgun.

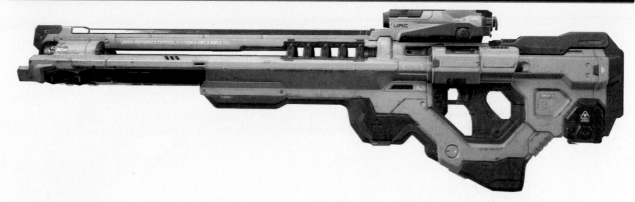

UNLOCKED AT LEVEL 1

PRIMARY: A precision long-range energy weapon with a magnified optic.

MODIFIER: Increases the magnification and charges to full power output. One second to fully charge. Max range of 4096 units.

VORTEX RIFLE: PRIMARY FIRE

DMG	ROF	SPLASH RADIUS	CRIT DMG	CRIT METHOD
30	1	-	45	Headshot

VORTEX RIFLE: WEAPON MOD

DMG	ROF	SPLASH RADIUS	CRIT DMG	CRIT METHOD
84	1	-	126	Headshot

The Vortex Rifle is an excellent sniping weapon, capable of precise shots from considerable distance. It features a scope that reveals the shooter's location with a laser that extends out from the rifle. An unmodified shot inflicts **30 DMG** (45 DMG on Critical Hits) and can be fired with only a slight delay between shots. The Vortex Rifle is best used against long-range enemies that are carrying imprecise weaponry or weapons that are best suited for close-range combat. Though the Vortex Rifle is one of the best sniper rifles available, DOOM is not a game conducive for camping out and sniping enemies. Maps like Excavation provide ample opportunity to get up high and target distant, distracted enemies, but you will be exposed. Take your shot, and immediately relocate! If your skills don't allow for sniping on the run, use the Alarm Hack Module (or Threat Sensor), and seek out areas where you're at least covered from two or three sides.

Enabling the Weapon Modifier with the Vortex Rifle amplifies the magnification, effectively giving you a terrific scope. The enhanced optics definitely help, but the Weapon Modifier's main benefit is the increased damage. Continue enabling the Weapon Modifier to charge the Vortex Rifle's energy to full power for an attack that can inflict **84 DMG** (126 on Critical Hits). Best of all, you need not fully charge the weapon until the reticle flashes yellow to gain a damage boost. Partially charged shots inflict a minimum of **39 DMG**.

The Vortex Rifle is a great weapon to use both when you're hanging back from teammates picking off a distracted opponent or when you're one-on-one in Clan Arena or Freeze Tag. Keep your distance, charge up your shot, and go for the headshot! Consider pairing this weapon with a Super Shotgun, Combat Shotgun, or something with a very high rate of fire, such as the Plasma Rifle. The Vortex Rifle is particularly useful on Excavation. Grab the Quad Damage powerup, charge up the rifle, and go for a Critical Hit to deliver **378 DMG**! Talk about a demon slayer!

UNLOCKED AT LEVEL 1

PRIMARY: Fully automatic assault rifle with a digital scope.

MODIFIER: Enables the digital scope for extended range combat. Movement speed reduced to 75% when using scope.

HEAVY ASSAULT RIFLE: PRIMARY FIRE

DMG	ROF	SPLASH RADIUS	CRIT DMG	CRIT METHOD
9	7.35	-	13	Headshot

HEAVY ASSAULT RIFLE: WEAPON MOD

DMG	ROF	SPLASH RADIUS	CRIT DMG	CRIT METHOD
-	-	-	-	-

The Heavy Assault Rifle fires a barrage of precision-aimed bullets at a fast rate of fire. Unfortunately, each bullet inflicts only **9 DMG** (13 on Critical Hits). This means that you'll need to engage your enemy in a drawn-out fight in order to finish him off with just this weapon. Nevertheless, the Heavy Assault Rifle is an adequate all-around weapon, provided you shoot from the hip, aim for the head, and stay on the move at all times. Circle-strafe, jump, and sidestep back and forth to avoid incoming attacks while peppering your adversary. This is the only way to bring down a healthy foe with just the Heavy Assault Rifle.

The Heavy Assault Rifle's Weapon Modifier is a digital scope that narrows your field of vision, zooms in on the distance, and allows for greater accuracy over long range. The weapon's projectiles will not inflict greater damage, but you'll be able to more accurately target your enemy from afar. This is useful when assisting a distant teammate or trying to provide support to a contested Control Point. Enabling the Weapon Modifier in medium- or close-range situations is not recommended.

The Heavy Assault Rifle can be an adequate primary weapon, but it's more useful as a secondary weapon that you can use to finish off weakened enemies. Consider pairing it with a Rocket Launcher or Vortex Rifle. Similarly, the Heavy Assault Rifle works well with the Siphon Grenade and Tesla Rocket. Use these other weapons while you move into a medium distance with the Heavy Assault Rifle. Remember that despite the Heavy Assault Rifle's high rate of fire and accuracy, it doesn't have quite the potency of several other weapons at close range. Use it on the run, and pick your shots—and your enemies—carefully.

UNLOCKED AT LEVEL 6

PRIMARY: An advanced semi-automatic Argent Energy weapon.

MODIFIER: Fires an incendiary round that burns targets on impact.

HELLSHOT: PRIMARY FIRE

DMG	ROF	SPLASH RADIUS	CRIT DMG	CRIT METHOD
20	2.86	-	35	Headshot

HELLSHOT: WEAPON MOD

DMG	ROF	SPLASH RADIUS	CRIT DMG	CRIT METHOD
48 / 4 secs	0.2	-	-	-

The Hellshot is an excellent all-purpose weapon that inflicts **20 DMG** per shot (35 on Critical Hits) and has above-average precision. The Hellshot's one downside is its relatively slow rate of fire—on par with the Vortex Rifle—but you can overcome this with strategic use of its Weapon Modifier.

Activating the Weapon Modifier with the Hellshot fires an incendiary projectile that continues to burn the struck target. The enemy will suffer burn damage while you pepper him with primary Hellshot fire or even another weapon. The Weapon Modifier inflicts a total of **48 DMG** over time and takes **5.5 seconds to recharge**. Hit the foe with the incendiary round, then open fire with the semi-automatic primary fire while the Weapon Modifier recharges.

The Hellshot's primary fire is accurate at medium to long range. The Weapon Modifier's incendiary round is fired in a slight arc (not as dramatic as the Combat Shotgun) and is best used against short- to medium-range enemies, given its slower velocity. The Hellshot doesn't deliver splash damage, so make sure that you are accurate with all attacks. Set an adversary on fire and circle-strafe around him while he burns, either switching to a Super Shotgun or using the Hellshot itself to finish him off. You can use the Hellshot as a primary or secondary weapon; it's recommended to match it with a Plasma Rifle or Super Shotgun for close-quarters situations.

UNLOCKED AT LEVEL 11

PRIMARY: A pump-action shotgun with a tight spread of buckshot.

MODIFIER: Loads the shotgun with lethal high-explosive mortar shells. Takes 0.5 seconds to ready a mortar shell.

COMBAT SHOTGUN: PRIMARY FIRE

DMG	ROF	SPLASH RADIUS	CRIT DMG	CRIT METHOD
45	1.18	-	-	High Damage

COMBAT SHOTGUN: WEAPON MOD

DMG	ROF	SPLASH RADIUS	CRIT DMG	CRIT METHOD
40	0.5	220	50	Direct Hit

The Combat Shotgun can't inflict as much damage as the Super Shotgun per squeeze of the trigger, but its higher rate of fire and tighter spread make it a bit more versatile. As with the other shotgun, the damage dealt depends entirely on how much of the buckshot hits its mark, and how much of it hits the enemy's head for a Critical Hit. It's possible to inflict as much as **44 DMG** per squeeze of the trigger. The Combat Shotgun is an effective weapon for close-range combat because it can be fired at approximately one shot per second.

Enabling the Weapon Modifier loads the Combat Shotgun with a mortar shell. The reticle will change and flash white when ready to fire. The mortar shell doesn't have quite the range of a plasma orb or the Hellshot's incendiary round, but it can inflict up to **50 DMG** on direct hits. It also inflicts splash damage within a tight radius. You can fire the mortar shell approximately every 1.5 seconds, so you will suffer a slight time penalty trying to rely on the weapon's alternate fire.

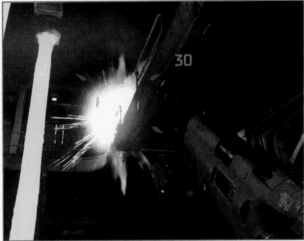

The Combat Shotgun is a very good secondary weapon to have equipped for those times when the combat moves to close quarters. While it's okay to fire a mortar shell down upon distant enemies from an elevated position, it's best to use the standard fire mode when engaging foes directly. Strafe, jump, and move erratically while pumping the Combat Shotgun's buckshot into the upper torso of your target. This is a good weapon to pair with the Vortex Rifle, Rocket Launcher, or Static Rifle, as it ensures that you are covered in any situation.

UNLOCKED AT LEVEL 14

PRIMARY: Short-range energy weapon that fires a constant stream of electricity.

MODIFIER: Creates an electrified field upon hitting a surface that can damage multiple targets. Consumes 2 ammo with each shot.

LIGHTNING GUN: PRIMARY FIRE

DMG	ROF	SPLASH RADIUS	CRIT DMG	CRIT METHOD
8	10	-	10	Consecutive Hits

LIGHTNING GUN: WEAPON MOD

DMG	ROF	SPLASH RADIUS	CRIT DMG	CRIT METHOD
5	10	150	7	Consecutive Hits

The Lightning Gun fires a continual stream of energy that delivers small amounts of damage in constant rapid doses. The Lightning Gun's primary attack inflicts **8 DMG** every split second (10 DMG on Critical Hits) for as long as you manage to keep the electricity stream aimed at the enemy. The Lightning Gun has above-average accuracy and can be used from short to medium distances without difficulty. Keep the trigger pulled, and watch the damage pile up.

The Lightning Gun's alternate fire creates an electric field that electrifies surfaces and inflicts damage to all enemies within a small radius. The Weapon Modifier takes no time to charge, consumes the same amount of ammunition as the primary fire mode, and can be used to deliver smaller increments of damage (**2 to 7 DMG,** depending on the enemy's proximity to where the gun is being aimed).

The Weapon Modifier is best employed when you're offering support fire against a number of opponents or when you are on the run (or at a longer range) and can't be as accurate. One of the best uses for the Lightning Gun's Weapon Modifier is to shoot at the floor and electrocute adversaries hiding behind cover and around corners. This is a great way for you to stay clear of their attacks while still damaging them.

The Lightning Gun inflicts death through a thousand paper cuts. Though each jolt of damage is minor, the rate of fire is extremely fast. Whether you're aiming at the floor near a group of enemies or keeping the primary stream aimed squarely at a single target, the Lightning Gun can bring down all but the healthiest and most armor-clad foes in no time at all. The Lightning Gun is, in some ways, a more precise Chaingun that has the capability of inflicting steady splash damage when the Weapon Modifier is enabled. It's a fine weapon that makes your climb to Level 14 all the more worthwhile. If the Lightning Gun has any drawbacks, it's that it's impossible to use without everyone in the area being able to trace the electricity to its source. There will be no doubt where you are when using this weapon, so sniping is out of the question.

UNLOCKED AT LEVEL 16

PRIMARY: A precision weapon that gains power when in constant motion and drains while idle. Takes 3.6 seconds to fully charge.

MODIFIER: Zooms the weapon for better precision at long range.

STATIC RIFLE: PRIMARY FIRE

DMG	ROF	SPLASH RADIUS	CRIT DMG	CRIT METHOD
20-60	1.18	-	26-79	Headshot

STATIC RIFLE: WEAPON MOD

DMG	ROF	SPLASH RADIUS	CRIT DMG	CRIT METHOD
-	-		-	

The Static Rifle is a precision long-range rifle that inflicts varying amounts of damage based on the level of charge when the trigger is pulled. Both in primary fire mode and when the Weapon Modifier is enabled, the weapon continues to charge while you are in motion. Even if you are just moving side to side, the weapon will charge, and the circular display on the reticle will fill. Shooting an enemy while stationary inflicts **20 DMG** (26 on Critical Hits), whereas hitting an adversary with a fully charged shot inflicts **60 DMG** (79 on Critical Hits). The weapon can be fired with a partial charge and will deal an amount of damage proportional to the level of charge. The Static Rifle requires **4 seconds** of continuous movement to charge.

The Weapon Modifier zooms the weapon in for more precise long-distance targeting. Unfortunately, this drastically slows your movement speed and narrows your field of vision considerably. While advantageous for sniping, the Weapon Modifier does not increase the damage dealt. And since you must still be moving to charge the weapon and deal greater damage, this tends to negate any advantages of concealed sniping that may be conducive with the Vortex Rifle. Enable the Weapon Modifier when your enemy's position is known and you are within a safe distance and/or can move slightly back and forth while waiting for him to round a corner or step out from behind cover. Consider using the Manhunt Hack Module for this purpose.

The Static Rifle is perfect for those who have the gameplay skill to accurately fire a precision weapon while on the move. The weapon need not be fully charged (or even partially charged) to fire at a rate of once every second. However, it's best to stay on the move, look for cover and health and ammo pickups while charging the Static Rifle, then turn and inflict heavy damage. Standing your ground while slowly doling out minimum damage with an uncharged Static Rifle is guaranteed to get you gunned down. Pick your shots, keep the weapon charged, and finish off weakened foes. Another worthwhile tactic is to combine the Static Rifle with the Super Shotgun or Combat Shotgun. Inflict heavy damage with the Static Rifle, then switch to a shotgun to finish off your foe. Note that the Static Rifle only begins to charge after equipping it; it will not be fully charged if you switch to it while on the move.

POWER WEAPONS

Power weapons spawn on the map after **1:45** and respawn **1:45** after their ammo is depleted.

Each map has one power weapon (BFG, Chainsaw, or Gauss Cannon) that will spawn in a specific location after a set period of time (10 seconds after the Demon Rune spawns). These weapons are extremely powerful but have very limited ammunition. They can tilt the battle in favor of the team that secures the weapon, but care must be taken when going for the pickup, as you can be sure that the opposition will have their guns pointed at the spawn point. Power weapons, particularly the BFG and Gauss Cannon, can greatly assist in taking down a demon.

Power weapons do not replace your loadout weapons. Switching to a different weapon will cause you to drop the power weapon on the floor, where another player can acquire it. Ammo for power weapons cannot be replenished. Listen for the announcer to alert players to the Demon Rune having spawned, and know that the power weapon will appear in 10 seconds.

ENEMY DETECTED!

Power weapons all share the same Weapon Modifier ability: a brief wall-penetrating scan of the area in front of you that highlights your foes' positions. Enable the Weapon Modifier, and watch for enemy positions highlighted in red. They appear for only one second, but this helps you hunt them down.

BFG 9000

Fire a giant burst of Argent Plasma that explodes on impact and untethers itself when fired to hit all enemies near its path. Tendril beams deal **15 damage** and have a range of 450 units.

MAPS AVAILABLE: Excavation, Heatwave, and Perdition

AMMO CAPACITY: 4

BFG 9000

DMG	ROF	SPLASH RADIUS	CRIT DMG	CRIT METHOD
200	0.67	432	275	Direct Hit

The BFG—a very large gun—fires a projectile that not only inflicts **275 DMG** to an enemy directly hit by the weapon's Argent Plasma, but also deals varying damage to all adversaries along its path. The BFG is an exceptional weapon to use in corridors or relatively confined spaces where numerous foes have gathered, as even those enemies on the periphery of the weapon's range will repeatedly suffer at least **15 DMG** as the projectile passes.

Most will perish! Unlike the Gauss Cannon, the BFG does not require much accuracy when you're firing it. Unfortunately, the BFG does have a slower firing rate than the Gauss Cannon. Avoid firing the BFG at close-range enemies or into nearby obstacles or walls, as the blast could be self-damaging.

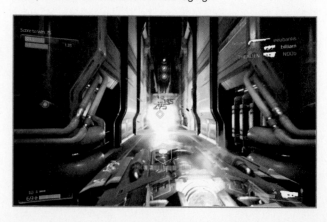

CHAINSAW

Rips enemy players to shreds! Each use grants the player the ability to automatically Glory Kill any enemy it hits. Increases movement speed by 22%.

MAPS AVAILABLE: Disposal, Helix, and Infernal

AMMO CAPACITY: 6

CHAINSAW

DMG	ROF	SPLASH RADIUS	CRIT DMG	CRIT METHOD
120	1.67	-	-	-

Securing the Chainsaw grants you a large movement bonus, making it that much easier to chase down enemies for a melee kill. Pull the trigger to rev and swing the Chainsaw when close to an adversary for a guaranteed Glory Kill. Holding the trigger swings the Chainsaw back and forth in a crisscross pattern, Glory Killing any foe within close range. Each swing of the Chainsaw consumes one of its ammo blocks. The Chainsaw is a lot of fun to use—and highly effective—but you must remember that you are defenseless against attacks from enemies at range. Move erratically and use the speed boost that the weapon confers to close the gap quickly. Seek out opponents who are unaware of your position, as well as those who are wielding long-range weapons.

GAUSS CANNON

Fires a high-velocity concentrated beam. An extremely powerful weapon but requires precision to be used effectively. Projectiles continue on through enemies.

MAPS AVAILABLE: Beneath, Chasm, and Sacrilegious

AMMO CAPACITY: 4

GAUSS CANNON

DMG	ROF	SPLASH RADIUS	CRIT DMG	CRIT METHOD
125	0.8	75	150	Direct Hit

The Gauss Cannon can inflict **150 DMG** on a direct hit, making it capable of delivering a one-shot kill to any enemy who didn't just acquire a Mega-Health pickup. Unlike the BFG, the Gauss Cannon fires a very narrow beam that must be aimed accurately to be effective. Fortunately, the Gauss Cannon has a moderate rate of fire (semi-automatic) and can be aimed on the move without difficulty. You can use the Gauss Cannon to hit foes at any range, and it is particularly effective against demons. Though not as devastating to multiple opponents as the BFG, the higher rate of fire and lack of splash damage risk to self makes the Gauss Cannon a worthy alternative.

EQUIPMENT

Each of your loadouts has a slot available for one of seven types of equipment. Unlike weaponry, which has an ammunition supply that must be replenished through pickups, equipment has a recharge timer. Equipment is available to use at the start of the match and takes **20 seconds** to recharge between uses. Your choice in equipment is every bit as important as your weapon selection. When deciding what to bring, consider the game mode that you're playing and the map where the battle is taking place. And above all, experiment!

FRAG GRENADE

UNLOCKED AT LEVEL 1

An anti-personnel fragmentation grenade that detonates **1 second** after impact against the floor.

The Frag Grenade is your basic high-explosive device that can be thrown once every 20 seconds. It explodes violently shortly after hitting the floor and deals up to **100 DMG** to those in the immediate vicinity. Hitting an enemy with the thrown Frag Grenade inflicts **10 DMG** from contact. The key to using the Frag Grenade effectively is to toss it onto the floor near multiple opponents. The damage inflicted depends on your foes' proximity to the explosion, so try to bounce it at their feet. The Frag Grenade is particularly useful in Domination and Warpath modes when multiple adversaries are attacking or defending a Control Point.

SHIELD WALL

UNLOCKED AT LEVEL 10

The Shield Wall allows allies to pass through but is impermeable to all projectiles and enemies.

When deployed, the Shield Wall creates a large barrier that can protect you and your team from incoming attacks (blue for allies and red for enemies). Though you cannot fire through it, your team is able to advance through the wall to rush the opposition. The Shield Wall remains active for a maximum of **8 seconds**, although the length of time is shortened with heavy damage. When encountering an enemy's Shield Wall, attack it with a Rocket Launcher or other heavy weaponry to disable it before it fades away on its own. The Shield Wall is a great defensive piece of equipment that can save your life if you're low on health. However, you can also use it to blockade opponents from reaching a Demon Rune or power weapon, or from getting to a Control Point in time to contest the area.

TESLA ROCKET

UNLOCKED AT LEVEL 4

A variable-speed energy device that slows down to strike targets it passes with bolts of energy.

Toss this hovering rocket down a corridor, and watch it repeatedly zap nearby enemies for **9 DMG** with each jolt as it passes by. The Tesla Rocket can inflict moderate to heavy damage in short time to numerous opponents. Though 9 DMG may not seem like much, the Tesla Rockets strike so rapidly that a single Tesla Rocket is capable of finishing off multiple weakened foes simultaneously. Consider using it with the Lightning Gun's modified attack to spread electricity across the floor and finish off those enemies being hit by the Tesla Rocket. Similarly, a well-aimed Rocket Launcher can also work well with a Tesla Rocket. Beware that the Tesla Rocket can also inflict damage upon you if you happen to throw it toward the floor or against a nearby wall. Be sure that it has plenty of room to fly before deploying it!

SIPHON GRENADE

UNLOCKED AT LEVEL 8

The siphon field created on impact leaches health from enemies and returns it to the thrower.

The Siphon Grenade erupts in a wide-reaching pink siphon field that quickly collapses, damaging all enemies in the field. Foes hit by the Siphon Grenade rapidly lose health in **5 DMG** increments. The siphon field quickly shrinks, but adversaries who are nearest to where the Siphon Grenade is thrown may suffer as much as **50 DMG**. This damage is returned to the user in the form of health, making the Siphon Grenade an effective way to drain health from multiple enemies and bestow healing powers, as well! The siphon field is only active for a little over a second, so be sure to throw it where it can do the most harm—and only when you are not at full health or (better still) engaged in a firefight with the enemy you are targeting. As with the Tesla Rocket, the Siphon Grenade complements splash damage weaponry such as the Rocket Launcher and the Combat Shotgun's mortar shells. This grenade is very useful in Clan Area, since there's no other way to regain health without pickups.

HOLOGRAM

UNLOCKED AT LEVEL 15

Creates a holographic copy of yourself. Once deployed, you can toggle the Hologram's behavior between running and remaining stationary.

The Hologram is a distraction technique that lasts for **6 seconds** with each use. Upon being deployed, the Hologram runs forward along a straight path, slowly firing a rifle in an effort to distract the enemy. Press the Equipment button a second time to make the Hologram stand still. You can continue toggling between these two behaviors for the length of the effect. The Hologram is best used in a chaotic firefight when there are multiple enemies and allies, as it's more likely for the Hologram to truly deceive someone in such a situation. The Hologram is less effective in one-on-one skirmishes, as a skilled opponent will quickly realize that the Hologram is a decoy.

THREAT SENSOR

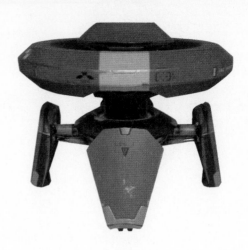

UNLOCKED AT LEVEL 13

A reflected energy device that tunnels through walls to highlight obscured enemies.

Toss the Threat Sensor on the ground and listen for its high-pitched alarm. The alarm will sound when an enemy is in the vicinity, at which time you should be able to spot the foe's skeleton through walls and other obstacles, thanks to the energy device. The Threat Sensor remains active for a total of **40 seconds** with each use, though you can deploy a second Threat Sensor after the customary 20-second recharge. The first Threat Sensor will disappear from the map as soon as the second one has been deployed. The Threat Sensor is best used when you have decided to "camp" an area like a Control Point or a power weapon spawn. The Threat Sensor is also useful for alerting you to adversaries while you're thawing allies in Freeze Tag matches, or for times when you simply want a quick notification if an enemy is in the vicinity.

EQUIPMENT DAMAGE

Threat Sensors and Personal Teleporters can be destroyed by enemies.

PERSONAL TELEPORTER

UNLOCKED AT LEVEL 1

A thrown device that teleports the user to its location. After deployment, activate it again to teleport.

The Personal Teleporter is arguably the most powerful piece of equipment, but it's also the most difficult to master. Throw the Personal Teleporter against any surface within the game space, where it will stick and blink for **8 seconds**. Press the Equipment button a second time while it is active to instantly teleport to that device's location. You can use this to quickly escape to a safe position, drop on foes from the ceiling, or even teleport to an enemy's position for a "tele-frag" kill. When teleporting, you will instantly disappear and reappear where the device was located. Try placing the Personal Teleporter along a well-traveled path or behind a camped opponent so that you can teleport to his position. You'll instantly tele-frag the enemy upon appearing where he was, as two objects cannot occupy the same space. The Personal Teleporter requires considerable practice to use effectively, but the effort it takes to master this device is worth it.

MULTIPLAYER MAPS

:X BENEATH

Beneath is one of the only symmetrical maps in the game and has an exterior walkway that encircles a multi-level interior. Both the central area and exterior corners contain jump boosts to help players move quickly between the levels. The only environmental hazard is the potential to fall from the outer edge of the exterior.

LOCATION INTEL

POWER WEAPON: Gauss Cannon

POWERUP: Haste, Invisibility

SUICIDE RISK: Moderate

A	Armor		**MH**	Mega Health
A	Domination Capture A		Ⓝ	Powerup
B	Domination Capture B		**PW**	Power Weapon
C	Domination Capture C		**SP**	Spawn Point

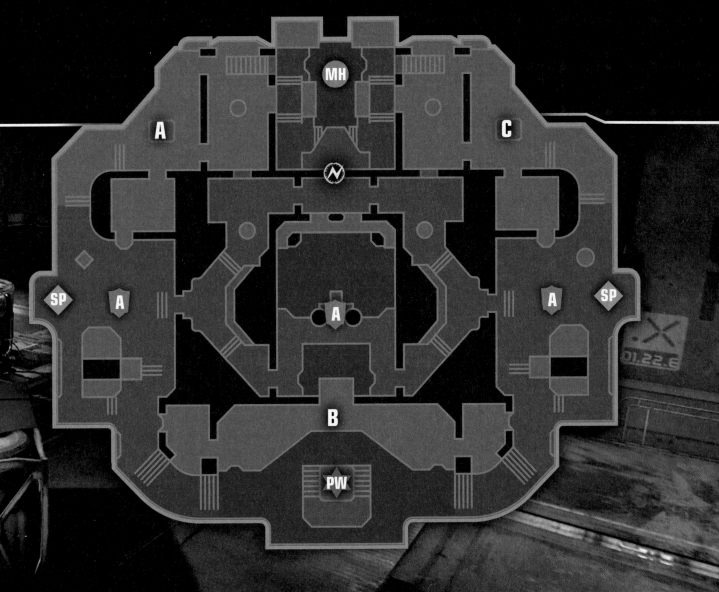

Teams spawn on the east and west sides of the map, identified by the colored stripe on the wall near their spawn. The path directly ahead leads to a V-shaped hallway. The team spawning on the red side of the map should enter this hallway and head right to quickly engage the enemy's front line. Those on the blue side can engage the enemy quickly by heading left inside the V-shaped corridor on their side. Those wanting to flank the enemy can go in the opposite direction and move along the upper walkway in the center of the interior space.

The northern and southern sides of the exterior drop down several flights of stairs and connect to the interior through a lower level tunnel. The Gauss Cannon is located on the southern side of the map, atop a platform that's accessible by stairs or by double jumping from the upper balcony. The Mega Health is atop a pillar on the northern side of the map, reachable only via a double jump. Grab the Mega Health, drop to the floor, and sprint inside to pick up the powerup in the lower hallway.

DEMONIC POSSESSION

The Prowler and Revenant are especially potent on Beneath due to the spacious exterior areas and multi-level interiors. Watch for enemies to congregate on the interior balcony near the Gauss Cannon. The Baron of Hell can also surprise numerous enemies in the hallways and gain instant Glory Kills without being shot from all directions.

OBJECTIVE BASED MODES

Initial team conflicts tend to take place between the balconies overlooking the lower level inside the center of the map. Consider flanking around to the side (via the other hallway) and catch your opponents in crossfire while your teammates shoot across the room. Much of the combat continues to coalesce around the central interior area, making it possible to freelance on the exterior, particularly in the direction of the Mega Health pickup.

Be extra careful around the area with the Gauss Cannon as there are multiple elevated positions that can target this coverless area. We recommend sprinting along a path that leads from the Armor pickups near the spawn points toward the Mega Health pickup and then to the powerup. From there, use a jump boost to the upper level of the interior and pick off enemies on either balcony as you cross the map back to the Gauss Cannon.

DOMINATION

Unlike in Team Deathmatch, the action in Domination is largely concentrated on the outer ring of the map. Those spawning near the red spawn can leave two teammates to secure Zone A while the rest of the squad hurries off to the right to contest Zone B. Another option is to forfeit Zone B and head along the outer path to the left to contest Zone C near the enemy's spawn. Those spawning near the blue side of the map can do this in reverse. Follow the outer edge of the map to the right to contest Zone A near the enemy spawn or head left (or through the interior) to fight over Zone B. The walkway above the powerup (directly across from the Mega Health) provides an excellent vantage point from which to lend support to teammates at any of the three Control Points.

ROUND BASED MODES

The initial clash is likely to take place across the interior, from one balcony to the other. Stick close to your team, but try to fall back and use the Vortex Rifle to snipe enemies across the gap, then fall back further, switch to the Chaingun, and watch for enemies flanking your position or those trying to assault your position via the jump boost.

We don't recommend heading along the exterior walkway to try to get the drop on your opponent as it's a very lengthy distance and the battle may well be decided by the time you reach your destination. Your running off may well cost your team the victory and though you may receive the Last Man Standing bonus, you'll likely be outnumbered.

:X CHASM

Chasm is arguably the most complicated and sprawling of all of the maps. This multi-level facility consists of numerous twisting corridors, narrow crawlspaces, stairs, and also the namesake canyon it's known for. The map is conducive for run-and-gun individual gameplay as it can be very difficult to coordinate attacks and even harder to verbally describe your position to teammates when calling for assistance. Many of the rooms are labeled within the map, but the complex geometry is sufficiently disorienting so as to make these labels only marginally helpful.

LOCATION INTEL

POWER WEAPON: Gauss Cannon

POWERUPS: Invisibility, Regeneration

SUICIDE RISK: Low

A	Armor		Powerup	
A	Domination Capture A	**PW**	Power Weapon	
B	Domination Capture B	**SP**	Spawn Point	
C	Domination Capture C			

Quickly look to the walls near where you spawn to see which room you're in. One team spawns in a room with a red stripe and "LR 3" on the wall. If this is where you begin, race straight ahead along the upper level and go through corridor "LR2" to where it overlooks the large central room. This is likely where the enemy is going to be by the time you get there, giving you an elevated position from which to shoot. If you begin in the gold-striped room with "LR6" on the wall, you're going to be tempted to advance toward the enemy in the center of the map—don't. Instead, sweep around the perimeter through the canyon.

Chasm is defined by rooms with large scientific pieces of equipment and numerous ledges and crates. Keep to the edges of the hallways and leap to the ledges that run along the walls to continuously collect Armor and Health pickups. There are two powerups on this map and three larger Armor pickups, but no Mega Health. The only place on the map that poses an environmental hazard is inside the namesake chasm. Be careful with your jumps here when going for the Gauss Cannon to avoid Suicide. Lastly, stay on the lookout for crawlspaces high in the walls that lead from one room to another (and even out into the canyon area). These tiny passageways are often lined with Health and Armor pickups and can provide a suitable place from which to launch your attack, particularly with the Invisible powerup.

DEMONIC POSSESSION

With so much ground to cover and so many places to hide, it's important to choose a demon that moves quickly. The Revenant and Prowler can accomplish this, as can the Baron of Hell. We're particularly fond of the Prowler on this map as you can use its Pounce ability to fling yourself down lengthy corridors and attack an enemy rounding the corner before it even knows you're coming. The Baron of Hell's Ground Pound attack is also quite destructive on this map.

OBJECTIVE BASED MODES

The initial clash between the two teams often takes place in the center of the map with the team that spawns in the red-striped room having an elevated advantage from which to shoot. If your team spawns in this location, take advantage of your good fortune and advance straight ahead to the gold-striped room where the enemy may be lurking. If, on the other hand, you spawn in the gold-striped room, you should instruct your team to ascend quickly via the hallways to the left. Get to the upper level where you can engage the enemy on equal footing and, possibly, by surprise!

After the initial clash, you're likely going to be separated from your teammates (especially after a respawn) and it can be very difficult to regroup on this map due to the complex geometry. Chasm is a map that, perhaps more than any other, rewards the team with the best individual players. Extend your life—and your effectiveness—by staying on the move and leaping/running in an erratic pattern from one trail of Health and Armor pickups to the next. Loop the perimeter of the lower level to collect the Invisibility or Regeneration powerup (and the Gauss Cannon, if possible) while trying to stay one step ahead of the enemy. Move to the upper level once in the center of the map, then use Frag Grenades and Tesla Rockets to weaken the enemies you encounter.

DOMINATION

If spawning near Zone C, quickly capture the point with one or two teammates, then continue along the perimeter of the map, keeping to the right, in a counter-clockwise manner and use the jump boost to reach the upper level. This puts you directly above Zone B just in time to contest the central location. The team that spawns near Zone A can secure the nearby Control Point with a single player while sending the rest of the team straight ahead along the lower level to Zone B. Be prepared for an attack from above and use the crates and nearby jump boosts to reach the

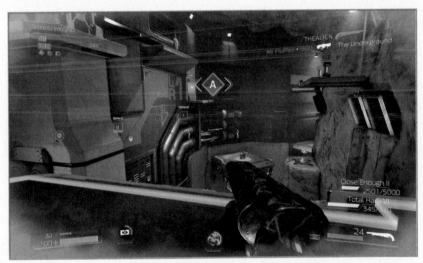

upper level to defend this point with everything you've got. Securing two of the three points at the start of the match can be a distance maker. Later in the match, once the Demon Rune and Gauss Cannon have spawned, do yourself a favor and only go for the Gauss Cannon if you're sure there are no enemies near Zone A.

ROUND BASED MODES

Much of the battle in Clan Arena and Freeze Tag is going to take place in and around the center of the map, in the room labeled "LR6." This map is so large that you may well never regroup with your teammates if you go off in a different direction. Instead, stick with the group and try to overwhelm the enemy as soon as the battle begins. Target isolated enemies with rifle fire and use explosives and other weapons that deal splash damage against groups of enemies.

One technique that can work well is to get on the same level of your opponent to flank them. When spawning on the red-striped upper level, advance to the curved hallway with your team, then veer left and descend the stairs to the lower level where you can engage the enemy as they are distracted. Similarly, the team spawning on the lower room should avoid the death-trap that awaits straight ahead and instead move through the canyon to circle the enemy or immediately ascend to the upper level via the jump boosts and crates on the left.

:X DISPOSAL

If you've ever wondered where the UAC's toxic waste ends up, here it is! Disposal is a moderately large map with several hallways and corridors that lead through a facility perched on the edge of a cliff. The central area has a room with a pool of toxic waste in it, there's a canyon you can fall into, and scattered throughout the map are small canisters that explode if shot, releasing poisonous gas into the area. Action predominantly takes place indoors, but you must watch where you step even there! There are several medium and large Armor powerups, an Invisibility powerup, and, best of all, the Chainsaw!

LOCATION INTEL

POWER WEAPON: Chainsaw

POWERUPS: Invisibility

SUICIDE RISK: Moderate

A Armor	**MH** Mega Health
A Domination Capture A	**⊘** Powerup
B Domination Capture B	**PW** Power Weapon
C Domination Capture C	**SP** Spawn Point

This is one of the easier maps to understand where you are when you spawn because one of the spawn points is outdoors, on the sandy cliff, and the other is inside. Nevertheless, teams tend to meet quickly in the room with the semi-circular wall (and the Mega Health) or in the room with the green toxic sludge flowing beneath the walkway. Most of the areas with two levels have stairs or can be climbed. For all of its corridors and staircases one is never far from the action in Disposal. The grimy, dank interior has a habit of leading players into one another, whether in the room with the toxic soup or the sandy exterior, bullets will certainly be flying! Unlike some maps which appear even larger and more complex than they are, Disposal can, at first, feel a bit small. It's not!

Consider following the upper perimeter wall in a clockwise direction to learn the map's main path. This leads you through rooms overlooking the Invisibility and Mega Health (two hotly-contested rooms) and then outside to the cliff area where the central pillar contains a Chainsaw. Double jump carefully or pay the price! Back inside, familiarize yourself with the inner ring that connects the room with the toxic waste on the floor with the room where the Mega Health is and the Invisibility powerup. These three rooms form an inner circle connected by several walkways and stairways leading to the outer loop. Lastly, note that there's a smaller exit leading outside in the southeast corner of the map that demons cannot fit through. To pursue enemies outside as the demon, you must use the larger doorway at the north end of the area.

DEMONIC POSSESSION

The larger rooms and shorter, good sight-lines make this a good map for Mancubus's rockets and Vent attack. It's also helpful to be the Revenant here as there are several areas where the Revenant can hover above the fray and rain rockets down on the enemies, particularly as they go for the powerup. As mentioned previously, demons cannot fit through the southwest passageway leading outside to the cliff area, so you must use the corridor to the north to get back inside if the Demon Rune spawns outside.

OBJECTIVE BASED MODES

Those spawning on the inside of the facility should be careful to avoid the toxic sludge in the adjacent room as they head toward the center of the map. The enemy is likely to approach from the right-hand side of the room with the Mega Health in it, so either join your teammates in engaging them when they appear or head to the left and ascend to the area overlooking the rooms with the Invisibility and the Mega Health. On the other hand, the team that spawns outside can often bait the enemy into funneling through the doorway leading into the room where the Mega Health is. Take partial cover behind the semi-circular wall and concentrate heavy firepower through the doorway as they come into view.

Try to maintain communication with your team and ask them to guide you to either the cliff, the toxic waste room or the room with the semi-circular wall. These are good landmarks that should be easy to navigate quickly to once you learn the map. Be sure to return to the inner spawn point periodically to collect the Armor that spawns there. This is a convenient item to grab on your way to the Invisibility and the Mega Health. Scan the area around the cliffs for enemies and never go for the Chainsaw without first shooting the green canister of toxic gas. Wait for the fumes to dissipate before making your move for the Chainsaw.

DOMINATION

Zone C is near the interior spawn and Zone A encircles the pile of crates and supplies by the outside spawn point. Since both of these are quite far from one another, they can be captured easily with just a single person while the rest of your team fights to secure Zone B, located where the Mega Health spawns. Zone B, perhaps even more than usual, is very hard to hold given its location on the map and its lack of cover. Coordinate with your teammates to have two people go for the capture while at least one other patrols the walkway overlooking the Control Point and provides fire from above. Another useful tactic on Disposal, regardless of where you spawn, is to focus your efforts on taking Zone C as it tends to be easier to defend than the other zones. Use the platform above the Control Point along with the narrow ledge above the Armor pickup to pick off unsuspecting enemies as they enter the Control Point from the room with the toxic waste.

ROUND BASED MODES

In games where the teams just rush one another, the major clashes tend to occur in the hallway connecting the room with the semi-circular wall and the hallway with the exposed toxic sludge. If you're on the team that spawns inside the facility, double jump across the toxic pool and come across the control terminal from the left to catch the enemy in crossfire. On the other hand, if you spawn outside, climb onto the upper ledge directly behind the storage tanks, duck inside on the second level and double jump across the gap so you can reach the windows looking down above the semi-circular room. This puts you in prime position to pick off the enemies from above. Consider lobbing a Tesla Rocket or Frag Grenade down at them along with your Rocket Launcher's rockets.

Playing Freeze Tag on this map does come with a slightly greater risk as frozen players can be shoved about (with gunfire) into the toxic pools. This makes them harder to thaw. If your ally is frozen near a cliff, then shoot them to knock them into the abyss. This allows them to respawn safely unfrozen.

EXCAVATION

Excavation is a large wide-open map with several caves on the south side and industrial hallways on the north, but is mostly one giant construction site, complete with dormant machinery. This is a map with great sight-lines, elevated ledges and several hidden tunnels and passageways to make it possible to sneak around. There are also several explosive canisters that can be detonated with a well-aimed round or two!

LOCATION INTEL

POWER WEAPON: BFG

POWERUP: Haste, Quad Damage

SUICIDE RISK: Low

A	Armor	MH	Mega Health	PW	Power Weapon
A	Domination Capture A	1	Portals in	SP	Spawn Point
B	Domination Capture B	1	Portals out		
C	Domination Capture C		Powerup		

As with Disposal, it's easy to know which side of the map you are on as soon as you spawn: if you're in the cave, you are on the south side and if you're outside, then you're in the northeast. Either way, you're going to want to stick to the perimeter of the map and collect the smaller Armor pickups while the larger ones wait to spawn. All of the valuable pickups, including the Haste pickup and the BFG, are located outside, along with the two larger Armor pickups and the Mega Health. All of these items are visible from the main construction site.

The most unique feature to Excavation is the presence of a large grinder in the north-central portion of this map. Stepping or falling into the grinder results in a Suicide, so be careful when approaching the large swirling portal behind it. That portal provides an instant transport to the southeast cave. Grab the Mega Health, run up the conveyor belt to grab the Haste pickup, then drop down and take the portal to the cave near the BFG.

DEMONIC POSSESSION

It's hard to beat the Revenant on this map as the ability to rain down rockets while hovering above the fray is just too good to pass up. But, if you want to mix things up, the Mancubus is also quite useful here as its rockets can reach enemies from considerable distance, making it possible to stick to the perimeter where there's some cover, and pick off distracted foes from afar.

OBJECTIVE BASED MODES

The initial clash at Excavation tends to occur in the middle east-west span across the construction site, in the area where the bridge is. This is a large area with plenty of pickups, and while the team on the east side has easier access to the BFG when it spawns, the team to the west has easier access to the Mega Health and Haste. And, of course, the portal leading to the BFG. Use the upper ledges and various obstacles for cover and try to stay clear of the open area in the center where you can be shot from multiple directions. Instead, coordinate with teammates to gang up on isolated opponents or stick to the periphery and lend a hand to your teammates.

Both the cave to the south and the industrial corridors on the north have multiple levels and small passages that can be scaled for stealth purposes. Make use of these off-the-beaten-path routes every now and then to see if they can nab you a surprise kill or two, but don't stay in one place for too long. Similarly, never hang out on the bridge or atop the conveyor belt as the field-of-view is quite wide and you will be seen.

DOMINATION

Quickly lay claim to the Zone nearest your spawn and then make your way to Zone B. Though it might seem that the team spawning near Zone A can get there faster, the other team can match their speed by using the portal. If you spawn near Zone C, try to coordinate so that two of your members capture Zone C while two double back through the caves to Zone B and the other two use the portal. This should surprise the opposition from two directions at once. On the other hand, if you are near Zone A at the start of the match, leave one person to capture it while the rest contest Zone B—with your eyes up at the rocky ledge in the corner of the cave to catch the enemies when they teleport in! Pay attention for powerup availability on this map and look to use the BFG to clear out contested zones. And while the Haste pickup may not be as critical in Domination, you'd better believe the Quad Damage pickup is. Look for it atop the conveyor belt!

ROUND BASED MODES

The quickest way to confront the other team is in the southwest corner cave, near the BFG spawn point. If you spawn in the cave, just head along the path to the right and you'll get there in moments. If you spawn outside, just head left and continue past the BFG spawn point. But that's only if you want to clash in one quick skirmish. On a map with so much open real-estate it's better to fall back as a team, look for an elevated position, and wait for the opponent to spread out looking for you. You need only pick one or two enemies off to gain a significant advantage in Clan Arena.

It won't happen often, but look to knock frozen allies into the grinder while playing Freeze Tag to allow them to respawn safely unfrozen. This isn't a particularly common place for skirmishes to take place, but it can certainly happen in longer-lasting matches as players go for the powerup or try to use the portal to reach the BFG.

:X HEATWAVE

Return to the foundry for an epic battle above pools of molten ore. Run, climb, and leap across narrow platforms and spacious gaps where one wrong move can be your last. Heatwave boasts a number of twisting, multi-level corridors and side areas that ring a larger central area filled with flowing—and cascading—molten death! Join the battle for supremacy in the center of the map or slip along the perimeter to catch your enemy by surprise.

LOCATION INTEL

POWER WEAPON: BFG

POWERUP: Quad Damage, Invisibility

SUICIDE RISK: High

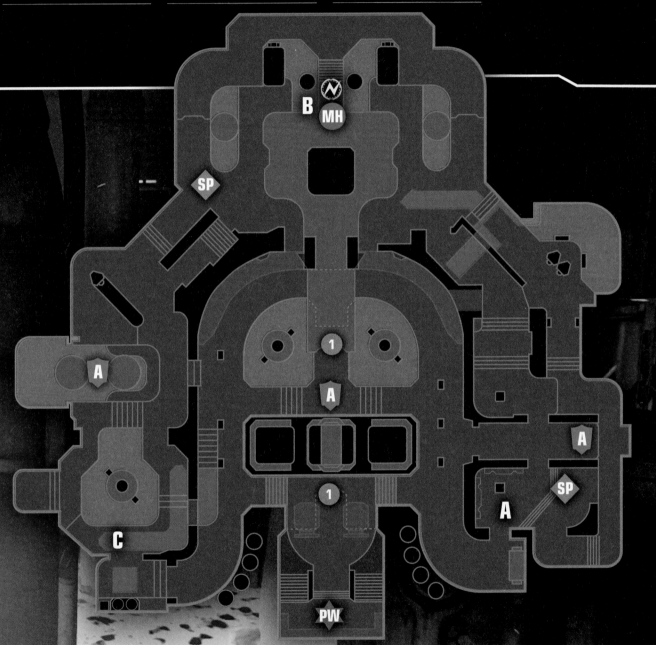

Legend

A	Armor	**C**	Domination Capture C	⊘	Powerup
A	Domination Capture A	**MH**	Mega Health	**PW**	Power Weapon
B	Domination Capture B	**1**	Portals (in/out)	**SP**	Spawn Point

Heatwave is larger than it first appears because so much of the battle takes place in the elongated central area where the BFG and powerups are spread out in a north-south line. Upon spawning into the map, check to see if you're in a control room or near a falling cascade of molten material. The team spawning in the control room is closer to the south side of the map and can quickly get to the lower portal and use it to reach the upper central area. The team spawning outside the control room is already close to the central area, but can fall back to the maze of hallways and paths that lead along the eastern side of the map.

The central area of Heatwave has a lengthy north-south series of ledges and walkways positioned at multiple elevations. Use the two-way portal to move between the lower and upper levels quickly and don't miss the large Armor pickup located in a sniper's perch directly above the upper portal. The Quad Damage powerup is atop the stairs at the north end of the map and can be clearly seen from afar. Try to time your approach so that you can claim the Mega Health located directly beneath the powerup, too! Double jump across the gap beneath the walkway to get the Mega Health, then loop around and nab the Quad Damage.

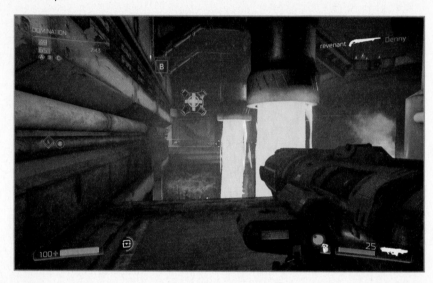

DEMONIC POSSESSION

With so many places to fall from solid ground, it really pays to have the Prowler on Heatwave. Use Pounce attacks to leap from one solid surface to the next, and line up your jumps with unsuspecting enemies. The other Demons can certainly rack up some kills on Heatwave, as well—even the slow-moving Mancubus can score plenty of kills so long as you're careful where you walk, but the Prowler's ability to guarantee safe purchase on any surface is worth considering.

OBJECTIVE BASED MODES

Much of the combat takes place around the center of the map, between the upper portal and where the Mega Health and powerup is located. If you're heading that way from your team's spawn point (regardless of which spawn that is), it's wise to snake through the hallways that lead to the right of your spawn so that your team can accumulate some Armor before heading into battle. Though the larger Armor pickups won't be ready just yet, there are plenty of smaller Armor pickups and Ammo Crates to gather on your way into battle. Consider having half of your team loop around to the north while the others head south so that you can catch the enemy in crossfire.

Be careful when making a run for the BFG as there may be an enemy located in the tower above the portals. Similarly, you may want to lob a Threat Detector near the BFG so that you can alert your team when someone is going for it. The Threat Detector's alarm will sound no matter how far away from it you are. Another equipment option is to use the Personal Teleporter to tele-frag an enemy player who is in the tower above the portals. That's a nice compact place where someone will try to camp out, making themselves extremely vulnerable to this special attack. Lastly, monitor your Health and Armor carefully and flee to the relative safety of the passages along the east and west sides of the map. There you'll find plenty of pickups, as well as some medium size Armor.

DOMINATION

Zones A and C are, as usual, close to the spawn points and can be captured quite easily. What makes this map different is that Zone B is so far away from the other Zones that A and C tend to be left unguarded as players fight to take and defend Zone B located near the Quad Damage powerup. This not only makes it possible for one player to sneak in and capture Zone A or C with little defense, but it also means that the BFG is sometimes forgotten all the way to the south end of the map. Depending on the situation and where you respawn, consider grabbing the BFG and using the lower portal to quickly reach the upper one. Turn around and climb the tower to where the Armor pickup is and use the BFG to take out any and all enemies near Zone B. Just be sure to let your team know you're going for this maneuver so they can be there to capture the Control Point right away.

ROUND BASED MODES

One of the most important factors in winning a Clan Arena or Freeze Tag match is making sure you don't Suicide. Players who try to repeatedly jump to make themselves a harder target sometimes leap over the railings to their death. Don't make this mistake. Stay close to your team as they make their way toward the center of the map and look for opportunities to flank the enemy and/or shoot your frozen allies into the molten ore when playing Freeze Tag to allow them to respawn safely unfrozen.

Should a game of Freeze Tag go long enough for the BFG, Demon Rune, and Quad Damage powerups to become a factor, resist the urge to run off by yourself to claim one. Stick together and move as a team to secure the powerup. Better yet, watch the clock and, after the first 1:15 has passed, make your way to the south end of the map and secure the area where the BFG will spawn.

:X HELIX

Helix is a scientific facility comprised of multiple specimen observation rooms where all manner of demons and oddities are kept in stasis tanks of various colors. This is an intimate map that forms a circle of sorts with several larger hub rooms in the center, making it possible to get anywhere quickly. Life is cheap at Helix where you're never more than a few steps from the business end of an enemy's weapon.

LOCATION INTEL

POWER WEAPON: Chainsaw

POWERUP: Quad Damage

SUICIDE RISK: Low

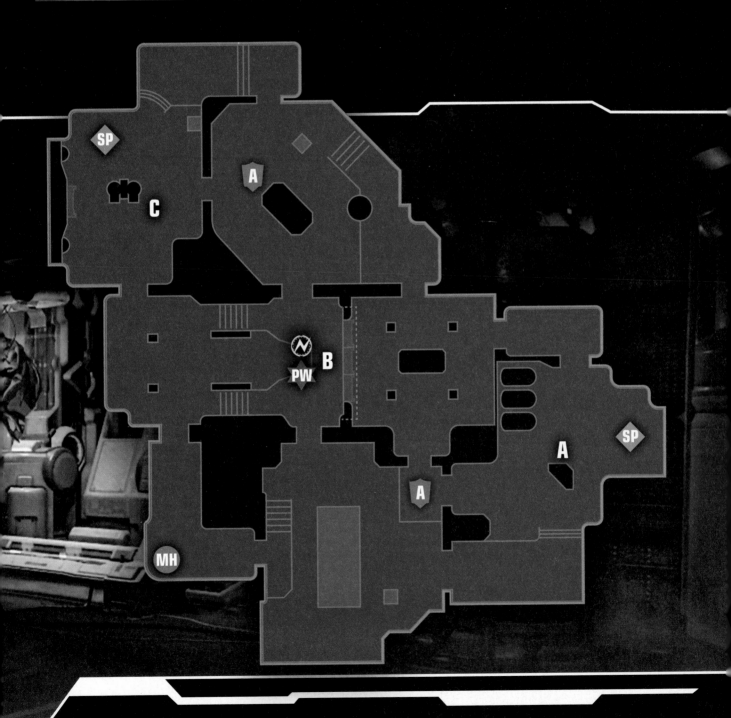

| | A | Armor | | B | Domination Capture B | | MH | Mega Health | | PW | Power Weapon |
| | A | Domination Capture A | | C | Domination Capture C | | | Powerup | | SP | Spawn Point |

AREA RECON

Familiarize yourself with the various rooms and learn a short code for describing them to your teammates to better coordinate attacks and calls for help. Teams spawn on opposite sides of the map, one in a room with blue-glowing stasis tanks and another with tanks illuminated in red light. The two largest rooms in the center of the map contain green-lit specimens and a larger testing room where a massive demon is being held in a device with a red laser. To the east of this is the delivery room where a large vehicle is parked. Hallways and staircases connect these rooms. You can leap through the observation windows between the room with the green-lit tanks and experiment room. It's also possible to run beneath the truck or atop it, though you're not advised to do the latter.

There are few special pickups on this smaller map and what truly sets it apart from others is that the Quad Damage powerup and Chainsaw spawn in the same place randomly. You may reach the experiment room and find a Quad Damage powerup or you may find the Chainsaw. Lastly, watch out for environmental damage from the red explosive canisters and laser.

DEMONIC POSSESSION

This tight map can be problematic for the Prowler, and even the Revenant may have trouble here. It's better to opt for the Mancubus or Baron of Hell and know that they at least have plenty of Health to withstand the bombardment that's sure to come your way!

OBJECTIVE BASED MODES

Soul Harvest and Team Deathmatch games often go quickly on Helix as the bodies can pile up here faster than most other maps. The initial clash usually takes place in the room with the green-lit sample tanks, but also on the upper walkway of the room to the north of it. Those spawning in the blue-lit room should consider flanking around to the room where the powerup is and shooting through the observation windows. Players spawning in the room with the red-lit stasis tanks should angle to the left and circle around through the room with the truck to catch the enemy by surprise from behind.

No matter how the beginning of the match goes, the action likely centers around the room with the truck and the one where the powerup spawns. Use the crates and various pieces of equipment for cover as best you can and look to make hit-and-run attacks from around corners. Target the explosive canisters whenever an enemy is nearby, especially if one happens to respawn behind him. There are very few places in this map where someone can't sneak up behind you, so stay on the move and choose your Hack Module selections wisely.

DOMINATION

Zone B is extraordinarily difficult to maintain control of on Helix, so you may want to consider focusing your efforts on Zones A and C. Though they are further apart and lack the nearby powerup spawn, they are easier to control thanks to their locations being further away from the center of the map. Nevertheless, when making a move on Zone B, try to attack it from both sides simultaneously. Collect the Armor near the truck and in the room between Zones C and B, then converge on the Control Point. It also really helps to pay attention to the clock on this map since the lone powerup spawns right next to Zone B. You don't want to show up late for it if you can avoid it. Since every second you can contest a Control Point is valuable to your team's success, arrive with Armor and stay alive. It takes less time to gather up some pickups than it does to become fodder that has to constantly wait to respawn.

ROUND BASED MODES

There aren't many tricks to perform on Helix when it comes to Clan Arena and Freeze Tag. Weapon choice matters, as does Hack Module, but it's going to come down to how well you can avoid damage and your team's ability to quickly whittle down the enemy's attackers. Much of the action is going to center around the room with the green tanks. Rocket Launchers, Frag Grenades, Siphon Grenades, and Plasma Rifles can quickly injure an entire enemy team if they stick too close together.

Hit the opposition hard with a concerted splash-damage attack, then fall back and finish them off as they funnel through the door. Clan Arena players won't have any Armor pickups to collect, but Freeze Tag players will—and there's one right near each spawn. Continue to use the Plasma Rifle's alternate attack to foul doorways and trap the enemy where they can take damage over time.

:X INFERNAL

Welcome to the largest, most complex, and goriest of all the DOOM maps. Infernal is dripping in blood—literally—and contains three separate portals in addition to multiple levels of passageways, bridges, and tunnels. There are places to fall to your death and blood-drenched waterfalls to ride to lower levels. Take your time learning the map and always remember to use the buddy system when wandering!

LOCATION INTEL

POWER WEAPON: Chainsaw

POWERUP: Quad Damage, Haste

SUICIDE RISK: High

A Armor	**1** Portals in
A Domination Capture A	**1** Portals out
B Domination Capture B	Ⓝ Powerup
C Domination Capture C	**PW** Power Weapon
MH Mega Health	**SP** Spawn Point

One of the teams spawns near an altar in the southwest corner of the map, within sight of the massive skull temple and bridge. The other spawns in the northeast corner, in a cave on the uppermost level of the map. Much of the action takes place on the south side of the map, near the large skull temple. It's not only where the Chainsaw and the Mega Health are located, but it's also where one of the portals teleports players to. This is the most dangerous area on the map due to the high Suicide risk and the incredible sightlines. If you're going to snipe, this is where you want to do it!

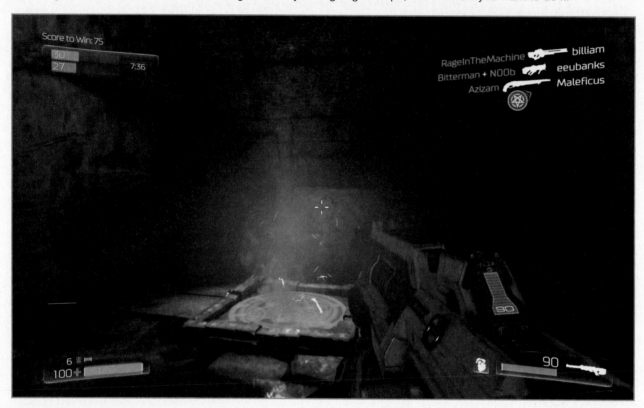

There are several larger Armor pickups throughout the map and a number of smaller Armor and Health pickups that line small holes in the floor and passages that you can safely navigate. Let the pickups be your guide! Stay on the lookout for small pools of green swirling energy as these are the portal entrances on this map. The portals here are not bi-directional, so check with the map to see where each portal leads. Speaking of portals, the easiest way to safely reach the Mega Health is by taking the portal in the middle of the map to the upper ledge above the Mega Health. You can reach it with a double jump from there. Likewise, let the Health pickups to the south of the Chainsaw lead you along the easiest path to the weapon. Leap from the stairs to the rock spire and then to the next closest one in order to reach the Chainsaw from behind it.

DEMONIC POSSESSION

The Mancubus and Baron of Hell can certainly come in handy during Domination matches, particularly if the Demon Rune is near a Control Point; otherwise, consider sticking with the more mobile Revenant and Prowler. There's a lot of ground to cover quickly to hunt down your prey on Infernal and the more agile Revenant and Prowler do well here.

OBJECTIVE BASED MODES

Stick close to your teammates for as long as you can; it's very easy to find yourself suddenly surrounded on this map. The team that spawns near the altar should forego the bridge area for the time being and instead make their way to the left, through the caves leading up the stairs in the direction of the other team's spawn in hopes of catching them unaware. Sweep south across the center of the map to use the portal that sends you to the upper ledge near the bridge in time to collect the Mega Health and, perhaps, the Chainsaw if it's already there.

Learn the whereabouts of the three portals and watch your back when entering them. Try to get in the habit of backing into the portals so you can see if someone is following you into it. There's nothing worse than exiting a portal and having someone appear right behind you and Super Shotgun you in the back! Since so much of the action takes place in the center and southern portions of the map, you'll likely be able to sneak away to get the powerup without much hassle. Grab it and drop through the hole due east of it to land near a portal that can deliver you to some nearby Armor. From there, head to the central portal to gain the upper perch overlooking the skull temple and bridge. You should have plenty of time to use your Quad Damage ability if you don't get derailed.

DOMINATION

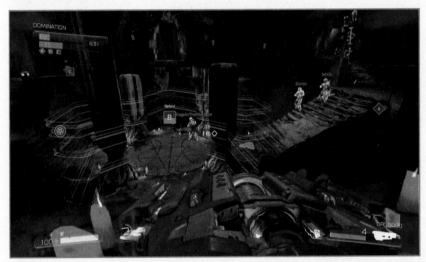

Zone C tends to get lost in the chaos during Domination matches on Infernal, so do your best to capture it early before the focus shifts to Zone B. Once you capture Zone C, especially if you spawn near the altar in the southwest corner, use the portal to reach the ledge overlooking Zone B and the Mega Health. Lob a Siphon Grenade or Frag Grenade down at the enemies there, then leap down and claim it. If your team spawns closer to Zone A, claim it quickly then try to station one or two players in the corner of the area and on the bridge above the Control Point. Zone A can be very hard to take if the other team mounts a coordinated defense and it takes only two players to defend it successfully. Zone B will likely trade hands throughout the match, so try to slip away and get the powerup or Chainsaw.

ROUND BASED MODES

It's easy to get split up from your team on a map of this size in Clan Arena and Freeze Tag and that's a surefire way to lose. Find out where the bulk of your team is headed and either join them or move to a semi-concealed position along their flank where you can perhaps surprise the enemy. Since much of the early action in Clan Arena is going to take place near the bridge you may have time to reach the portal that leads to the overlook, but don't be surprised if the other team is thinking the same thing. Instead, consider fanning out along the ledges and stairs in the area east of the bridge and letting the enemy come to you.

When playing Freeze Tag, it's important to avoid the bridge area (or better still, bait your enemy into crossing toward you). You can be frozen and shoved off the side into the pit below in this precarious location. Try to move in teams of two or three when playing Freeze Tag, especially if you see that the other team is also splitting up after the first round. Don't leave frozen enemies behind unattended—consider using a Threat Detector near a frozen foe to let you know if an enemy is trying to thaw them.

:X PERDITION

As the world fractures and falls apart, all that binds the ground beneath our feet are the roots of the mightiest organisms. The trees that sprout in this land of eternal damnation serve as guideposts on the way to salvation—or at least to the BFG or Regeneration powerup. Perdition is a foul land of suffering with numerous places to fall to your death and myriad altars upon which you can be slaughtered.

LOCATION INTEL

POWER WEAPON: BFG

POWERUP: Regeneration, Haste

SUICIDE RISK: High

LEGEND

A Armor	**B** Domination Capture B	⊘ Powerup	**SP** Spawn Point
A Domination Capture A	**C** Domination Capture C	**PW** Power Weapon	

This relatively small, circular map features an array of staircases, pillars, tunnels, and rock pedestals that make the area feel far larger and more complex than it actually is. The teams spawn directly across from one another and can quickly engage the opposition in the area in front of the totem with the pink-glowing stone sphere on the south side of the map. The pink tunnel lined in blood and flesh facing the totem leads through the center of the map to the area to the north where the BFG is located. Follow the trail of small Armor pickups for a valuable shortcut! This tunnel can be utilized in both directions.

Both the Regeneration powerup and the BFG are perched atop floating rock fragments that can be reached only with careful leaps. Engage the thrusters to double jump if necessary, but try to save the one-use thrusters in case you get shot and need to correct your trajectory while airborne. There is no Mega Health on this map, but there are numerous medium-sized Health pickups. Be aware that the Armor pickup atop the altar near the eastern spawn point is not there during Domination matches. It is replaced with a Haste powerup in that mode. There are also no portals on Perdition.

DEMONIC POSSESSION

Despite the numerous fragmented patches of ground, this map is conducive for all four demons. The Prowler and Revenant can certainly venture a bit wider afield than the Baron and Mancubus on this map, but you may find it safer to play as one of the larger, more resilient enemies as the narrow staircases and relatively cramped spaces of each of the map's various rooms forces enemies to get a bit closer than they may prefer when sharing quarters with other rampaging demons.

OBJECTIVE BASED MODES

Try to keep the enemy occupied on the south side of the map during the beginning of the match where there's more solid ground upon which to have the major clash. Sweep through the eastern side of the map to collect up the Armor pickup and move into position to claim the BFG when it spawns. The north, northwest, and southwest corners of the map pose the greatest risk of Suicide. Take into account where the battle is being fought when you have the opportunity to claim a Demon Rune and consider letting a teammate with the Revenant get the Demon Rune instead if the enemies are all near the more hazardous area of the map.

The shortcut that leads through the center of the map (the pink tunnel with the Armor pickups) provides a quick transit from the Regeneration powerup to the BFG and vice-versa. Use it to escape combat or to quickly lend support to your teammates. There aren't any portals on this map, but you can still get just about anywhere very quickly if you know the way. There's a central circle around the large mountain with the tunnel through it, as well as two smaller circular paths in the northwest and southeast corners. Your team needn't travel far and disperse themselves across the map, but can mow down the enemy by focusing on one of these smaller circular routes. The enemy will be on the move, looking for you, especially in Soul Harvest and Team Deathmatch, so move as a unit and focus your forces in one small area at a time. Then, once the Demon Rune spawns, get to that location fast.

DOMINATION

Zones A and C are easy to capture at the start of the match, one per team as is usual. Both of these Control Points are on solid ground with no risk of falling to your death when defending and attacking these places. This can't be said for Zone B, which is perched along the cliff where the BFG spawns. Listen for the Demon Rune spawn and get near Zone B with your teammates so you can time the pickup of the BFG as it spawns 10 seconds after the Demon Rune. The Haste pickup that replaces the Armor pickup near Zone C in Domination matches can help you beat the enemy to the Demon Rune or the BFG and shouldn't be overlooked. All of the Zones on Perdition can be approached from multiple directions and are all challenging to hold for long. Expect Control Points to change hands frequently on this map.

ROUND BASED MODES

The narrow brick-lined tunnels that help to form tighter, circular paths in the corners of the map can be helpful in quickly flanking your enemy. With no pickups available in Clan Arena, it's always wise to loop back around after picking off some enemies. As the action tends to congregate along the eastern side of the map in Clan Arena, you can use the area near the jump boost to evade and encircle enemies. This is particularly helpful if you find yourself outnumbered and the lone survivor on your team.

Freeze Tag matches can be a lot of fun on Perdition if the players dare take the battle to the far northern or southern edges of the map, near the powerups.

:X SACRILEGIOUS

Sacrilegious teeters on the edge of an abyss, where one wrong step could be your last. Bone-lined caves lead to pits of lava and floating rock pedestals where the environment is as threatening as your opposition. Sacrilegious is larger than it plays because many of the powerups are clustered in the southwest quadrant of the map. Monitor your Health and Armor carefully when venturing out alone or else your bones, too, will become part of the scenery.

LOCATION INTEL

POWER WEAPON: Gauss Cannon

POWERUP: Regeneration, Haste

SUICIDE RISK: High

A	Armor	B	Domination Capture B	MH	Mega Health	PW	Power Weapon
A	Domination Capture A	C	Domination Capture C	Ⓝ	Powerup	SP	Spawn Point

The teams spawn in opposite corners of the map, with one located in a lava-filled cave in the northeast corner and the other out in the open to the southwest. Teams commonly clash in the corridor near the stairs in the eastern portion of the map. The team spawning near the four pillars in the southeast can head to the right and sweep around the periphery of the map in a counter-clockwise direction to initiate contact with the enemy as they follow the perimeter south from their spawn point.

The center and western edge of the map have many obvious landmarks, including a series of floating rock pedestals where the Gauss Cannon can be found, along with an elevated platform that contains the powerup. One of the most dangerous areas on the map is the channel below the Mega Health. This narrow corridor located beneath the two upper ramps leading to the Mega Health is a shooter's gallery and should be avoided at all costs when enemies are present. The center portion of the map features numerous platform trails with small Health and Amor pickups—grab them by jumping from rock to rock. Those heading in the downslope direction from north to south can run across these pedestals without having to jump, making it safer and faster to collect these items.

DEMONIC POSSESSION

The Revenant and Baron of Hell really shine at Sacrilegious, but for different reasons. The Baron's ability to move quickly and take advantage of choke points makes him something to be feared on this map, provided you stay clear of the edges and lava pits. The Revenant can move quickly on foot like the Baron of Hell, but can also fly high above the lava and rain rockets down on enemies that may be focused on their footing in precarious locations of the map.

OBJECTIVE BASED MODES

Advance with your team toward the initial class in the southeast area of the map, then shift your focus to launching hit-and-run attacks throughout the map while trying to keep the enemy away from the Mega Health and Gauss Cannon spawns. Consider equipping Siphon Grenades and the Plasma Rifle for two attacks that can inflict damage over time across an area. Launch these attacks simultaneously against enemies caught in the channel beneath the Mega Health pickup or on the upper altar where the powerup (and often the Demon Rune) spawns.

Use the shortcuts that lead through the lava pits to collect small amounts of Health and Armor and to surprise enemies by climbing up from ledges they may not anticipate. The element of surprise can play a huge role on this map as there are numerous paths to take. Coordinate with your teammates to fall back to either spawn location (or the southeast corner) and regroup when you find yourselves getting too separated. Communication is also important when going for the Gauss Cannon as having multiple teammates so exposed, over such delicate footing, is a recipe for disaster. It wouldn't take much from the enemy to assist in your Suicide. Remember that the powerups are in positions that are highly exposed to enemy fire, so use the buddy system!

DOMINATION

Zones B and C are closer to one another than Zone A, resulting in the latter Control Point often going undefended. Claim it quickly if you spawn in the southwest corner, then split your forces and attack the other two Zones, both of which can be difficult to hold for long. Zone B is one of the more easily defended Control Points thanks to the nearby pit of lava and the upper ledges that offer a grand view of the area—and excellent sightlines for attacking approaching enemies. Zone C is out in the open at a crossroads of four paths and has the added disadvantage of being near the Gauss Cannon. Alert your teammates

if the Gauss Cannon is taken by the enemy and consider yielding Zone C to the enemy at once. Fall back to Zones B and A where you may be able to fortify your position or trade one Control Point for two.

ROUND BASED MODES

Those playing Freeze Tag here should be extra careful when charging the enemy near the center of the map or near the lava pits along the eastern edge as there are numerous barrier-free places to fall to your death. Try to keep to the upper ledges and bridge-like paths overlooking the channel beneath the Mega Health spawn or any of those atop staircases along the western side of the amp so that you are shooting from the higher ground.

For Clan Arena matches, consider equipping the Rocket Launcher, Siphon Grenade, and Vortex Rifle for the initial clash with the enemy. Lob the Siphon Grenade to offset any damage that you might be taking. Then either fire rockets at the crowd or fall back and snipe with the Vortex Rifle. The Burst Rifle can also be effective in this situation.

CHALLENGES, MEDALS, AND COMMENDATIONS

Multiplayer mode contains hundreds of Challenges, Medals, and Commendations for you to earn by playing DOOM against other human players. These various systems award bonus XP which, in turn, increases your level and Echelon and, more importantly, unlocks myriad customization options for your character and weaponry. Access the Profile screen within Multiplayer mode to view your progress.

:X CHALLENGES

The bar graph on the Challenges screen indicates how close you are to completing each of the Challenges within a particular category. Your performance is tracked across all game modes. With 2,727,000 XP needed to hit the ultimate level cap, you're going to need to complete as many of these Challenges and earn as many Medals and Commendations as possible to get there!

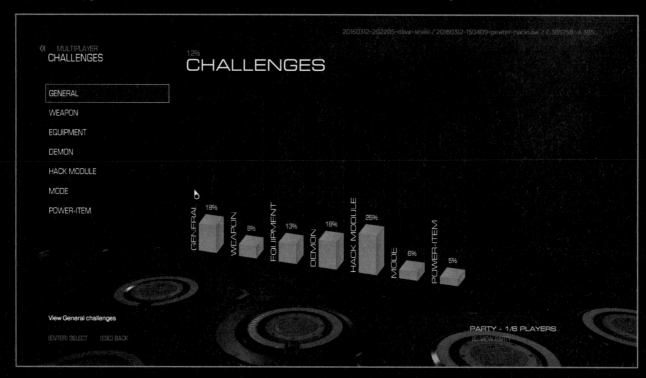

Each Challenge has 5-10 levels with ever-increasing XP rewards that help you reach that next Echelon. Nearly every single action you perform in Multiplayer, no matter how specific it is, goes toward completing a Challenge. Challenges track your kills, weapon mastery, skill in various modes, and even how well you interact with demons. There are also Challenges designed to reward players who earn a wealth of Medals and Commendations. Details for all of it are included in this chapter.

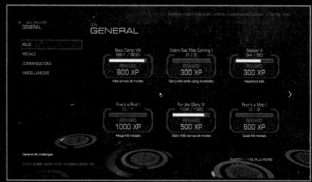

KILLS CHALLENGES

TITLE	DESCRIPTION	REWARD	UNLOCKED
Boot Camp I	Kills across all modes (25)	100 XP	-
Boot Camp II	Kills across all modes (75)	200 XP	-
Boot Camp III	Kills across all modes (150)	300 XP	-
Boot Camp IV	Kills across all modes (250)	400 XP	-
Boot Camp V	Kills across all modes (375)	500 XP	-
Boot Camp VI	Kills across all modes (525)	600 XP	-
Boot Camp VII	Kills across all modes (700)	700 XP	-
Boot Camp VIII	Kills across all modes (900)	800 XP	-
Boot Camp IX	Kills across all modes (1125)	900 XP	-
Boot Camp X	Kills across all modes (1375)	1000 XP	-
Boot Camp XI	Kills across all modes (1650)	1100 XP	-
Boot Camp XII	Kills across all modes (1950)	1200 XP	-
Boot Camp XIII	Kills across all modes (2275)	1300 XP	-
Boot Camp XIV	Kills across all modes (2625)	1400 XP	-
Boot Camp XV	Kills across all modes (3000)	1500 XP	-
Boot Camp XVI	Kills across all modes (3400)	1600 XP	-
Boot Camp XVII	Kills across all modes (3825)	1700 XP	-
Boot Camp XVIII	Kills across all modes (4275)	1800 XP	-
Boot Camp XIX	Kills across all modes (4750)	1900 XP	-
Boot Camp XX	Kills across all modes (5250)	2000 XP	-
Boot Camp XXI	Kills across all modes (5775)	2100 XP	-
Boot Camp XXII	Kills across all modes (6325)	2200 XP	-
Boot Camp XXIII	Kills across all modes (6900)	2300 XP	-
Boot Camp XXIV	Kills across all modes (7500)	2400 XP	-
Boot Camp XXV	Kills across all modes (8125)	2500 XP	-
For the Glory I	Glory Kills across all modes (5)	100 XP	-
For the Glory II	Glory Kills across all modes (10)	100 XP	-
For the Glory III	Glory Kills across all modes (20)	200 XP	-
For the Glory IV	Glory Kills across all modes (35)	300 XP	-
For the Glory V	Glory Kills across all modes (50)	300 XP	-
For the Glory VI	Glory Kills across all modes (65)	300 XP	-
For the Glory VII	Glory Kills across all modes (80)	300 XP	-
For the Glory VIII	Glory Kills across all modes (95)	300 XP	-
For the Glory IX	Glory Kills across all modes (120)	500 XP	-
For the Glory X	Glory Kills across all modes (150)	600 XP	-
Kill-a-holic I	Blood Bath medals (5)	250 XP	-
Kill-a-holic II	Blood Bath medals (10)	250 XP	-
Kill-a-holic III	Blood Bath medals (20)	500 XP	-
Kill-a-holic IV	Blood Bath medals (30)	500 XP	-
Kill-a-holic V	Blood Bath medals (40)	500 XP	-
Kill-a-holic VI	Blood Bath medals (50)	500 XP	-
Kill-a-holic VII	Blood Bath medals (60)	500 XP	-
Kill-a-holic VIII	Blood Bath medals (70)	500 XP	-
Kill-a-holic IX	Blood Bath medals (85)	750 XP	-
Kill-a-holic X	Blood Bath medals (100)	750 XP	-
Two's Company I	Double Kill medals (5)	150 XP	-
Two's Company II	Double Kill medals (10)	150 XP	-
Two's Company III	Double Kill medals (20)	300 XP	-
Two's Company IV	Double Kill medals (30)	300 XP	-

KILLS CHALLENGES CONT.

TITLE	DESCRIPTION	REWARD	UNLOCKED
Two's Company V	Double Kill medals (40)	300 XP	-
Two's Company VI	Double Kill medals (50)	300 XP	-
Two's Company VII	Double Kill medals (60)	300 XP	-
Two's Company VIII	Double Kill medals (70)	300 XP	-
Two's Company IX	Double Kill medals (85)	450 XP	-
Two's Company X	Double Kill medals (100)	450 XP	-
Scalper I	Headshot Kills (20)	200 XP	Echelon 1
Scalper II	Headshot Kills (50)	300 XP	Echelon 1
Scalper III	Headshot Kills (90)	400 XP	Echelon 1
Scalper IV	Headshot Kills (140)	500 XP	Echelon 1
Scalper V	Headshot Kills (200)	600 XP	Echelon 1
Scalper VI	Headshot Kills (270)	700 XP	Echelon 1
Scalper VII	Headshot Kills (350)	800 XP	Echelon 1
Scalper VIII	Headshot Kills (440)	900 XP	Echelon 1
Scalper IX	Headshot Kills (540)	1000 XP	Echelon 1
Scalper X	Headshot Kills (666)	1260 XP	Echelon 1
Three's a Crowd I	Triple Kill medals (3)	300 XP	Echelon 1
Three's a Crowd II	Triple Kill medals (6)	300 XP	Echelon 1
Three's a Crowd III	Triple Kill medals (10)	400 XP	Echelon 1
Three's a Crowd IV	Triple Kill medals (15)	500 XP	Echelon 1
Three's a Crowd V	Triple Kill medals (20)	500 XP	Echelon 1
Four's a Mob I	Quad Kill medals (3)	600 XP	Echelon 2
Four's a Mob II	Quad Kill medals (6)	600 XP	Echelon 2
Four's a Mob III	Quad Kill medals (10)	800 XP	Echelon 2
Four's a Mob IV	Quad Kill medals (15)	1000 XP	Echelon 2
Four's a Mob V	Quad Kill medals (20)	1000 XP	Echelon 2
Vindication I	Revenge medals (5)	100 XP	Echelon 2
Vindication II	Revenge medals (15)	200 XP	Echelon 2
Vindication III	Revenge medals (30)	300 XP	Echelon 2
Vindication IV	Revenge medals (50)	400 XP	Echelon 2
Vindication V	Revenge medals (75)	500 XP	Echelon 2
Five's a Riot I	Mega Kill medals (1)	1000 XP	Echelon 3
Five's a Riot II	Mega Kill medals (3)	2000 XP	Echelon 3
Five's a Riot III	Mega Kill medals (5)	2000 XP	Echelon 3
Five's a Riot IV	Mega Kill medals (7)	2000 XP	Echelon 3
Five's a Riot V	Mega Kill medals (10)	3000 XP	Echelon 3
See You in Hell I	Redemption medals (25)	500 XP	Echelon 3
See You in Hell II	Redemption medals (50)	500 XP	Echelon 3
See You in Hell III	Redemption medals (100)	1000 XP	Echelon 3
See You in Hell IV	Redemption medals (150)	1000 XP	Echelon 3
See You in Hell V	Redemption medals (200)	1000 XP	Echelon 3
MVP? More like LVP I	Kill the top enemy three times in a match (5)	500 XP	Echelon 5
MVP? More like LVP II	Kill the top enemy three times in a match (10)	500 XP	Echelon 5
MVP? More like LVP III	Kill the top enemy three times in a match (20)	1000 XP	Echelon 5
MVP? More like LVP IV	Kill the top enemy three times in a match (30)	1000 XP	Echelon 5
MVP? More like LVP V	Kill the top enemy three times in a match (40)	1000 XP	Echelon 5

TITLE	DESCRIPTION	REWARD	UNLOCKED
Comeback King I	Comeback medals (5)	125 XP	-
Comeback King II	Comeback medals (10)	125 XP	-
Comeback King III	Comeback medals (20)	250 XP	-
Comeback King IV	Comeback medals (30)	250 XP	-
Comeback King V	Comeback medals (40)	250 XP	-
Double Down I	Quick Draw medals (10)	120 XP	Echelon 1
Double Down II	Quick Draw medals (20)	120 XP	Echelon 1
Double Down III	Quick Draw medals (35)	180 XP	Echelon 1
Double Down IV	Quick Draw medals (50)	180 XP	Echelon 1
Double Down V	Quick Draw medals (75)	300 XP	Echelon 1
Double Down VI	Quick Draw medals (100)	300 XP	Echelon 1
Double Down VII	Quick Draw medals (150)	600 XP	Echelon 1
Double Down VIII	Quick Draw medals (200)	600 XP	Echelon 1
Double Down IX	Quick Draw medals (250)	250 XP	Echelon 1
Double Down X	Quick Draw medals (300)	300 XP	Echelon 1
Survivalist I	Survivor medals (5)	125 XP	Echelon 1
Survivalist II	Survivor medals (15)	250 XP	Echelon 1
Survivalist III	Survivor medals (30)	375 XP	Echelon 1
Survivalist IV	Survivor medals (50)	500 XP	Echelon 1
Survivalist V	Survivor medals (75)	625 XP	Echelon 1
Avenged I	Avenger medals (10)	250 XP	Echelon 2
Avenged II	Avenger medals (30)	500 XP	Echelon 2
Avenged III	Avenger medals (60)	750 XP	Echelon 2
Avenged IV	Avenger medals (100)	1000 XP	Echelon 2
Avenged V	Avenger medals (150)	1250 XP	Echelon 2
Hit the Kill Switch I	Power Down medals (5)	250 XP	Echelon 2
Hit the Kill Switch II	Power Down medals (15)	500 XP	Echelon 2
Hit the Kill Switch III	Power Down medals (30)	750 XP	Echelon 2
Hit the Kill Switch IV	Power Down medals (50)	1000 XP	Echelon 2
Hit the Kill Switch V	Power Down medals (75)	1250 XP	Echelon 2
Rampaging Disaster I	Carnage medals (3)	750 XP	Echelon 2
Rampaging Disaster II	Carnage medals (6)	750 XP	Echelon 2
Rampaging Disaster III	Carnage medals (10)	1000 XP	Echelon 2
Rampaging Disaster IV	Carnage medals (15)	1250 XP	Echelon 2
Rampaging Disaster V	Carnage medals (20)	1250 XP	Echelon 2
Jester I	Humiliation medals (25)	250 XP	Echelon 3
Jester II	Humiliation medals (50)	250 XP	Echelon 3
Jester III	Humiliation medals (100)	500 XP	Echelon 3
Jester IV	Humiliation medals (150)	500 XP	Echelon 3
Jester V	Humiliation medals (200)	500 XP	Echelon 3
Personal Hazard I	Hazardous medals (5)	250 XP	Echelon 3
Personal Hazard II	Hazardous medals (15)	500 XP	Echelon 3
Personal Hazard III	Hazardous medals (30)	750 XP	Echelon 3
Personal Hazard IV	Hazardous medals (50)	1000 XP	Echelon 3
Personal Hazard V	Hazardous medals (75)	1250 XP	Echelon 3
Bloodhound I	First Blood medals (5)	150 XP	Echelon 4
Bloodhound II	First Blood medals (15)	300 XP	Echelon 4
Bloodhound III	First Blood medals (30)	450 XP	Echelon 4
Bloodhound IV	First Blood medals (50)	600 XP	Echelon 4
Bloodhound V	First Blood medals (75)	750 XP	Echelon 4

TITLE	DESCRIPTION	REWARD	UNLOCKED
Everyone's a Critic I	Critical Chain medals (15)	300 XP	Echelon 4
Everyone's a Critic II	Critical Chain medals (30)	300 XP	Echelon 4
Everyone's a Critic III	Critical Chain medals (50)	400 XP	Echelon 4
Everyone's a Critic IV	Critical Chain medals (75)	500 XP	Echelon 4
Everyone's a Critic V	Critical Chain medals (100)	500 XP	Echelon 4
World Destroyer I	Massacre medals (1)	500 XP	Echelon 4
World Destroyer II	Massacre medals (3)	1000 XP	Echelon 4
World Destroyer III	Massacre medals (5)	1000 XP	Echelon 4
World Destroyer IV	Massacre medals (7)	1000 XP	Echelon 4
World Destroyer V	Massacre medals (10)	1500 XP	Echelon 4
Fallen Angel I	Upshot medals (10)	200 XP	Echelon 5
Fallen Angel II	Upshot medals (30)	400 XP	Echelon 5
Fallen Angel III	Upshot medals (60)	600 XP	Echelon 5
Fallen Angel IV	Upshot medals (100)	800 XP	Echelon 5
Fallen Angel V	Upshot medals (150)	1000 XP	Echelon 5
Overpowered I	Power Kill medals (20)	400 XP	Echelon 5
Overpowered II	Power Kill medals (60)	800 XP	Echelon 5
Overpowered III	Power Kill medals (120)	1200 XP	Echelon 5
Overpowered IV	Power Kill medals (200)	1600 XP	Echelon 5
Overpowered V	Power Kill medals (300)	2000 XP	Echelon 5
Angel of Death I	Extermination medals (1)	750 XP	Echelon 6
Angel of Death II	Extermination medals (3)	1500 XP	Echelon 6
Angel of Death III	Extermination medals (5)	1500 XP	Echelon 6
Angel of Death IV	Extermination medals (7)	1500 XP	Echelon 6
Angel of Death V	Extermination medals (10)	2250 XP	Echelon 6
Guardian I	Protection medals (10)	200 XP	Echelon 6
Guardian II	Protection medals (30)	400 XP	Echelon 6
Guardian III	Protection medals (60)	600 XP	Echelon 6
Guardian IV	Protection medals (100)	800 XP	Echelon 6
Guardian V	Protection medals (150)	1000 XP	Echelon 6
Sniper I	Longshot medals (10)	500 XP	Echelon 6
Sniper II	Longshot medals (25)	750 XP	Echelon 6
Sniper III	Longshot medals (50)	1250 XP	Echelon 6
Sniper IV	Longshot medals (75)	1250 XP	Echelon 6
Sniper V	Longshot medals (10)	1250 XP	Echelon 6
Booby Trap I	Rune Denied medals (5)	250 XP	Echelon 7
Booby Trap II	Rune Denied medals (10)	250 XP	Echelon 7
Booby Trap III	Rune Denied medals (20)	500 XP	Echelon 7
Booby Trap IV	Rune Denied medals (30)	500 XP	Echelon 7
Booby Trap V	Rune Denied medals (40)	500 XP	Echelon 7
Power Outage I	Shutdown medals (5)	250 XP	Echelon 7
Power Outage II	Shutdown medals (15)	500 XP	Echelon 7
Power Outage III	Shutdown medals (30)	750 XP	Echelon 7
Power Outage IV	Shutdown medals (50)	1000 XP	Echelon 7
Power Outage V	Shutdown medals (75)	1250 XP	Echelon 7
Deus Ex Machina I	Savior medals (3)	300 XP	Echelon 8
Deus Ex Machina II	Savior medals (6)	300 XP	Echelon 8
Deus Ex Machina III	Savior medals (10)	400 XP	Echelon 8
Deus Ex Machina IV	Savior medals (15)	500 XP	Echelon 8
Deus Ex Machina V	Savior medals (20)	500 XP	Echelon 8

MEDALS CHALLENGES CONT.

TITLE	DESCRIPTION	REWARD	UNLOCKED
Stain the Streak I	Show Stopper medals (5)	125 XP	Echelon 8
Stain the Streak II	Show Stopper medals (10)	125 XP	Echelon 8
Stain the Streak III	Show Stopper medals (20)	250 XP	Echelon 8
Stain the Streak IV	Show Stopper medals (30)	250 XP	Echelon 8
Stain the Streak V	Show Stopper medals (40)	250 XP	Echelon 8
Avoid the Crowd I	Untouchable medals (5)	200 XP	Echelon 9
Avoid the Crowd II	Untouchable medals (10)	200 XP	Echelon 9
Avoid the Crowd III	Untouchable medals (15)	200 XP	Echelon 9
Avoid the Crowd IV	Untouchable medals (20)	200 XP	Echelon 9
Avoid the Crowd V	Untouchable medals (25)	200 XP	Echelon 9
Maximum Destruction I	Mega Kill medals with power weapons (3)	600 XP	Echelon 9
Maximum Destruction II	Mega Kill medals with power weapons (6)	600 XP	Echelon 9
Maximum Destruction III	Mega Kill medals with power weapons (10)	800 XP	Echelon 9
Maximum Destruction IV	Mega Kill medals with power weapons (15)	1000 XP	Echelon 9
Maximum Destruction V	Mega Kill medals with power weapons (20)	1000 XP	Echelon 9
Leave None Alive I	Genocide medals (5)	1000 XP	Echelon 10
Leave None Alive II	Genocide medals (10)	1000 XP	Echelon 10
Leave None Alive III	Genocide medals (20)	2000 XP	Echelon 10
Leave None Alive IV	Genocide medals (30)	2000 XP	Echelon 10
Leave None Alive V	Genocide medals (40)	2000 XP	Echelon 10
Thresher of Flesh I	Annihilation medals (1)	1500 XP	Echelon 10
Thresher of Flesh II	Annihilation medals (2)	1500 XP	Echelon 10
Thresher of Flesh III	Annihilation medals (3)	1500 XP	Echelon 10
Thresher of Flesh IV	Annihilation medals (4)	1500 XP	Echelon 10
Thresher of Flesh V	Annihilation medals (5)	1500 XP	Echelon 10

COMMENDATIONS CHALLENGES

TITLE	DESCRIPTION	REWARD	UNLOCKED
Not Dead Yet I	Walking Wounded commendations (5)	300 XP	Echelon 1
Not Dead Yet II	Walking Wounded commendations (10)	300 XP	Echelon 1
Not Dead Yet III	Walking Wounded commendations (20)	600 XP	Echelon 1
Not Dead Yet IV	Walking Wounded commendations (30)	600 XP	Echelon 1
Not Dead Yet V	Walking Wounded commendations (40)	600 XP	Echelon 1
Blood Brother I	Assistant commendations (5)	300 XP	Echelon 2
Blood Brother II	Assistant commendations (15)	600 XP	Echelon 2
Blood Brother III	Assistant commendations (30)	900 XP	Echelon 2
Blood Brother IV	Assistant commendations (50)	1200 XP	Echelon 2
Blood Brother V	Assistant commendations (75)	1500 XP	Echelon 2
Olympiad I	Marathon Runner commendations (5)	250 XP	Echelon 2
Olympiad II	Marathon Runner commendations (10)	250 XP	Echelon 2
Olympiad III	Marathon Runner commendations (20)	500 XP	Echelon 2
Olympiad IV	Marathon Runner commendations (30)	500 XP	Echelon 2
Olympiad V	Marathon Runner commendations (40)	500 XP	Echelon 2
Bomber Man I	Explosive Expert commendations (5)	300 XP	Echelon 3
Bomber Man II	Explosive Expert commendations (10)	300 XP	Echelon 3
Bomber Man III	Explosive Expert commendations (20)	600 XP	Echelon 3
Bomber Man IV	Explosive Expert commendations (30)	600 XP	Echelon 3
Bomber Man V	Explosive Expert commendations (40)	600 XP	Echelon 3

COMMENDATIONS CHALLENGES CONT.

TITLE	DESCRIPTION	REWARD	UNLOCKED
Kangaroo I	Bunny Hopper commendations (5)	250 XP	Echelon 3
Kangaroo II	Bunny Hopper commendations (10)	250 XP	Echelon 3
Kangaroo III	Bunny Hopper commendations (20)	500 XP	Echelon 3
Kangaroo IV	Bunny Hopper commendations (30)	500 X	Echelon 3
Kangaroo V	Bunny Hopper commendations (40)	500 XP	Echelon 3
Something for Every Occasion I	Engineer commendations (5)	200 XP	Echelon 3
Something for Every Occasion II	Engineer commendations (10)	200 XP	Echelon 3
Something for Every Occasion III	Engineer commendations (20)	400 XP	Echelon 3
Something for Every Occasion IV	Engineer commendations (30)	400 XP	Echelon 3
Something for Every Occasion V	Engineer commendations (40)	400 XP	Echelon 3
Deadeye I	Marksman commendations (5)	500 XP	Echelon 4
Deadeye II	Marksman commendations (10)	500 XP	Echelon 4
Deadeye III	Marksman commendations (20)	1000 XP	Echelon 4
Deadeye IV	Marksman commendations (30)	1000 XP	Echelon 4
Deadeye V	Marksman commendations (40)	1000 XP	Echelon 4
I Don't Need a Gun to Kill You I	Glory Hound commendations (5)	600 XP	Echelon 4
I Don't Need a Gun to Kill You II	Glory Hound commendations (10)	600 XP	Echelon 4
I Don't Need a Gun to Kill You III	Glory Hound commendations (20)	1200 XP	Echelon 4
I Don't Need a Gun to Kill You IV	Glory Hound commendations (30)	1200 XP	Echelon 4
I Don't Need a Gun to Kill You V	Glory Hound commendations (40)	1200 XP	Echelon 4
Worst Nightmare I	Demonation commendations (5)	600 XP	Echelon 4
Worst Nightmare II	Demonation commendations (10)	600 XP	Echelon 4
Worst Nightmare III	Demonation commendations (20)	1200 XP	Echelon 4
Worst Nightmare IV	Demonation commendations (30)	1200 XP	Echelon 4
Worst Nightmare V	Demonation commendations (40)	1200 XP	Echelon 4
Bodyguard Extraordinaire I	Elite Escort commendations (5)	500 XP	Echelon 5
Bodyguard Extraordinaire II	Elite Escort commendations (10)	500 XP	Echelon 5
Bodyguard Extraordinaire III	Elite Escort commendations (20)	1000 XP	Echelon 5
Bodyguard Extraordinaire IV	Elite Escort commendations (30)	1000 XP	Echelon 5
Bodyguard Extraordinaire V	Elite Escort commendations (40)	1000 XP	Echelon 5
Challenger I	Controller commendations (5)	600 XP	Echelon 5
Challenger II	Controller commendations (10)	600 XP	Echelon 5
Challenger III	Controller commendations (20)	1200 XP	Echelon 5
Challenger IV	Controller commendations (30)	1200 XP	Echelon 5
Challenger V	Controller commendations (40)	1200 XP	Echelon 5
Winter's End I	Defroster commendations (5)	750 XP	Echelon 5
Winter's End II	Defroster commendations (10)	750 XP	Echelon 5
Winter's End III	Defroster commendations (20)	1500 XP	Echelon 5
Winter's End IV	Defroster commendations (30)	1500 XP	Echelon 5
Winter's End V	Defroster commendations (40)	1500 XP	Echelon 5
Every Bit Helps I	Tank commendations (5)	250 XP	Echelon 6
Every Bit Helps II	Tank commendations (10)	250 XP	Echelon 6
Every Bit Helps III	Tank commendations (20)	500 XP	Echelon 6
Every Bit Helps IV	Tank commendations (30)	500 XP	Echelon 6
Every Bit Helps V	Tank commendations (40)	500 XP	Echelon 6
Hell Fears Me I	Master Demon Slayer commendations (5)	500 XP	Echelon 6

TITLE	DESCRIPTION	REWARD	UNLOCKED
Hell Fears Me II	Master Demon Slayer commendations (10)	500 XP	Echelon 6
Hell Fears Me III	Master Demon Slayer commendations (20)	1000 XP	Echelon 6
Hell Fears Me IV	Master Demon Slayer commendations (30)	1000 XP	Echelon 6
Hell Fears Me V	Master Demon Slayer commendations (40)	1000 XP	Echelon 6
Soul Keeper I	Soul Preserver commendations (5)	250 XP	Echelon 6
Soul Keeper I	Soul Preserver commendations (10)	250 XP	Echelon 6
Soul Keeper III	Soul Preserver commendations (20)	500 XP	Echelon 6
Soul Keeper IV	Soul Preserver commendations (30)	500 X	Echelon 6
Soul Keeper V	Soul Preserver commendations (40)	500 XP	Echelon 6
Atlas I	Overachiever commendations (5)	600 XP	Echelon 7
Atlas II	Overachiever commendations (10)	600 XP	Echelon 7
Atlas III	Overachiever commendations (20)	1200 XP	Echelon 7
Atlas IV	Overachiever commendations (30)	1200 XP	Echelon 7
Atlas V	Overachiever commendations (40)	1200 XP	Echelon 7
Hate the Player I	Hater commendations (5)	500 XP	Echelon 7
Hate the Player II	Hater commendations (10)	500 XP	Echelon 7
Hate the Player III	Hater commendations (20)	1000 XP	Echelon 7
Hate the Player IV	Hater commendations (30)	1000 XP	Echelon 7
Hate the Player V	Hater commendations (40)	1000 XP	Echelon 7
Prince of the Universe I	Immortal commendations (5)	500 XP	Echelon 7
Prince of the Universe II	Immortal commendations (10)	500 XP	Echelon 7
Prince of the Universe III	Immortal commendations (20)	1000 XP	Echelon 7
Prince of the Universe IV	Immortal commendations (30)	1000 XP	Echelon 7
Prince of the Universe V	Immortal commendations (40)	1000 XP	Echelon 7
Territorial I	Defensive commendations (5)	750 XP	Echelon 8
Territorial II	Defensive commendations (10)	750 XP	Echelon 8
Territorial III	Defensive commendations (20)	1500 XP	Echelon 8
Territorial IV	Defensive commendations (30)	1500 XP	Echelon 8
Territorial V	Defensive commendations (40)	1500 XP	Echelon 8
Here Comes the Juggernaut I	Juggernaut commendations (3)	450 XP	Echelon 8
Here Comes the Juggernaut II	Juggernaut commendations (6)	450 XP	Echelon 8
Here Comes the Juggernaut III	Juggernaut commendations (10)	600 XP	Echelon 8
Here Comes the Juggernaut IV	Juggernaut commendations (15)	750 XP	Echelon 8
Here Comes the Juggernaut V	Juggernaut commendations (20)	750 XP	Echelon 8
Overkill Master I	Pain Merchant commendations (5)	600 XP	Echelon 8
Overkill Master II	Pain Merchant commendations (10)	600 XP	Echelon 8
Overkill Master III	Pain Merchant commendations (20)	1200 XP	Echelon 8
Overkill Master IV	Pain Merchant commendations (30)	1200 XP	Echelon 8
Overkill Master V	Pain Merchant commendations (40)	1200 XP	Echelon 8
Bulletproof I	Hard to Kill commendations (5)	750 XP	Echelon 9
Bulletproof II	Hard to Kill commendations (10)	750 XP	Echelon 9
Bulletproof III	Hard to Kill commendations (20)	1500 XP	Echelon 9
Bulletproof IV	Hard to Kill commendations (30)	1500 XP	Echelon 9
Bulletproof V	Hard to Kill commendations (40)	1500 XP	Echelon 9
Inventive Display I	Gadgeteer commendations (5)	600 XP	Echelon 9
Inventive Display II	Gadgeteer commendations (10)	600 XP	Echelon 9
Inventive Display III	Gadgeteer commendations (20)	1200 XP	Echelon 9
Inventive Display IV	Gadgeteer commendations (30)	1200 XP	Echelon 9

TITLE	DESCRIPTION	REWARD	UNLOCKED
Inventive Display V	Gadgeteer commendations (40)	1200 XP	Echelon 9
Pickup Artist I	Master Thief commendations (5)	600 XP	Echelon 9
Pickup Artist II	Master Thief commendations (10)	600 XP	Echelon 9
Pickup Artist III	Master Thief commendations (20)	1200 XP	Echelon 9
Pickup Artist IV	Master Thief commendations (30)	1200 XP	Echelon 9
Pickup Artist V	Master Thief commendations (40)	1200 XP	Echelon 9
Fearless Leader I	Clan Leader commendations (5)	750 XP	Echelon 10
Fearless Leader II	Clan Leader commendations (10)	750 XP	Echelon 10
Fearless Leader III	Clan Leader commendations (20)	1500 XP	Echelon 10
Fearless Leader IV	Clan Leader commendations (30)	1500 XP	Echelon 10
Fearless Leader V	Clan Leader commendations (40)	1500 XP	Echelon 10
Siegemaster I	Invader commendations (5)	750 XP	Echelon 10
Siegemaster II	Invader commendations (10)	750 XP	Echelon 10
Siegemaster III	Invader commendations (20)	1500 XP	Echelon 10
Siegemaster IV	Invader commendations (30)	1500 XP	Echelon 10
Siegemaster V	Invader commendations (40)	1500 XP	Echelon 10
1337 I	MVP commendations (3)	900 XP	Echelon 10
1337 II	MVP commendations (6)	900 XP	Echelon 10
1337 III	MVP commendations (10)	1200 XP	Echelon 10
1337 IV	MVP commendations (15)	1500 XP	Echelon 10
1337 V	MVP commendations (20)	1500 XP	Echelon 10

MISCELLANEOUS CHALLENGES

TITLE	DESCRIPTION	REWARD	UNLOCKED
Beyond Fit I	Collect mega-health pickups (5)	150 XP	-
Beyond Fit II	Collect mega-health pickups (15)	300 XP	-
Beyond Fit III	Collect mega-health pickups (30)	450 XP	-
Beyond Fit IV	Collect mega-health pickups (50)	600 XP	-
Beyond Fit V	Collect mega-health pickups (75)	750 XP	-
Bombs Away I	Splash damage dealt with weapons and equipment (1000)	150 XP	-
Bombs Away II	Splash damage dealt with weapons and equipment (2500)	225 XP	-
Bombs Away III	Splash damage dealt with weapons and equipment (5000)	375 XP	-
Bombs Away IV	Splash damage dealt with weapons and equipment (7500)	375 XP	-
Bombs Away V	Splash damage dealt with weapons and equipment (10000)	375 XP	-
Bombs Away VI	Splash damage dealt with weapons and equipment (12500)	375 XP	-
Bombs Away VII	Splash damage dealt with weapons and equipment (15000)	375 XP	-
Bombs Away VIII	Splash damage dealt with weapons and equipment (17500)	375 XP	-
Bombs Away IX	Splash damage dealt with weapons and equipment (20000)	375 XP	-
Bombs Away X	Splash damage dealt with weapons and equipment (25000)	750 XP	-
Self-Improvement I	Collect health and armor pickups (2000)	100 XP	-
Self-Improvement II	Collect health and armor pickups (6000)	200 XP	-
Self-Improvement III	Collect health and armor pickups (12000)	300 XP	-
Self-Improvement IV	Collect health and armor pickups (20000)	400 XP	-
Self-Improvement V	Collect health and armor pickups (30000)	500 XP	-

TITLE	DESCRIPTION	REWARD	UNLOCKED
Self-Improvement VI	Collect health and armor pickups (42000)	600 XP	-
Self-Improvement VII	Collect health and armor pickups (56000)	700 XP	-
Self-Improvement VIII	Collect health and armor pickups (72000)	800 XP	-
Self-Improvement IX	Collect health and armor pickups (90000)	900 XP	-
Self-Improvement X	Collect health and armor pickups (110000)	1000 XP	-
Number Won I	Win matches across all modes (10)	250 XP	-
Number Won II	Win matches across all modes (20)	250 XP	-
Number Won III	Win matches across all modes (35)	375 XP	-
Number Won IV	Win matches across all modes (50)	375 XP	-
Number Won V	Win matches across all modes (75)	625 XP	-
Number Won VI	Win matches across all modes (100)	625 XP	-
Number Won VII	Win matches across all modes (150)	1250 XP	-
Number Won VIII	Win matches across all modes (200)	1250 XP	-
Number Won IX	Win matches across all modes (250)	1250 XP	-
Number Won X	Win matches across all modes (300)	1250 XP	-
Pride Goeth Before the Fall I	Silencer medals (5)	250 XP	Echelon 7
Pride Goeth Before the Fall II	Silencer medals (10)	250 XP	Echelon 7
Pride Goeth Before the Fall III	Silencer medals (20)	500 XP	Echelon 7
Pride Goeth Before the Fall IV	Silencer medals (30)	500 XP	Echelon 7
Pride Goeth Before the Fall V	Silencer medals (40)	500 XP	Echelon 7

WEAPON

ROCKET LAUNCHER CHALLENGES

TITLE	DESCRIPTION	REWARD	UNLOCKED
Rocket Launcher Mastery I	Rocket Launcher kills (20)	250 XP	-
Rocket Launcher Mastery II	Rocket Launcher kills (50)	375 XP	-
Rocket Launcher Mastery III	Rocket Launcher kills (90)	500 XP	-
Rocket Launcher Mastery IV	Rocket Launcher kills (140)	625 XP	-
Rocket Launcher Mastery V	Rocket Launcher kills (200)	750 XP	-
Rocket Launcher Mastery VI	Rocket Launcher kills (270)	875 XP	-
Rocket Launcher Mastery VII	Rocket Launcher kills (350)	1000 XP	-
Rocket Launcher Mastery VIII	Rocket Launcher kills (440)	1125 XP	-
Rocket Launcher Mastery IX	Rocket Launcher kills (540)	1250 XP	-
Rocket Launcher Mastery X	Rocket Launcher kills (666)	1575 XP	-
Shredded with Shrapnel I	Splash damage dealt with the Rocket Launcher (1000)	200 XP	-
Shredded with Shrapnel II	Splash damage dealt with the Rocket Launcher (3000)	400 XP	-
Shredded with Shrapnel III	Splash damage dealt with the Rocket Launcher (5000)	400 XP	-
Shredded with Shrapnel IV	Splash damage dealt with the Rocket Launcher (7500)	500 XP	-
Shredded with Shrapnel V	Splash damage dealt with the Rocket Launcher (10000)	500 XP	-
Flak Cannon I	Kills with the Rocket Launcher's manual detonate (10)	400 XP	Echelon 2
Flak Cannon II	Kills with the Rocket Launcher's manual detonate (25)	600 XP	Echelon 2

TITLE	DESCRIPTION	REWARD	UNLOCKED
Flak Cannon III	Kills with the Rocket Launcher's manual detonate (50)	1000 XP	Echelon 2
Flak Cannon IV	Kills with the Rocket Launcher's manual detonate (75)	1000 XP	Echelon 2
Flak Cannon V	Kills with the Rocket Launcher's manual detonate (100)	1000 XP	Echelon 2
Rocket Launcher Overkill I	Rocket Launcher critical kills (10)	200 XP	Echelon 4
Rocket Launcher Overkill II	Rocket Launcher critical kills (30)	400 XP	Echelon 4
Rocket Launcher Overkill III	Rocket Launcher critical kills (60)	600 XP	Echelon 4
Rocket Launcher Overkill IV	Rocket Launcher critical kills (100)	800 XP	Echelon 4
Rocket Launcher Overkill V	Rocket Launcher critical kills (150)	1000 XP	Echelon 4
Because Rockets I	Multi-kills with the Rocket Launcher (10)	800 XP	Echelon 8
Because Rockets II	Multi-kills with the Rocket Launcher (25)	1200 XP	Echelon 8
Because Rockets III	Multi-kills with the Rocket Launcher (50)	2000 XP	Echelon 8
Because Rockets IV	Multi-kills with the Rocket Launcher (75)	2000 XP	Echelon 8
Because Rockets V	Multi-kills with the Rocket Launcher (100)	2000 XP	Echelon 8

PLASMA RIFLE CHALLENGES

TITLE	DESCRIPTION	REWARD	UNLOCKED
Plasma Rifle Mastery I	Plasma Rifle kills (20)	250 XP	-
Plasma Rifle Mastery II	Plasma Rifle kills (50)	375 XP	-
Plasma Rifle Mastery III	Plasma Rifle kills (90)	500 XP	-
Plasma Rifle Mastery IV	Plasma Rifle kills (140)	625 XP	-
Plasma Rifle Mastery V	Plasma Rifle kills (200)	750 XP	-
Plasma Rifle Mastery VI	Plasma Rifle kills (270)	875 XP	-
Plasma Rifle Mastery VII	Plasma Rifle kills (350)	1000 XP	-
Plasma Rifle Mastery VIII	Plasma Rifle kills (440)	1125 XP	-
Plasma Rifle Mastery IX	Plasma Rifle kills (540)	1250 XP	-
Plasma Rifle Mastery X	Plasma Rifle kills (666)	1575 XP	-
Radioactive I	Damage dealt with Plasma Rifle pools (1000)	200 XP	-
Radioactive II	Damage dealt with Plasma Rifle pools (3000)	400 XP	-
Radioactive III	Damage dealt with Plasma Rifle pools (5000)	400 XP	-
Radioactive IV	Damage dealt with Plasma Rifle pools (7500)	500 XP	-
Radioactive V	Damage dealt with Plasma Rifle pools (10000)	500 XP	-
Plasma Rifle Overkill I	Critical kills with the Plasma Rifle (10)	200 XP	Echelon 2
Plasma Rifle Overkill II	Critical kills with the Plasma Rifle (30)	400 XP	Echelon 2
Plasma Rifle Overkill III	Critical kills with the Plasma Rifle (60)	600 XP	Echelon 2
Plasma Rifle Overkill IV	Critical kills with the Plasma Rifle (100)	800 XP	Echelon 2
Plasma Rifle Overkill V	Critical kills with the Plasma Rifle (150)	1000 XP	Echelon 2
Wasteland I	Kills with Plasma Rifle pools (5)	300 XP	Echelon 4
Wasteland II	Kills with Plasma Rifle pools (15)	600 XP	Echelon 4
Wasteland III	Kills with Plasma Rifle pools (30)	900 XP	Echelon 4
Wasteland IV	Kills with Plasma Rifle pools (50)	1200 XP	Echelon 4
Wasteland V	Kills with Plasma Rifle pools (75)	1500 XP	Echelon 4
Plasma Donation I	Multi-kills with the Plasma Rifle (10)	800 XP	Echelon 8
Plasma Donation II	Multi-kills with the Plasma Rifle (25)	1200 XP	Echelon 8
Plasma Donation III	Multi-kills with the Plasma Rifle (50)	2000 XP	Echelon 8
Plasma Donation IV	Multi-kills with the Plasma Rifle (75)	2000 XP	Echelon 8
Plasma Donation V	Multi-kills with the Plasma Rifle (100)	2000 XP	Echelon 8

SUPER SHOTGUN CHALLENGES

TITLE	DESCRIPTION	REWARD	UNLOCKED
Close Enough I	Super Shotgun critical damage (2000)	500 XP	-
Close Enough II	Super Shotgun critical damage (5000)	750 XP	-
Close Enough III	Super Shotgun critical damage (10000)	1250 XP	-
Close Enough IV	Super Shotgun critical damage (17000)	1750 XP	-
Close Enough V	Super Shotgun critical damage (26000)	2250 XP	-
Super Shotgun Mastery I	Super Shotgun kills (20)	250 XP	-
Super Shotgun Mastery II	Super Shotgun kills (50)	375 XP	-
Super Shotgun Mastery III	Super Shotgun kills (90)	500 XP	-
Super Shotgun Mastery IV	Super Shotgun kills (140)	625 XP	-
Super Shotgun Mastery V	Super Shotgun kills (200)	750 XP	-
Super Shotgun Mastery VI	Super Shotgun kills (270)	875 XP	-
Super Shotgun Mastery VII	Super Shotgun kills (350)	1000 XP	-
Super Shotgun Mastery VIII	Super Shotgun kills (440)	1125 XP	-
Super Shotgun Mastery IX	Super Shotgun kills (540)	1250 XP	-
Super Shotgun Mastery X	Super Shotgun kills (666)	1575 XP	-
Up Close and Personal I	Close range kills with the Super Shotgun (15)	300 XP	Echelon 2
Up Close and Personal II	Close range kills with the Super Shotgun (30)	300 XP	Echelon 2
Up Close and Personal III	Close range kills with the Super Shotgun (50)	400 XP	Echelon 2
Up Close and Personal IV	Close range kills with the Super Shotgun 75)	500 XP	Echelon 2
Up Close and Personal V	Close range kills with the Super Shotgun (100)	500 XP	Echelon 2
Super Shotgun Overkill I	Super Shotgun critical kills (10)	200 XP	Echelon 4
Super Shotgun Overkill II	Super Shotgun critical kills (30)	400 XP	Echelon 4
Super Shotgun Overkill III	Super Shotgun critical kills (60)	600 XP	Echelon 4
Super Shotgun Overkill IV	Super Shotgun critical kills (100)	800 XP	Echelon 4
Super Shotgun Overkill V	Super Shotgun critical kills (150)	1000 XP	Echelon 4
Down the Barrel I	Kill two players with a single Super Shotgun blast (1)	800 XP	Echelon 8
Down the Barrel II	Kill two players with a single Super Shotgun blast (3)	1600 XP	Echelon 8
Down the Barrel III	Kill two players with a single Super Shotgun blast (5)	1600 XP	Echelon 8
Down the Barrel IV	Kill two players with a single Super Shotgun blast (7)	1600 XP	Echelon 8
Down the Barrel V	Kill two players with a single Super Shotgun blast (10)	2400 XP	Echelon 8

CHAINGUN CHALLENGES

TITLE	DESCRIPTION	REWARD	UNLOCKED
Chaingun Mastery I	Chaingun kills (20)	250 XP	-
Chaingun Mastery II	Chaingun kills (50)	375 XP	-
Chaingun Mastery III	Chaingun kills (90)	500 XP	-
Chaingun Mastery IV	Chaingun kills (140)	625 XP	-
Chaingun Mastery V	Chaingun kills (200)	750 XP	-
Chaingun Mastery VI	Chaingun kills (270)	875 XP	-
Chaingun Mastery VII	Chaingun kills (350)	1000 XP	-
Chaingun Mastery VIII	Chaingun kills (440)	1125 XP	-
Chaingun Mastery IX	Chaingun kills (540)	1250 XP	-
Chaingun Mastery X	Chaingun kills (666)	1575 XP	-
Spray and Pray I	Kills with the Chaingun fully spun up (15)	600 XP	-
Spray and Pray II	Kills with the Chaingun fully spun up (40)	1000 XP	-

CHAINGUN CHALLENGES CONT.

TITLE	DESCRIPTION	REWARD	UNLOCKED
Spray and Pray III	Kills with the Chaingun fully spun up (75)	1400 XP	-
Spray and Pray IV	Kills with the Chaingun fully spun up (120)	1800 XP	-
Spray and Pray V	Kills with the Chaingun fully spun up (200)	3200 XP	-
A Home for Every Bullet I	Chaingun critical damage (2000)	500 XP	Echelon 2
A Home for Every Bullet II	Chaingun critical damage (5000)	750 XP	Echelon 2
A Home for Every Bullet III	Chaingun critical damage (10000)	1250 XP	Echelon 2
A Home for Every Bullet IV	Chaingun critical damage (17000)	1750 XP	Echelon 2
A Home for Every Bullet V	Chaingun critical damage (26000)	2250 XP	Echelon 2
Prepper I	Time with the Chaingun fully spun up (150)	300 XP	Echelon 4
Prepper II	Time with the Chaingun fully spun up (300)	300 XP	Echelon 4
Prepper III	Time with the Chaingun fully spun up (500)	400 XP	Echelon 4
Prepper IV	Time with the Chaingun fully spun up (750)	500 XP	Echelon 4
Prepper V	Time with the Chaingun fully spun up (1000)	500 XP	Echelon 4
Chaingun Overkill I	Chaingun critical kills (20)	500 XP	Echelon 8
Chaingun Overkill II	Chaingun critical kills (40)	500 XP	Echelon 8
Chaingun Overkill III	Chaingun critical kills (60)	500 XP	Echelon 8
Chaingun Overkill IV	Chaingun critical kills (80)	500 XP	Echelon 8
Chaingun Overkill V	Chaingun critical kills (120)	1000 XP	Echelon 8

VORTEX RIFLE CHALLENGES

TITLE	DESCRIPTION	REWARD	UNLOCKED
Vortex Rifle Mastery I	Vortex Rifle kills (20)	250 XP	-
Vortex Rifle Mastery II	Vortex Rifle kills (50)	375 XP	-
Vortex Rifle Mastery III	Vortex Rifle kills (90)	500 XP	-
Vortex Rifle Mastery IV	Vortex Rifle kills (140)	625 XP	-
Vortex Rifle Mastery V	Vortex Rifle kills (200)	750 XP	-
Vortex Rifle Mastery VI	Vortex Rifle kills (270)	875 XP	-
Vortex Rifle Mastery VII	Vortex Rifle kills (350)	1000 XP	-
Vortex Rifle Mastery VIII	Vortex Rifle kills (440)	1125 XP	-
Vortex Rifle Mastery IX	Vortex Rifle kills (540)	1250 XP	-
Vortex Rifle Mastery X	Vortex Rifle kills (666)	1575 XP	-
Whites of Their Eyes I	Kills using the Vortex Rifle's scope (50)	300 XP	-
Whites of Their Eyes II	Kills using the Vortex Rifle's scope (125)	450 XP	-
Whites of Their Eyes III	Kills using the Vortex Rifle's scope (200)	450 XP	-
Whites of Their Eyes IV	Kills using the Vortex Rifle's scope (275)	450 XP	-
Whites of Their Eyes V	Kills using the Vortex Rifle's scope (350)	450 XP	-
One Shot, One Kill I	Kills with Vortex Rifle shots that deal at least 100 damage (15)	600 XP	Echelon 2
One Shot, One Kill II	Kills with Vortex Rifle shots that deal at least 100 damage (30)	600 XP	Echelon 2
One Shot, One Kill III	Kills with Vortex Rifle shots that deal at least 100 damage (50)	800 XP	Echelon 2
One Shot, One Kill IV	Kills with Vortex Rifle shots that deal at least 100 damage (75)	1000 XP	Echelon 2
One Shot, One Kill V	Kills with Vortex Rifle shots that deal at least 100 damage (100)	1000 XP	Echelon 2
Vortex Rifle Overkill I	Vortex Rifle critical kills (10)	200 XP	Echelon 4
Vortex Rifle Overkill II	Vortex Rifle critical kills (30)	400 XP	Echelon 4
Vortex Rifle Overkill III	Vortex Rifle critical kills (60)	600 XP	Echelon 4
Vortex Rifle Overkill IV	Vortex Rifle critical kills (100)	800 XP	Echelon 4

VORTEX RIFLE CHALLENGES CONT.

TITLE	DESCRIPTION	REWARD	UNLOCKED
Vortex Rifle Overkill V	Vortex Rifle critical kills (150)	1000 XP	Echelon 4
Maelstrom I	Longshot medals with the Vortex Rifle (10)	800 XP	Echelon 8
Maelstrom II	Longshot medals with the Vortex Rifle (25)	1200 XP	Echelon 8
Maelstrom III	Longshot medals with the Vortex Rifle (50)	2000 XP	Echelon 8
Maelstrom IV	Longshot medals with the Vortex Rifle (75)	2000 XP	Echelon 8
Maelstrom V	Longshot medals with the Vortex Rifle (100)	2000 XP	Echelon 8

HEAVY ASSAULT RIFLE CHALLENGES

TITLE	DESCRIPTION	REWARD	UNLOCKED
Heavily Damaged I	Heavy Assault Rifle damage dealt (2500)	150 XP	-
Heavily Damaged II	Heavy Assault Rifle damage dealt (5000)	150 XP	-
Heavily Damaged III	Heavy Assault Rifle damage dealt (10000)	300 XP	-
Heavily Damaged IV	Heavy Assault Rifle damage dealt (20000)	600 XP	-
Heavily Damaged V	Heavy Assault Rifle damage dealt (35000)	900 XP	-
Heavy Assault Rifle Mastery I	Heavy Assault Rifle kills (20)	250 XP	-
Heavy Assault Rifle Mastery II	Heavy Assault Rifle kills (50)	375 XP	-
Heavy Assault Rifle Mastery III	Heavy Assault Rifle kills (90)	500 XP	-
Heavy Assault Rifle Mastery IV	Heavy Assault Rifle kills (140)	625 XP	-
Heavy Assault Rifle Mastery V	Heavy Assault Rifle kills (200)	750 XP	-
Heavy Assault Rifle Mastery VI	Heavy Assault Rifle kills (270)	875 XP	-
Heavy Assault Rifle Mastery VII	Heavy Assault Rifle kills (350)	1000 XP	-
Heavy Assault Rifle Mastery VIII	Heavy Assault Rifle kills (440)	1125 XP	-
Heavy Assault Rifle Mastery IX	Heavy Assault Rifle kills (540)	1250 XP	-
Heavy Assault Rifle Mastery X	Heavy Assault Rifle kills (666)	1575 XP	-
Critical Assault I	Heavy Assault Rifle critical damage (500)	400 XP	Echelon 2
Critical Assault II	Heavy Assault Rifle critical damage (1000)	400 XP	Echelon 2
Critical Assault III	Heavy Assault Rifle critical damage (2000)	800 XP	Echelon 2
Critical Assault IV	Heavy Assault Rifle critical damage (4000)	1600 XP	Echelon 2
Critical Assault V	Heavy Assault Rifle critical damage (7500)	2800 XP	Echelon 2
Unending Assault I	Multi-kills with the Heavy Assault Rifle (10)	800 XP	Echelon 4
Unending Assault II	Multi-kills with the Heavy Assault Rifle (25)	1200 XP	Echelon 4
Unending Assault III	Multi-kills with the Heavy Assault Rifle (50)	2000 XP	Echelon 4
Unending Assault IV	Multi-kills with the Heavy Assault Rifle (75)	20000 XP	Echelon 4
Unending Assault V	Multi-kills with the Heavy Assault Rifle (100)	2000 XP	Echelon 4
Heavy Assault Rifle Overkill I	Heavy Assault Rifle critical kills (10)	200 XP	Echelon 8
Heavy Assault Rifle Overkill II	Heavy Assault Rifle critical kills (30)	400 XP	Echelon 8
Heavy Assault Rifle Overkill III	Heavy Assault Rifle critical kills (600)	600 XP	Echelon 8
Heavy Assault Rifle Overkill IV	Heavy Assault Rifle critical kills (100)	800 XP	Echelon 8
Heavy Assault Rifle Overkill V	Heavy Assault Rifle critical kills (150)	1000 XP	Echelon 8

LIGHTNING GUN CHALLENGES

TITLE	DESCRIPTION	REWARD	UNLOCKED
Lightning Gun Mastery I	Lightning Gun kills (20)	250 XP	-
Lightning Gun Mastery II	Lightning Gun kills (50)	375 XP	-
Lightning Gun Mastery III	Lightning Gun kills (90)	500 XP	-
Lightning Gun Mastery IV	Lightning Gun kills (140)	625 XP	-
Lightning Gun Mastery V	Lightning Gun kills (200)	750 XP	-
Lightning Gun Mastery VI	Lightning Gun kills (270)	875 XP	-
Lightning Gun Mastery VII	Lightning Gun kills (350)	1000 XP	-
Lightning Gun Mastery VIII	Lightning Gun kills (440)	1125 XP	-
Lightning Gun Mastery IX	Lightning Gun kills (540)	1250 XP	-
Lightning Gun Mastery X	Lightning Gun kills (666)	1575 XP	-
Thunderstorm I	Damage dealt with the Lightning Gun's splash field (1000)	200 XP	-
Thunderstorm II	Damage dealt with the Lightning Gun's splash field (3000)	200 XP	-
Thunderstorm III	Damage dealt with the Lightning Gun's splash field (5000)	400 XP	-
Thunderstorm IV	Damage dealt with the Lightning Gun's splash field (7500)	500 XP	-
Thunderstorm V	Damage dealt with the Lightning Gun's splash field (10000)	500 XP	-
Lightning Gun Overkill I	Lightning Gun critical kills (25)	375 XP	Echelon 2
Lightning Gun Overkill II	Lightning Gun critical kills (50)	375 XP	Echelon 2
Lightning Gun Overkill III	Lightning Gun critical kills (100)	750 XP	Echelon 2
Lightning Gun Overkill IV	Lightning Gun critical kills (150)	750 XP	Echelon 2
Lightning Gun Overkill V	Lightning Gun critical kills (200)	750 XP	Echelon 2
Explosive Shock I	Kills with the Lightning Gun's splash field (10)	250 XP	Echelon 4
Explosive Shock II	Kills with the Lightning Gun's splash field (25)	375 XP	Echelon 4
Explosive Shock III	Kills with the Lightning Gun's splash field (50)	625 XP	Echelon 4
Explosive Shock IV	Kills with the Lightning Gun's splash field (75)	625 XP	Echelon 4
Explosive Shock V	Kills with the Lightning Gun's splash field (100)	625 XP	Echelon 4
My Lightning Strikes Twice I	Multi-kills with the Lightning Gun (10)	800 XP	Echelon 8
My Lightning Strikes Twice II	Multi-kills with the Lightning Gun (25)	1200 XP	Echelon 8
My Lightning Strikes Twice III	Multi-kills with the Lightning Gun (50)	2000 XP	Echelon 8
My Lightning Strikes Twice IV	Multi-kills with the Lightning Gun (75)	2000 XP	Echelon 8
My Lightning Strikes Twice V	Multi-kills with the Lightning Gun (100)	2000 XP	Echelon 8

COMBAT SHOTGUN CHALLENGES

TITLE	DESCRIPTION	REWARD	UNLOCKED
Combat Shotgun Mastery I	Combat Shotgun kills (20)	250 XP	-
Combat Shotgun Mastery II	Combat Shotgun kills (50)	375 XP	-
Combat Shotgun Mastery III	Combat Shotgun kills (90)	500 XP	-
Combat Shotgun Mastery IV	Combat Shotgun kills (140)	625 XP	-
Combat Shotgun Mastery V	Combat Shotgun kills (200)	750 XP	-
Combat Shotgun Mastery VI	Combat Shotgun kills (270)	875 XP	-
Combat Shotgun Mastery VII	Combat Shotgun kills (350)	1000 XP	-
Combat Shotgun Mastery VIII	Combat Shotgun kills (440)	1125 XP	-
Combat Shotgun Mastery IX	Combat Shotgun kills (540)	1250 XP	-
Combat Shotgun Mastery X	Combat Shotgun kills (666)	1575 XP	-

COMBAT SHOTGUN CHALLENGES CONT.

TITLE	DESCRIPTION	REWARD	UNLOCKED
Pop Rocketeer I	Damaged dealt with the Combat Shotgun's mortar shells (500)	250 XP	-
Pop Rocketeer II	Damaged dealt with the Combat Shotgun's mortar shells (1000)	250 XP	-
Pop Rocketeer III	Damaged dealt with the Combat Shotgun's mortar shells (1750)	375 XP	-
Pop Rocketeer IV	Damaged dealt with the Combat Shotgun's mortar shells (2600)	425 XP	-
Pop Rocketeer V	Damaged dealt with the Combat Shotgun's mortar shells (3600)	500 XP	-
Combat Shotgun Overkill I	Combat Shotgun critical kills (20)	500 XP	Echelon 2
Combat Shotgun Overkill II	Combat Shotgun critical kills (40)	500 XP	Echelon 2
Combat Shotgun Overkill III	Combat Shotgun critical kills (60)	500 XP	Echelon 2
Combat Shotgun Overkill IV	Combat Shotgun critical kills (80)	500 XP	Echelon 2
Combat Shotgun Overkill V	Combat Shotgun critical kills (120)	1000 XP	Echelon 2
Pop Shot I	Kills with the Combat Shotgun's mortar shells (10)	300 XP	Echelon 4
Pop Shot II	Kills with the Combat Shotgun's mortar shells (30)	600 XP	Echelon 4
Pop Shot III	Kills with the Combat Shotgun's mortar shells (60)	900 XP	Echelon 4
Pop Shot IV	Kills with the Combat Shotgun's mortar shells (100)	1200 XP	Echelon 4
Pop Shot V	Kills with the Combat Shotgun's mortar shells (150)	1500 XP	Echelon 4
Lead Buckets I	Multi-kills with the Combat Shotgun (10)	800 XP	Echelon 8
Lead Buckets II	Multi-kills with the Combat Shotgun (25)	1200 XP	Echelon 8
Lead Buckets III	Multi-kills with the Combat Shotgun (50)	2000 XP	Echelon 8
Lead Buckets IV	Multi-kills with the Combat Shotgun (75)	2000 XP	Echelon 8
Lead Buckets V	Multi-kills with the Combat Shotgun (100)	2000 XP	Echelon 8

HELLSHOT CHALLENGES

TITLE	DESCRIPTION	REWARD	UNLOCKED
Fire Starter I	Damage dealt with Hellshot Incendiary rounds (2000)	500 XP	-
Fire Starter II	Damage dealt with Hellshot Incendiary rounds (5000)	750 XP	-
Fire Starter III	Damage dealt with Hellshot Incendiary rounds (10000)	1250 XP	-
Fire Starter IV	Damage dealt with Hellshot Incendiary rounds (17000)	1750 XP	-
Fire Starter V	Damage dealt with Hellshot Incendiary rounds (26000)	2250 XP	-
Hellshot Mastery I	Hellshot kills (20)	250 XP	-
Hellshot Mastery II	Hellshot kills (50)	375 XP	-
Hellshot Mastery III	Hellshot kills (90)	500 XP	-
Hellshot Mastery IV	Hellshot kills (140)	625 XP	-
Hellshot Mastery V	Hellshot kills (200)	750 XP	-
Hellshot Mastery VI	Hellshot kills (270)	875 XP	-
Hellshot Mastery VII	Hellshot kills (350)	1000 XP	-
Hellshot Mastery VIII	Hellshot kills (440)	1125 XP	-
Hellshot Mastery IX	Hellshot kills (540)	1250 XP	-
Hellshot Mastery X	Hellshot kills (666)	1575 XP	-
Hellshot Overkill I	Hellshot critical kills (5)	200 XP	Echelon 2
Hellshot Overkill II	Hellshot critical kills (15)	400 XP	Echelon 2
Hellshot Overkill III	Hellshot critical kills (30)	600 XP	Echelon 2
Hellshot Overkill IV	Hellshot critical kills (50)	800 XP	Echelon 2

HELLSHOT CHALLENGES CONT.

TITLE	DESCRIPTION	REWARD	UNLOCKED
Hellshot Overkill V	Hellshot critical kills (75)	1000 XP	Echelon 2
Burn, Baby, Burn I	Kills with Hellshot incendiary rounds (5)	150 XP	Echelon 4
Burn, Baby, Burn II	Kills with Hellshot incendiary rounds (15)	300 XP	Echelon 4
Burn, Baby, Burn III	Kills with Hellshot incendiary rounds (30)	450 XP	Echelon 4
Burn, Baby, Burn IV	Kills with Hellshot incendiary rounds (50)	600 XP	Echelon 4
Burn, Baby, Burn V	Kills with Hellshot incendiary rounds (75)	750 XP	Echelon 4
First Aid I	Heal Hellshot burns with health pickups (5)	1000 XP	Echelon 8
First Aid II	Heal Hellshot burns with health pickups (10)	1000 XP	Echelon 8
First Aid III	Heal Hellshot burns with health pickups (20)	2000 XP	Echelon 8
First Aid IV	Heal Hellshot burns with health pickups (30)	2000 XP	Echelon 8
First Aid V	Heal Hellshot burns with health pickups (40)	2000 XP	Echelon 8

STATIC RIFLE CHALLENGES

TITLE	DESCRIPTION	REWARD	UNLOCKED
Capacitor I	Time with the Static Rifle fully charged (400)	240 XP	-
Capacitor II	Time with the Static Rifle fully charged (1000)	360 XP	
Capacitor III	Time with the Static Rifle fully charged (1750)	450 XP	
Capacitor IV	Time with the Static Rifle fully charged (2600)	510 XP	
Capacitor V	Time with the Static Rifle fully charged (3300)	600 XP	
Static Rifle Mastery I	Static Rifle kills (20)	250 XP	-
Static Rifle Mastery II	Static Rifle kills (50)	375 XP	-
Static Rifle Mastery III	Static Rifle kills (90)	500 XP	-
Static Rifle Mastery IV	Static Rifle kills (140)	625 XP	-
Static Rifle Mastery V	Static Rifle kills (200)	750 XP	-
Static Rifle Mastery VI	Static Rifle kills (270)	875 XP	-
Static Rifle Mastery VII	Static Rifle kills (350)	1000 XP	-
Static Rifle Mastery VIII	Static Rifle kills (440)	1125 XP	-
Static Rifle Mastery IX	Static Rifle kills (540)	1250 XP	-
Static Rifle Mastery X	Static Rifle kills (666)	1575 XP	-
Overcharge I	Static Rifle critical damage (1000)	500 XP	Echelon 4
Overcharge II	Static Rifle critical damage (4000)	1500 XP	Echelon 4
Overcharge III	Static Rifle critical damage (7000)	1500 XP	Echelon 4
Overcharge IV	Static Rifle critical damage (10000)	1500 XP	Echelon 4
Overcharge V	Static Rifle critical damage (13000)	1500 XP	Echelon 4
Static Rifle Overkill I	Static Rifle critical kills (10)	200 XP	Echelon 4
Static Rifle Overkill II	Static Rifle critical kills (30)	400 XP	Echelon 4
Static Rifle Overkill III	Static Rifle critical kills (60)	600 XP	Echelon 4
Static Rifle Overkill IV	Static Rifle critical kills (100)	800 XP	Echelon 4
Static Rifle Overkill V	Static Rifle critical kills (150)	1000 XP	Echelon 4
Static Shock I	Longshot medals with the Static Rifle (5)	1000 XP	Echelon 8
Static Shock II	Longshot medals with the Static Rifle (10)	1000 XP	Echelon 8
Static Shock III	Longshot medals with the Static Rifle (20)	2000 XP	Echelon 8
Static Shock IV	Longshot medals with the Static Rifle (30)	2000 XP	Echelon 8
Static Shock V	Longshot medals with the Static Rifle (40)	2000 XP	Echelon 8

BURST RIFLE CHALLENGES

TITLE	DESCRIPTION	REWARD	UNLOCKED
Burst Rifle Mastery I	Burst Rifle kills (20)	250 XP	-
Burst Rifle Mastery II	Burst Rifle kills (50)	375 XP	-
Burst Rifle Mastery III	Burst Rifle kills (90)	500 XP	-
Burst Rifle Mastery IV	Burst Rifle kills (140)	625 XP	-
Burst Rifle Mastery V	Burst Rifle kills (200)	750 XP	-
Burst Rifle Mastery VI	Burst Rifle kills (270)	875 XP	-
Burst Rifle Mastery VII	Burst Rifle kills (350)	1000 XP	-
Burst Rifle Mastery VIII	Burst Rifle kills (440)	1125 XP	-
Burst Rifle Mastery IX	Burst Rifle kills (540)	1250 XP	-
Burst Rifle Mastery X	Burst Rifle kills (666)	1575 XP	-
Repeated Beatdown I	Burst Rifle critical damage (1000)	650 XP	-
Repeated Beatdown II	Burst Rifle critical damage (3000)	1300 XP	-
Repeated Beatdown III	Burst Rifle critical damage (5000)	1300 XP	-
Repeated Beatdown IV	Burst Rifle critical damage (7500)	1625 XP	-
Repeated Beatdown V	Burst Rifle critical damage (10000)	1625 XP	-
Fine-Grained Fire I	Kills with the Burst Rifle's semi-auto mode (10)	200 XP	Echelon 2
Fine-Grained Fire II	Kills with the Burst Rifle's semi-auto mode (25)	300 XP	Echelon 2
Fine-Grained Fire III	Kills with the Burst Rifle's semi-auto mode (50)	500 XP	Echelon 2
Fine-Grained Fire IV	Kills with the Burst Rifle's semi-auto mode (75)	500 XP	Echelon 2
Fine-Grained Fire V	Kills with the Burst Rifle's semi-auto mode (100)	500 XP	Echelon 2
Burst Rifle Overkill I	Burst Rifle critical kills (10)	200 XP	Echelon 4
Burst Rifle Overkill II	Burst Rifle critical kills (30)	400 XP	Echelon 4
Burst Rifle Overkill III	Burst Rifle critical kills (60)	600 XP	Echelon 4
Burst Rifle Overkill IV	Burst Rifle critical kills (100)	800 XP	Echelon 4
Burst Rifle Overkill V	Burst Rifle critical kills (150)	1000 XP	Echelon 4
Head Full of Lead I	Critical kills with the Burt Rifle's burst mode (10)	800 XP	Echelon 8
Head Full of Lead II	Critical kills with the Burt Rifle's burst mode (25)	1200 XP	Echelon 8
Head Full of Lead III	Critical kills with the Burt Rifle's burst mode (50)	2000 XP	Echelon 8
Head Full of Lead IV	Critical kills with the Burt Rifle's burst mode (75)	2000 XP	Echelon 8
Head Full of Lead V	Critical kills with the Burt Rifle's burst mode (100)	2000 XP	Echelon 8

EQUIPMENT

FRAG GRENADE CHALLENGES

TITLE	DESCRIPTION	REWARD	UNLOCKED
Grenadier I	Frag Grenade kills (25)	250 XP	-
Grenadier II	Frag Grenade kills (50)	250 XP	-
Grenadier III	Frag Grenade kills (100)	500 XP	-
Grenadier IV	Frag Grenade kills (150)	500 XP	-
Grenadier V	Frag Grenade kills (200)	500 XP	-
Blast Zone I	Frag Grenade damage dealt (2000)	200 XP	-
Blast Zone II	Frag Grenade damage dealt (4000)	200 XP	-
Blast Zone III	Frag Grenade damage dealt (7000)	300 XP	-
Blast Zone IV	Frag Grenade damage dealt (11000)	400 XP	-
Blast Zone V	Frag Grenade damage dealt (16000)	500 XP	-

PERSONAL TELEPORTER CHALLENGES

TITLE	DESCRIPTION	REWARD	UNLOCKED
Surprise! I	Quick kills after using a Personal Teleporter (10)	500 XP	-
Surprise! II	Quick kills after using a Personal Teleporter (30)	1000 XP	-
Surprise! III	Quick kills after using a Personal Teleporter (60)	1500 XP	-
Surprise! IV	Quick kills after using a Personal Teleporter (100)	2000 XP	-
Surprise! V	Quick kills after using a Personal Teleporter (150)	2500 XP	-
That's My Spot I	Telefrags with the Personal Teleporter (3)	300 XP	-
That's My Spot II	Telefrags with the Personal Teleporter (6)	300 XP	-
That's My Spot III	Telefrags with the Personal Teleporter (10)	400 XP	-
That's My Spot IV	Telefrags with the Personal Teleporter (15)	500 XP	-
That's My Spot V	Telefrags with the Personal Teleporter (20)	500 XP	-

SIPHON GRENADE CHALLENGES

TITLE	DESCRIPTION	REWARD	UNLOCKED
Soul Siphon I	Siphon Grenade damage dealt (1000)	250 XP	-
Soul Siphon II	Siphon Grenade damage dealt (3000)	500 XP	-
Soul Siphon III	Siphon Grenade damage dealt (5000)	500 XP	-
Soul Siphon IV	Siphon Grenade damage dealt (7500)	625 XP	-
Soul Siphon V	Siphon Grenade damage dealt (10000)	625 XP	-
Vampire I	Siphon Grenade kills (10)	250 XP	-
Vampire II	Siphon Grenade kills (25)	375 XP	-
Vampire III	Siphon Grenade kills (50)	625 XP	-
Vampire IV	Siphon Grenade kills (75)	625 XP	-
Vampire V	Siphon Grenade kills (100)	625 XP	-

HOLOGRAM CHALLENGES

TITLE	DESCRIPTION	REWARD	UNLOCKED
Deceiver I	Distraction medals (10)	250 XP	-
Deceiver II	Distraction medals (30)	500 XP	-
Deceiver III	Distraction medals (60)	750 XP	-
Deceiver IV	Distraction medals (100)	1000 XP	-
Deceiver V	Distraction medals (150)	1250 XP	-

SHIELD WALL CHALLENGES

TITLE	DESCRIPTION	REWARD	UNLOCKED
Best Defense I	Kill enemies while using the Shield Wall (20)	300 XP	-
Best Defense II	Kill enemies while using the Shield Wall (60)	600 XP	-
Best Defense III	Kill enemies while using the Shield Wall (120)	900 XP	-
Best Defense IV	Kill enemies while using the Shield Wall (200)	1200 XP	-
Best Defense V	Kill enemies while using the Shield Wall (300)	1500 XP	-
Personal Fortress I	Absorb damage with the Shield Wall (500)	250 XP	-
Personal Fortress II	Absorb damage with the Shield Wall (1000)	250 XP	-

SHIELD WALL CHALLENGES CONT.

TITLE	DESCRIPTION	REWARD	UNLOCKED
Personal Fortress III	Absorb damage with the Shield Wall (1750)	375 XP	-
Personal Fortress IV	Absorb damage with the Shield Wall (2600)	425 XP	-
Personal Fortress V	Absorb damage with the Shield Wall (3600)	500 XP	-

TESLA ROCKET CHALLENGES

TITLE	DESCRIPTION	REWARD	UNLOCKED
Electric Boogaloo I	Tesla Rocket damage dealt (500)	250 XP	-
Electric Boogaloo II	Tesla Rocket damage dealt (1000)	250 XP	-
Electric Boogaloo III	Tesla Rocket damage dealt (2000)	500 XP	-
Electric Boogaloo IV	Tesla Rocket damage dealt (4000)	1000 XP	-
Electric Boogaloo V	Tesla Rocket damage dealt (7500)	1750 XP	-
Lightning Baller I	Tesla Rocket kills (5)	300 XP	-
Lightning Baller II	Tesla Rocket kills (15)	600 XP	-
Lightning Baller III	Tesla Rocket kills (30)	900 XP	-
Lightning Baller IV	Tesla Rocket kills (50)	1200 XP	-
Lightning Baller V	Tesla Rocket kills (75)	1500 XP	-

THREAT SENSOR CHALLENGES

TITLE	DESCRIPTION	REWARD	UNLOCKED
Threat Eliminated I	Kill enemies while using the Threat Sensor (25)	250 XP	-
Threat Eliminated II	Kill enemies while using the Threat Sensor (50)	250 XP	-
Threat Eliminated III	Kill enemies while using the Threat Sensor (100)	500 XP	-
Threat Eliminated IV	Kill enemies while using the Threat Sensor (150)	500 XP	-
Threat Eliminated V	Kill enemies while using the Threat Sensor (200)	500 XP	-
Threat Spotted I	Detect enemies with the Threat Sensor (50)	300 XP	-
Threat Spotted II	Detect enemies with the Threat Sensor (125)	450 XP	-
Threat Spotted III	Detect enemies with the Threat Sensor (200)	450 XP	-
Threat Spotted IV	Detect enemies with the Threat Sensor (275)	450 XP	-
Threat Spotted V	Detect enemies with the Threat Sensor (350)	450 XP	-

DEMON

GENERAL DEMON CHALLENGES

TITLE	DESCRIPTION	REWARD	UNLOCKED
Demon Hunter I	Enemy demons killed (10)	500 XP	-
Demon Hunter II	Enemy demons killed (25)	750 XP	-
Demon Hunter III	Enemy demons killed (50)	1250 XP	-
Demon Hunter IV	Enemy demons killed (75)	1250 XP	-
Demon Hunter V	Enemy demons killed (100)	1250 XP	-
Demonology I	Times transformed into a demon (5)	250 XP	-
Demonology II	Times transformed into a demon (10)	250 XP	-
Demonology III	Times transformed into a demon (20)	500 XP	-
Demonology IV	Times transformed into a demon (35)	750 XP	-

GENERAL DEMON CHALLENGES CONT.

TITLE	DESCRIPTION	REWARD	UNLOCKED
Demonology V	Times transformed into a demon (50)	750 XP	-
Demonology VI	Times transformed into a demon (65)	750 XP	-
Demonology VII	Times transformed into a demon (80)	750 XP	-
Demonology VIII	Times transformed into a demon (95)	750 XP	-
Demonology IX	Times transformed into a demon (120)	1250 XP	-
Demonology X	Times transformed into a demon (150)	1500 XP	-
Exorcist I	Glory killed demons (5)	750 XP	-
Exorcist II	Glory killed demons (10)	750 XP	-
Exorcist III	Glory killed demons (20)	1500 XP	-
Exorcist IV	Glory killed demons (30)	1500 XP	-
Exorcist V	Glory killed demons (40)	1500 XP	-
Armageddon I	Earn Carnage medals while playing as a demon (3)	750 XP	Echelon 3
Armageddon II	Earn Carnage medals while playing as a demon (6)	750 XP	Echelon 3
Armageddon III	Earn Carnage medals while playing as a demon (10)	1000 XP	Echelon 3
Armageddon IV	Earn Carnage medals while playing as a demon (15)	1250 XP	Echelon 3
Armageddon V	Earn Carnage medals while playing as a demon (20)	1250 XP	Echelon 3
Can't Fight the Power I	Transform into a demon twice in one life (1)	250 XP	Echelon 5
Can't Fight the Power II	Transform into a demon twice in one life (3)	500 XP	Echelon 5
Can't Fight the Power III	Transform into a demon twice in one life (5)	500 XP	Echelon 5
Can't Fight the Power IV	Transform into a demon twice in one life (7)	500 XP	Echelon 5
Can't Fight the Power V	Transform into a demon twice in one life (10)	750 XP	Echelon 5
Ultimate Demon Slayer I	Kill three demons in a single match (3)	1500 XP	Echelon 10
Ultimate Demon Slayer I	Kill three demons in a single match (6)	1500 XP	Echelon 10
Ultimate Demon Slayer I	Kill three demons in a single match (10)	2000 XP	Echelon 10
Ultimate Demon Slayer I	Kill three demons in a single match (15)	2500 XP	Echelon 10
Ultimate Demon Slayer I	Kill three demons in a single match (20)	2500 XP	Echelon 10

BARON CHALLENGES

TITLE	DESCRIPTION	REWARD	UNLOCKED
Earthquake I	Ground Pound multi-kills as the Baron (5)	500 XP	-
Earthquake II	Ground Pound multi-kills as the Baron (15)	1000 XP	-
Earthquake III	Ground Pound multi-kills as the Baron (30)	1500 XP	-
Earthquake IV	Ground Pound multi-kills as the Baron (50)	2000 XP	-
Earthquake V	Ground Pound multi-kills as the Baron (75)	2500 XP	-
No Escaping the Baron I	Glory kills as the Baron (25)	200 XP	-
No Escaping the Baron II	Glory kills as the Baron (50)	200 XP	-
No Escaping the Baron III	Glory kills as the Baron (100)	400 XP	-
No Escaping the Baron IV	Glory kills as the Baron (150)	400 XP	-
No Escaping the Baron V	Glory kills as the Baron (200)	400 XP	-
Red Baron I	Kill enemies while playing as the Baron (10)	250 XP	-
Red Baron II	Kill enemies while playing as the Baron (20)	250 XP	-
Red Baron III	Kill enemies while playing as the Baron (35)	375 XP	-
Red Baron IV	Kill enemies while playing as the Baron (50)	375 XP	-
Red Baron V	Kill enemies while playing as the Baron (75)	625 XP	-
Red Baron VI	Kill enemies while playing as the Baron (100)	625 XP	-
Red Baron VII	Kill enemies while playing as the Baron (150)	1250 XP	-

BARON CHALLENGES CONT.

TITLE	DESCRIPTION	REWARD	UNLOCKED
Red Baron VIII	Kill enemies while playing as the Baron (200)	1250 XP	-
Red Baron IX	Kill enemies while playing as the Baron (250)	1250 XP	-
Red Baron X	Kill enemies while playing as the Baron (300)	1250 XP	-
Regicide I	Barons killed (5)	250 XP	Echelon 1
Regicide II	Barons killed (15)	500 XP	Echelon 1
Regicide III	Barons killed (30)	750 XP	Echelon 1
Regicide IV	Barons killed (50)	1000 XP	Echelon 1
Regicide V	Barons killed (75)	1250 XP	Echelon 1
Oppression I	Multi-kills as the Baron (15)	900 XP	Echelon 2
Oppression II	Multi-kills as the Baron (30)	900 XP	Echelon 2
Oppression III	Multi-kills as the Baron (50)	1200 XP	Echelon 2
Oppression IV	Multi-kills as the Baron (75)	1500 XP	Echelon 2
Oppression V	Multi-kills as the Baron (100)	1500 XP	Echelon 2

REVENANT CHALLENGES

TITLE	DESCRIPTION	REWARD	UNLOCKED
Grounded I	Revenant jetpacks disabled (5)	250 XP	-
Grounded II	Revenant jetpacks disabled (15)	500 XP	-
Grounded III	Revenant jetpacks disabled (30)	750 XP	-
Grounded IV	Revenant jetpacks disabled (50)	1000 XP	-
Grounded V	Revenant jetpacks disabled (75)	1250 XP	-
Ravenous I	Blood Bath medals as the Revenant (5)	200 XP	-
Ravenous II	Blood Bath medals as the Revenant (10)	200 XP	-
Ravenous III	Blood Bath medals as the Revenant (20)	400 XP	-
Ravenous IV	Blood Bath medals as the Revenant (30)	400 XP	-
Reaver I	Kill enemies while playing as the Revenant (10)	250 XP	-
Reaver II	Kill enemies while playing as the Revenant (20)	250 XP	-
Reaver III	Kill enemies while playing as the Revenant (35)	375 XP	-
Reaver IV	Kill enemies while playing as the Revenant (50)	375 XP	-
Reaver V	Kill enemies while playing as the Revenant (75)	625 XP	-
Reaver VI	Kill enemies while playing as the Revenant (100)	625 XP	-
Reaver VII	Kill enemies while playing as the Revenant (150)	1250 XP	-
Reaver VIII	Kill enemies while playing as the Revenant (200)	1250 XP	-
Reaver IX	Kill enemies while playing as the Revenant (250)	1250 XP	-
Reaver X	Kill enemies while playing as the Revenant (300)	1250 XP	-
Undertaker I	Revenants killed (5)	250 XP	Echelon 1
Undertaker II	Revenants killed (15)	500 XP	Echelon 1
Undertaker III	Revenants killed (30)	750 XP	Echelon 1
Undertaker IV	Revenants killed (50)	1000 XP	Echelon 1
Undertaker V	Revenants killed (75)	1250 XP	Echelon 1
Air Strike I	Double Kill medals while airborne as the Revenant (10)	1000 XP	Echelon 2
Air Strike II	Double Kill medals while airborne as the Revenant (25)	1500 XP	Echelon 2
Air Strike III	Double Kill medals while airborne as the Revenant (50)	2500 XP	Echelon 2
Air Strike IV	Double Kill medals while airborne as the Revenant (75)	2500 XP	Echelon 2
Air Strike V	Double Kill medals while airborne as the Revenant (100)	2500 XP	Echelon 2

MANCUBUS CHALLENGES

TITLE	DESCRIPTION	REWARD	UNLOCKED
Artillery Master I	Longshot medals as the Mancubus (5)	400 XP	-
Artillery Master II	Longshot medals as the Mancubus (10)	400 XP	-
Artillery Master III	Longshot medals as the Mancubus (20)	800 XP	-
Artillery Master IV	Longshot medals as the Mancubus (30)	800 XP	-
Artillery Master V	Longshot medals as the Mancubus (40)	800 XP	-
Bring the Heat I	Kill enemies with the Mancubus's steam vent (5)	200 XP	-
Bring the Heat II	Kill enemies with the Mancubus's steam vent (10)	200 XP	-
Bring the Heat III	Kill enemies with the Mancubus's steam vent (20)	400 XP	-
Bring the Heat IV	Kill enemies with the Mancubus's steam vent (30)	400 XP	-
Bring the Heat V	Kill enemies with the Mancubus's steam vent (40)	400 XP	-
Hit by a Bus I	Kill enemies while playing as the Mancubus (10)	250 XP	-
Hit by a Bus II	Kill enemies while playing as the Mancubus (20)	250 XP	-
Hit by a Bus III	Kill enemies while playing as the Mancubus (35)	375 XP	-
Hit by a Bus IV	Kill enemies while playing as the Mancubus (50)	375 XP	-
Hit by a Bus V	Kill enemies while playing as the Mancubus (75)	625 XP	-
Hit by a Bus VI	Kill enemies while playing as the Mancubus (100)	625 XP	-
Hit by a Bus VII	Kill enemies while playing as the Mancubus (150)	1250 XP	-
Hit by a Bus VIII	Kill enemies while playing as the Mancubus (200)	1250 XP	-
Hit by a Bus IX	Kill enemies while playing as the Mancubus (250)	1250 XP	-
Hit by a Bus X	Kill enemies while playing as the Mancubus (300)	1250 XP	-
Bunker Buster I	Mancubi killed (5)	250 XP	Echelon 1
Bunker Buster II	Mancubi killed (15)	500 XP	Echelon 1
Bunker Buster III	Mancubi killed (30)	750 XP	Echelon 1
Bunker Buster IV	Mancubi killed (50)	1000 XP	Echelon 1
Bunker Buster V	Mancubi killed (75)	1250 XP	Echelon 1
Stay Outta My Kitchen I	Double Kill medals with the Mancubus's steam vent (3)	450 XP	Echelon 2
Stay Outta My Kitchen II	Double Kill medals with the Mancubus's steam vent (6)	450 XP	Echelon 2
Stay Outta My Kitchen III	Double Kill medals with the Mancubus's steam vent (10)	600 XP	Echelon 2
Stay Outta My Kitchen IV	Double Kill medals with the Mancubus's steam vent (15)	750 XP	Echelon 2
Stay Outta My Kitchen V	Double Kill medals with the Mancubus's steam vent (20)	750 XP	Echelon 2

PROWLER CHALLENGES

TITLE	DESCRIPTION	REWARD	UNLOCKED
Creeper I	Kill enemies while playing as the Prowler (10)	250 XP	-
Creeper II	Kill enemies while playing as the Prowler (20)	250 XP	-
Creeper III	Kill enemies while playing as the Prowler (35)	375 XP	-
Creeper IV	Kill enemies while playing as the Prowler (50)	375 XP	-
Creeper V	Kill enemies while playing as the Prowler (75)	625 XP	-
Creeper VI	Kill enemies while playing as the Prowler (100)	625 XP	-
Creeper VII	Kill enemies while playing as the Prowler (150)	1250 XP	-
Creeper VIII	Kill enemies while playing as the Prowler (200)	1250 XP	-
Creeper IX	Kill enemies while playing as the Prowler (250)	1250 XP	-
Creeper X	Kill enemies while playing as the Prowler (300)	1250 XP	-

PROWLER CHALLENGES CONT.

TITLE	DESCRIPTION	REWARD	UNLOCKED
Death from Above I	Time spent off the ground as the Prowler (150)	180 XP	-
Death from Above II	Time spent off the ground as the Prowler (300)	180 XP	-
Death from Above III	Time spent off the ground as the Prowler (500)	240 XP	-
Death from Above IV	Time spent off the ground as the Prowler (750)	300 XP	-
Death from Above V	Time spent off the ground as the Prowler (1000)	300 XP	-
Prowling Demise I	Kill enemies with the Prowler's pounce (10)	200 XP	-
Prowling Demise II	Kill enemies with the Prowler's pounce (30)	200 XP	-
Prowling Demise III	Kill enemies with the Prowler's pounce (60)	400 XP	-
Prowling Demise IV	Kill enemies with the Prowler's pounce (100)	400 XP	-
Prowling Demise V	Kill enemies with the Prowler's pounce (150)	400 XP	-
Prowler Befouler I	Prowlers killed (5)	250 XP	Echelon 1
Prowler Befouler II	Prowlers killed (15)	500 XP	Echelon 1
Prowler Befouler III	Prowlers killed (30)	750 XP	Echelon 1
Prowler Befouler IV	Prowlers killed (50)	1000 XP	Echelon 1
Prowler Befouler V	Prowlers killed (75)	1250 XP	Echelon 1
Ninja Assassin I	Multi-kills as the Prowler (10)	1000 XP	Echelon 2
Ninja Assassin II	Multi-kills as the Prowler (25)	1500 XP	Echelon 2
Ninja Assassin III	Multi-kills as the Prowler (50)	2500 XP	Echelon 2
Ninja Assassin IV	Multi-kills as the Prowler (75)	2500 XP	Echelon 2
Ninja Assassin V	Multi-kills as the Prowler (100)	2500 XP	Echelon 2

HACK MODULE

KILLS CHALLENGES

TITLE	DESCRIPTION	REWARD	UNLOCKED
Total Hack I	Kill enemies while using hack modules (20)	200 XP	Echelon 1
Total Hack II	Kill enemies while using hack modules (50)	300 XP	Echelon 1
Total Hack III	Kill enemies while using hack modules (100)	500 XP	Echelon 1
Total Hack IV	Kill enemies while using hack modules (170)	700 XP	Echelon 1
Total Hack V	Kill enemies while using hack modules (260)	900 XP	Echelon 1
Total Hack VI	Kill enemies while using hack modules (370)	1100 XP	Echelon 1
Total Hack VII	Kill enemies while using hack modules (500)	1300 XP	Echelon 1
Total Hack VIII	Kill enemies while using hack modules (650)	1500 XP	Echelon 1
Total Hack IX	Kill enemies while using hack modules (820)	1700 XP	Echelon 1
Total Hack X	Kill enemies while using hack modules (1000)	1800 XP	Echelon 1
Anti-Virus I	Kill enemies that are using hack modules (30)	250 XP	Echelon 3
Anti-Virus II	Kill enemies that are using hack modules (100)	585 XP	Echelon 3
Anti-Virus III	Kill enemies that are using hack modules (225)	1040 XP	Echelon 3
Anti-Virus IV	Kill enemies that are using hack modules (400)	1460 XP	Echelon 3
Anti-Virus V	Kill enemies that are using hack modules (666)	2215 XP	Echelon 3

MODE

TEAM DEATHMATCH CHALLENGES

TITLE	DESCRIPTION	REWARD	UNLOCKED
Matched with Death I	Team Deathmatch score (5000)	150 XP	-
Matched with Death II	Team Deathmatch score (15000)	300 XP	-
Matched with Death III	Team Deathmatch score (30000)	450 XP	-
Matched with Death IV	Team Deathmatch score (50000)	600 XP	-
Matched with Death V	Team Deathmatch score (75000)	750 XP	-
Matched with Death VI	Team Deathmatch score (10000)	750 XP	-
Matched with Death VII	Team Deathmatch score (125000)	750 XP	-
Matched with Death VIII	Team Deathmatch score (150000)	750 XP	-
Matched with Death IX	Team Deathmatch score (175000)	750 XP	-
Matched with Death X	Team Deathmatch score (200000)	750 XP	-
Team Deathmatch Master I	Win Team Deathmatch matches (5)	500 XP	Echelon 1
Team Deathmatch Master II	Win Team Deathmatch matches (10)	500 XP	Echelon 1
Team Deathmatch Master III	Win Team Deathmatch matches (20)	1000 XP	Echelon 1
Team Deathmatch Master IV	Win Team Deathmatch matches (35)	1500 XP	Echelon 1
Team Deathmatch Master V	Win Team Deathmatch matches (50)	1500 XP	Echelon 1
Team Deathmatch Master VI	Win Team Deathmatch matches (65)	1500 XP	Echelon 1
Team Deathmatch Master VII	Win Team Deathmatch matches (80)	1500 XP	Echelon 1
Team Deathmatch Master VIII	Win Team Deathmatch matches (95)	1500 XP	Echelon 1
Team Deathmatch Master IX	Win Team Deathmatch matches (120)	2500 XP	Echelon 1
Team Deathmatch Master X	Win Team Deathmatch matches (150)	3000 XP	Echelon 1
Lord of the Fangs I	Kills in Team Deathmatch (20)	150 XP	Echelon 3
Lord of the Fangs II	Kills in Team Deathmatch (60)	300 XP	Echelon 3
Lord of the Fangs III	Kills in Team Deathmatch (120)	450 XP	Echelon 3
Lord of the Fangs IV	Kills in Team Deathmatch (200)	600 XP	Echelon 3
Lord of the Fangs V	Kills in Team Deathmatch (300)	750 XP	Echelon 3
Precision Killer I	Critical Kill medals in Team Deathmatch (10)	150 XP	Echelon 5
Precision Killer II	Critical Kill medals in Team Deathmatch (25)	225 XP	Echelon 5
Precision Killer III	Critical Kill medals in Team Deathmatch (50)	375 XP	Echelon 5
Precision Killer IV	Critical Kill medals in Team Deathmatch (85)	525 XP	Echelon 5
Precision Killer V	Critical Kill medals in Team Deathmatch (130)	675 XP	Echelon 5
Efficient Player I	Multi-kills in Team Deathmatch (10)	400 XP	Echelon 7
Efficient Player II	Multi-kills in Team Deathmatch (25)	600 XP	Echelon 7
Efficient Player III	Multi-kills in Team Deathmatch (50)	1000 XP	Echelon 7
Efficient Player IV	Multi-kills in Team Deathmatch (75)	1000 XP	Echelon 7
Efficient Player V	Multi-kills in Team Deathmatch (100)	1000 XP	Echelon 7
Match Survivor I	Survivor medals in Team Deathmatch (5)	500 XP	Echelon 9
Match Survivor I	Survivor medals in Team Deathmatch (15)	1000 XP	Echelon 9
Match Survivor I	Survivor medals in Team Deathmatch (30)	1500 XP	Echelon 9
Match Survivor I	Survivor medals in Team Deathmatch (50)	2000 XP	Echelon 9
Match Survivor I	Survivor medals in Team Deathmatch (75)	2500 XP	Echelon 9

CLAN ARENA CHALLENGES

TITLE	DESCRIPTION	REWARD	UNLOCKED
Clan Life I	Clan Arena score (5000)	150 XP	-
Clan Life II	Clan Arena score (15000)	300 XP	-
Clan Life III	Clan Arena score (30000)	450 XP	-
Clan Life IV	Clan Arena score (50000)	600 XP	-
Clan Life V	Clan Arena score (75000)	750 XP	-
Clan Life VI	Clan Arena score (10000)	750 XP	-
Clan Life VII	Clan Arena score (125000)	750 XP	-
Clan Life VIII	Clan Arena score (150000)	750 XP	-
Clan Life IX	Clan Arena score (175000)	750 XP	-
Clan Life X	Clan Arena score (200000)	750 XP	-
All in the Family I	Win Clan Arena matches (5)	500 XP	Echelon 1
All in the Family II	Win Clan Arena matches (10)	500 XP	Echelon 1
All in the Family III	Win Clan Arena matches (20)	1000 XP	Echelon 1
All in the Family IV	Win Clan Arena matches (30)	1000 XP	Echelon 1
All in the Family V	Win Clan Arena matches (40)	1000 XP	Echelon 1
All in the Family VI	Win Clan Arena matches (50)	1000 XP	Echelon 1
All in the Family VII	Win Clan Arena matches (60)	1000 XP	Echelon 1
All in the Family VIII	Win Clan Arena matches (70)	1000 XP	Echelon 1
All in the Family IX	Win Clan Arena matches (85)	1500 XP	Echelon 1
All in the Family X	Win Clan Arena matches (100)	1500 XP	Echelon 1
Clan Assassin I	Critical Kill medals in Clan Arena (10)	250 XP	Echelon 3
Clan Assassin II	Critical Kill medals in Clan Arena (25)	375 XP	Echelon 3
Clan Assassin III	Critical Kill medals in Clan Arena (50)	625 XP	Echelon 3
Clan Assassin IV	Critical Kill medals in Clan Arena (75)	625 XP	Echelon 3
Clan Assassin V	Critical Kill medals in Clan Arena (100)	625 XP	Echelon 3
Clan Guard I	Protection medals in Clan Arena (3)	300 XP	Echelon 5
Clan Guard II	Protection medals in Clan Arena (6)	300 XP	Echelon 5
Clan Guard III	Protection medals in Clan Arena (10)	400 XP	Echelon 5
Clan Guard IV	Protection medals in Clan Arena (15)	500 XP	Echelon 5
Clan Guard V	Protection medals in Clan Arena (20)	500 XP	Echelon 5
Not a Scratch I	Win Clan Arena rounds without taking any damage (3)	600 XP	Echelon 7
Not a Scratch II	Win Clan Arena rounds without taking any damage (6)	600 XP	Echelon 7
Not a Scratch III	Win Clan Arena rounds without taking any damage (10)	800 XP	Echelon 7
Not a Scratch IV	Win Clan Arena rounds without taking any damage (15)	1000 XP	Echelon 7
Not a Scratch V	Win Clan Arena rounds without taking any damage (20)	1000 XP	Echelon 7
Underdog I	Win Clan Arena rounds as the last remaining team member (3)	1500 XP	Echelon 9
Underdog II	Win Clan Arena rounds as the last remaining team member (6)	1500 XP	Echelon 9
Underdog III	Win Clan Arena rounds as the last remaining team member (10)	2000 XP	Echelon 9
Underdog IV	Win Clan Arena rounds as the last remaining team member (15)	2500 XP	Echelon 9
Underdog V	Win Clan Arena rounds as the last remaining team member (20)	2500 XP	Echelon 9

WARPATH CHALLENGES

TITLE	DESCRIPTION	REWARD	UNLOCKED
Ride the Line I	Warpath score (5000)	150 XP	-
Ride the Line II	Warpath score (15000)	300 XP	-
Ride the Line III	Warpath score (30000)	450 XP	-
Ride the Line IV	Warpath score (50000)	600 XP	-
Ride the Line V	Warpath score (75000)	750 XP	-
Ride the Line VI	Warpath score (10000)	750 XP	-
Ride the Line VII	Warpath score (125000)	750 XP	-
Ride the Line VIII	Warpath score (150000)	750 XP	-
Ride the Line IX	Warpath score (175000)	750 XP	-
Ride the Line X	Warpath score (200000)	750 XP	-
Conveyed I	Win Warpath matches (5)	500 XP	Echelon 1
Conveyed II	Win Warpath matches (10)	500 XP	Echelon 1
Conveyed III	Win Warpath matches (20)	1000 XP	Echelon 1
Conveyed IV	Win Warpath matches (30)	1000 XP	Echelon 1
Conveyed V	Win Warpath matches (40)	1000 XP	Echelon 1
Conveyed VI	Win Warpath matches (50)	1000 XP	Echelon 1
Conveyed VII	Win Warpath matches (60)	1000 XP	Echelon 1
Conveyed VIII	Win Warpath matches (70)	1000 XP	Echelon 1
Conveyed IX	Win Warpath matches (85)	1500 XP	Echelon 1
Conveyed X	Win Warpath matches (100)	1500 XP	Echelon 1
Convoy Collector I	Captures in Warpath (5)	125 XP	Echelon 3
Convoy Collector II	Captures in Warpath (15)	250 XP	Echelon 3
Convoy Collector III	Captures in Warpath (30)	375 XP	Echelon 3
Convoy Collector IV	Captures in Warpath (50)	500 XP	Echelon 3
Convoy Collector V	Captures in Warpath (75)	625 XP	Echelon 3
Bandit I	Offense kills in Warpath (25)	175 XP	Echelon 5
Bandit II	Offense kills in Warpath (50)	175 XP	Echelon 5
Bandit III	Offense kills in Warpath (100)	350 XP	Echelon 5
Bandit IV	Offense kills in Warpath (175)	525 XP	Echelon 5
Bandit V	Offense kills in Warpath (275)	700 XP	Echelon 5
Get Off My Train I	Defender medals in Warpath (25)	500 XP	Echelon 7
Get Off My Train I	Defender medals in Warpath (50)	500 XP	Echelon 7
Get Off My Train I	Defender medals in Warpath (100)	1000 XP	Echelon 7
Get Off My Train I	Defender medals in Warpath (150)	1000 XP	Echelon 7
Get Off My Train I	Defender medals in Warpath (200)	1000 XP	Echelon 7
Survived the Raid I	Survivor medals while inside a Warpath control point (5)	1250 XP	Echelon 9
Survived the Raid II	Survivor medals while inside a Warpath control point (10)	1250 XP	Echelon 9
Survived the Raid III	Survivor medals while inside a Warpath control point (20)	2500 XP	Echelon 9
Survived the Raid IV	Survivor medals while inside a Warpath control point (30)	2500 XP	Echelon 9
Survived the Raid V	Survivor medals while inside a Warpath control point (40)	2500 XP	Echelon 9

FREEZE TAG CHALLENGES

TITLE	DESCRIPTION	REWARD	UNLOCKED
Blizzard I	Freeze Tag score (5000)	150 XP	-
Blizzard II	Freeze Tag score (15000)	300 XP	-
Blizzard III	Freeze Tag score (30000)	450 XP	-
Blizzard IV	Freeze Tag score (50000)	600 XP	-
Blizzard V	Freeze Tag score (75000)	750 XP	-
Blizzard VI	Freeze Tag score (10000)	750 XP	-
Blizzard VII	Freeze Tag score (125000)	750 XP	-
Blizzard VIII	Freeze Tag score (150000)	750 XP	-
Blizzard IX	Freeze Tag score (175000)	750 XP	-
Blizzard X	Freeze Tag score (200000)	750 XP	-
Ice King I	Win Freeze Tag matches (5)	500 XP	Echelon 1
Ice King II	Win Freeze Tag matches (10)	500 XP	Echelon 1
Ice King III	Win Freeze Tag matches (20)	1000 XP	Echelon 1
Ice King IV	Win Freeze Tag matches (30)	1000 XP	Echelon 1
Ice King V	Win Freeze Tag matches (40)	1000 XP	Echelon 1
Ice King VI	Win Freeze Tag matches (50)	1000 XP	Echelon 1
Ice King VII	Win Freeze Tag matches (60)	1000 XP	Echelon 1
Ice King VIII	Win Freeze Tag matches (70)	1000 XP	Echelon 1
Ice King IX	Win Freeze Tag matches (85)	1500 XP	Echelon 1
Ice King X	Win Freeze Tag matches (100)	1500 XP	Echelon 1
Global Warming I	Thaw medals in Freeze Tag (10)	200 XP	Echelon 3
Global Warming II	Thaw medals in Freeze Tag (30)	400 XP	Echelon 3
Global Warming III	Thaw medals in Freeze Tag (60)	600 XP	Echelon 3
Global Warming IV	Thaw medals in Freeze Tag (100)	800 XP	Echelon 3
Global Warming V	Thaw medals in Freeze Tag (150)	1000 XP	Echelon 3
Stay Frosty I	Kill enemies that are thawing their teammates in Freeze Tag (5)	250 XP	Echelon 5
Stay Frosty II	Kill enemies that are thawing their teammates in Freeze Tag (10)	250 XP	Echelon 5
Stay Frosty III	Kill enemies that are thawing their teammates in Freeze Tag (20)	500 XP	Echelon 5
Stay Frosty IV	Kill enemies that are thawing their teammates in Freeze Tag (30)	500 XP	Echelon 5
Stay Frosty V	Kill enemies that are thawing their teammates in Freeze Tag (40)	500 XP	Echelon 5
Central Heating I	Multi-Thaw medals (5)	500 XP	Echelon 7
Central Heating II	Multi-Thaw medals (10)	500 XP	Echelon 7
Central Heating III	Multi-Thaw medals (20)	1000 XP	Echelon 7
Central Heating IV	Multi-Thaw medals (30)	1000 XP	Echelon 7
Central Heating V	Multi-Thaw medals (40)	1000 XP	Echelon 7
Cold Determination I	Survivor medals while thawing teammates in Freeze Tag (3)	1500 XP	Echelon 9
Cold Determination II	Survivor medals while thawing teammates in Freeze Tag (6)	1500 XP	Echelon 9
Cold Determination III	Survivor medals while thawing teammates in Freeze Tag (10)	2000 XP	Echelon 9
Cold Determination IV	Survivor medals while thawing teammates in Freeze Tag (15)	2500 XP	Echelon 9
Cold Determination V	Survivor medals while thawing teammates in Freeze Tag (20)	2500 XP	Echelon 9

SOUL HARVEST CHALLENGES

TITLE	DESCRIPTION	REWARD	UNLOCKED
Bloodthirsty I	Soul Harvest score (5000)	150 XP	-
Bloodthirsty II	Soul Harvest score (15000)	300 XP	-
Bloodthirsty III	Soul Harvest score (30000)	450 XP	-
Bloodthirsty IV	Soul Harvest score (50000)	600 XP	-
Bloodthirsty V	Soul Harvest score (75000)	750 XP	-
Bloodthirsty VI	Soul Harvest score (10000)	750 XP	-
Bloodthirsty VII	Soul Harvest score (125000)	750 XP	-
Bloodthirsty VIII	Soul Harvest score (150000)	750 XP	-
Bloodthirsty IX	Soul Harvest score (175000)	750 XP	-
Bloodthirsty X	Soul Harvest score (200000)	750 XP	-
Unquenchable Thirst I	Win Soul Harvest matches (5)	500 XP	Echelon 1
Unquenchable Thirst II	Win Soul Harvest matches (10)	500 XP	Echelon 1
Unquenchable Thirst III	Win Soul Harvest matches (20)	1000 XP	Echelon 1
Unquenchable Thirst IV	Win Soul Harvest matches (35)	1500 XP	Echelon 1
Unquenchable Thirst V	Win Soul Harvest matches (50)	1500 XP	Echelon 1
Unquenchable Thirst VI	Win Soul Harvest matches (65)	1500 XP	Echelon 1
Unquenchable Thirst VII	Win Soul Harvest matches (80)	1500 XP	Echelon 1
Unquenchable Thirst VIII	Win Soul Harvest matches (95)	1500 XP	Echelon 1
Unquenchable Thirst IX	Win Soul Harvest matches (120)	2500 XP	Echelon 1
Unquenchable Thirst X	Win Soul Harvest matches (150)	3000 XP	Echelon 1
Soul Reaper I	Capture souls in Soul Harvest (50)	500 XP	Echelon 3
Soul Reaper II	Capture souls in Soul Harvest (125)	750 XP	Echelon 3
Soul Reaper III	Capture souls in Soul Harvest (200)	750 XP	Echelon 3
Soul Reaper IV	Capture souls in Soul Harvest (275)	750 XP	Echelon 3
Soul Reaper V	Capture souls in Soul Harvest (350)	750 XP	Echelon 3
Bloodletter I	Critical Kill medals in Soul Harvest (10)	150 XP	Echelon 5
Bloodletter II	Critical Kill medals in Soul Harvest (25)	225 XP	Echelon 5
Bloodletter III	Critical Kill medals in Soul Harvest (50)	375 XP	Echelon 5
Bloodletter IV	Critical Kill medals in Soul Harvest (85)	525 XP	Echelon 5
Bloodletter V	Critical Kill medals in Soul Harvest (130)	675 XP	Echelon 5
Plausible Deniability I	Souls denied in Soul Harvest (10)	400 XP	Echelon 7
Plausible Deniability II	Souls denied in Soul Harvest (25)	600 XP	Echelon 7
Plausible Deniability III	Souls denied in Soul Harvest (50)	1000 XP	Echelon 7
Plausible Deniability IV	Souls denied in Soul Harvest (75)	1000 XP	Echelon 7
Plausible Deniability V	Souls denied in Soul Harvest (100)	1000 XP	Echelon 7
Cursed Blood I	First Blood medals in Soul Harvest (3)	1500 XP	Echelon 9
Cursed Blood II	First Blood medals in Soul Harvest (6)	1500 XP	Echelon 9
Cursed Blood III	First Blood medals in Soul Harvest (10)	2000 XP	Echelon 9
Cursed Blood IV	First Blood medals in Soul Harvest (15)	2500 XP	Echelon 9
Cursed Blood V	First Blood medals in Soul Harvest (20)	2500 XP	Echelon 9

DOMINATION CHALLENGES

TITLE	DESCRIPTION	REWARD	UNLOCKED
Dominator I	Domination score (5000)	150 XP	-
Dominator II	Domination score (15000)	300 XP	-
Dominator III	Domination score (30000)	450 XP	-
Dominator IV	Domination score (50000)	600 XP	-
Dominator V	Domination score (75000)	750 XP	-
Dominator VI	Domination score (10000)	750 XP	-
Dominator VII	Domination score (125000)	750 XP	-
Dominator VIII	Domination score (150000)	750 XP	-
Dominator IX	Domination score (175000)	750 XP	-
Dominator X	Domination score (200000)	750 XP	-
Total Domination I	Win Domination matches (5)	500 XP	Echelon 1
Total Domination II	Win Domination matches (10)	500 XP	Echelon 1
Total Domination III	Win Domination matches (20)	1000 XP	Echelon 1
Total Domination IV	Win Domination matches (35)	1500 XP	Echelon 1
Total Domination V	Win Domination matches (50)	1500 XP	Echelon 1
Total Domination VI	Win Domination matches (65)	1500 XP	Echelon 1
Total Domination VII	Win Domination matches (80)	1500 XP	Echelon 1
Total Domination VIII	Win Domination matches (95)	1500 XP	Echelon 1
Total Domination IX	Win Domination matches (120)	2500 XP	Echelon 1
Total Domination X	Win Domination matches (150)	3000 XP	Echelon 1
Imperialism I	Captures in Domination (10)	250 XP	Echelon 3
Imperialism II	Captures in Domination (30)	500 XP	Echelon 3
Imperialism III	Captures in Domination (60)	750 XP	Echelon 3
Imperialism IV	Captures in Domination (100)	1000 XP	Echelon 3
Imperialism V	Captures in Domination (150)	1250 XP	Echelon 3
Your Home is My Castle I	Offense kills in Domination (10)	150 XP	Echelon 5
Your Home is My Castle II	Offense kills in Domination (30)	300 XP	Echelon 5
Your Home is My Castle III	Offense kills in Domination (60)	450 XP	Echelon 5
Your Home is My Castle IV	Offense kills in Domination (100)	600 XP	Echelon 5
Your Home is My Castle V	Offense kills in Domination (150)	750 XP	Echelon 5
Castle Doctrine I	Defender medals in Domination (25)	500 XP	Echelon 7
Castle Doctrine II	Defender medals in Domination (50)	500 XP	Echelon 7
Castle Doctrine III	Defender medals in Domination (100)	1000 XP	Echelon 7
Castle Doctrine IV	Defender medals in Domination (150)	1000 XP	Echelon 7
Castle Doctrine V	Defender medals in Domination (200)	1000 XP	Echelon 7
Remember the Alamo I	Survivor medals while inside a Domination control point (3)	1500 XP	Echelon 9
Remember the Alamo II	Survivor medals while inside a Domination control point (6)	1500 XP	Echelon 9
Remember the Alamo III	Survivor medals while inside a Domination control point (10)	2000 XP	Echelon 9
Remember the Alamo IV	Survivor medals while inside a Domination control point (15)	2500 XP	Echelon 9
Remember the Alamo V	Survivor medals while inside a Domination control point (20)	2500 XP	Echelon 9

POWER-ITEM

BFG CHALLENGES

TITLE	DESCRIPTION	REWARD	UNLOCKED
Infernal Injuries I	BFG kills (10)	600 XP	Echelon 4
Infernal Injuries II	BFG kills (25)	900 XP	Echelon 4
Infernal Injuries III	BFG kills (50)	1500 XP	Echelon 4
Infernal Injuries IV	BFG kills (75)	1500 XP	Echelon 4
Infernal Injuries V	BFG kills (100)	1500 XP	Echelon 4
Green Fire Bomb I	Multi-kills with the BFG (5)	500 XP	Echelon 8
Green Fire Bomb II	Multi-kills with the BFG (15)	1000 XP	Echelon 8
Green Fire Bomb III	Multi-kills with the BFG (30)	1500 XP	Echelon 8
Green Fire Bomb IV	Multi-kills with the BFG (50)	2000 XP	Echelon 8
Green Fire Bomb V	Multi-kills with the BFG (75)	2500 XP	Echelon 8

CHAINSAW CHALLENGES

TITLE	DESCRIPTION	REWARD	UNLOCKED
Timber! I	Chainsaw kills (10)	600 XP	Echelon 4
Timber! II	Chainsaw kills (25)	900 XP	Echelon 4
Timber! III	Chainsaw kills (50)	1500 XP	Echelon 4
Timber! IV	Chainsaw kills (75)	1500 XP	Echelon 4
Timber! V	Chainsaw kills (100)	1500 XP	Echelon 4
Industrial Logging I	Double Kill medals with the Chainsaw (2)	600 XP	Echelon 6
Industrial Logging II	Double Kill medals with the Chainsaw (4)	600 XP	Echelon 6
Industrial Logging III	Double Kill medals with the Chainsaw (7)	900 XP	Echelon 6
Industrial Logging IV	Double Kill medals with the Chainsaw (11)	1200 XP	Echelon 6
Industrial Logging V	Double Kill medals with the Chainsaw (16)	1500 XP	Echelon 6
Chain the Chainsaw I	Three Chainsaw kills in a match (5)	500 XP	Echelon 8
Chain the Chainsaw II	Three Chainsaw kills in a match (10)	500 XP	Echelon 8
Chain the Chainsaw III	Three Chainsaw kills in a match (20)	1000 XP	Echelon 8
Chain the Chainsaw IV	Three Chainsaw kills in a match (30)	1000 XP	Echelon 8
Chain the Chainsaw V	Three Chainsaw kills in a match (40)	1000 XP	Echelon 8

GAUSS CANNON CHALLENGES

TITLE	DESCRIPTION	REWARD	UNLOCKED
Nice Shot, Kid I	Gauss Cannon kills (10)	600 XP	Echelon 4
Nice Shot, Kid II	Gauss Cannon kills (25)	900 XP	Echelon 4
Nice Shot, Kid III	Gauss Cannon kills (50)	1500 XP	Echelon 4
Nice Shot, Kid IV	Gauss Cannon kills (75)	1500 XP	Echelon 4
Nice Shot, Kid V	Gauss Cannon kills (100)	1500 XP	Echelon 4
Gauss the Distance I	Longshot medals with the Gauss Rifle (5)	1000 XP	Echelon 8
Gauss the Distance II	Longshot medals with the Gauss Rifle (10)	1000 XP	Echelon 8
Gauss the Distance III	Longshot medals with the Gauss Rifle (20)	2000 XP	Echelon 8
Gauss the Distance IV	Longshot medals with the Gauss Rifle (30)	2000 XP	Echelon 8
Gauss the Distance V	Longshot medals with the Gauss Rifle (40)	2000 XP	Echelon 8

:X MEDALS

Medals are awarded at the end of a match to any player who performs a specific action, as required by the Medal. It's not only possible for multiple players to earn the same Medal, but you may even earn multiple copies of the same Medal in a single match! For example, every time you Glory Kill an enemy, you receive a Glorious medal. Each of these counts toward progress on the "For the Glory" Challenge. You will likely earn hundreds of the same Medal over the course of your time with DOOM.

TITLE	DESCRIPTION	ICON
Glorious	Glory kill an enemy.	
Savior	Kill an enemy mid-glory-kill.	
Double Kill	Kill 2 enemies within a short span.	
Triple Kill	Kill 3 enemies within a short span.	
Quad Kill	Kill 4 enemies within a short span.	
Mega Kill	Kill 5 enemies within a short span.	
Insanity	Kill 6 enemies within a short span.	
Blood Bath	5 kills in a single life.	
Carnage	10 kills in a single life.	
Massacre	15 kills in a single life.	
Extermination	20 kills in a single life.	
Annihilation	30 kills in a single life.	
Genocide	Kill every enemy team member in a single life.	

TITLE	DESCRIPTION	ICON
Upshot	Kill an airborne enemy.	
Redemption	Kill from beyond the grave.	
Revenge Kill	Kill the enemy who last killed you.	
Avenger	Avenge the death of a teammate.	
Protection	Kill an enemy attacking your teammates.	
Grenade Kill	Frag Grenade kill.	
Comeback	Record a kill following three deaths in a row.	
Show Stopper	End an enemy's killstreak.	
Untouchable	Kill three enemies without taking any damage.	
Longshot	Long-range kill.	
Silencer	Kill an enemy who is taunting.	
Survivor	Barely survive a firefight.	
Assisted Suicide	Knock an enemy into a hazard.	

TITLE	DESCRIPTION	ICON
Power Kill	Powerup kill.	
Power Down	Kill an enemy who has a powerup.	
Humiliation	Celebrate a kill by taunting.	
Shutdown	Kill an enemy who has a power down.	
Excessive	Power weapon kill.	
Rune Denied	Kill an enemy about to collect a demon rune.	
Quick Draw	Kill an enemy with both your weapons.	
Supremacy	Capture three control points in a single life.	
Critical Chain	Follow up a critical kill with another critical kill.	
First Blood	First kill of the match.	
Critical Kill	Kill an enemy with a critical hit.	
Assist	Help a teammate kill an enemy.	
Telefrag	Telefrag an enemy.	
Drained	Siphon Grenade kill.	
High Voltage	Tesla Rocket Kill.	
Distraction	Kill an enemy while your Hologram is active.	
Marked	Use the Threat Sensor to hunt down an enemy.	
Off the Wall	Kill an enemy while your Shield Wall is active.	
Demon Slayer	Kill a demon.	
Defender	Defend a control point.	

TITLE	DESCRIPTION	ICON
Offense Kill	Assault a control point.	
Denied	Kill an enemy about to collect a soul.	
Thawed Teammate	Thaw a frozen teammate.	
Multi-Thaw	Thaw two frozen teammates within a short span.	
Permafrost	Freeze three enemies as the only survivor on your team (Freeze Tag).	
Clan Survivor	Kill three enemies as the only survivor on your team (Clan Arena)	
Capture	Capture a control point.	
Bounty I	Earn Bounty I bonus.	
Bounty II	Earn Bounty II bonus.	
Bounty III	Earn Bounty III bonus.	
Wingman I	Earn Wingman I bonus.	
Wingman II	Earn Wingman II bonus.	
Wingman III	Earn Wingman III bonus.	
Manhunt I	Earn Manhunt I bonus.	
Manhunt II	Earn Manhunt II bonus.	
Manhunt III	Earn Manhunt III bonus.	
Osmosis I	Earn Osmosis I bonus.	
Osmosis II	Earn Osmosis II bonus.	
Osmosis III	Earn Osmosis III bonus.	

:X COMMENDATIONS

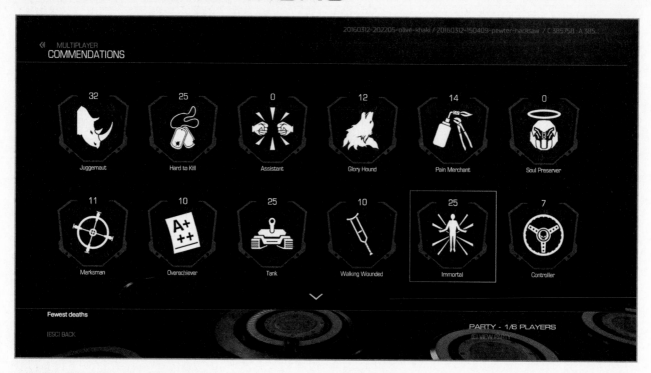

« MULTIPLAYER
COMMENDATIONS

20160312-202205-olive-khaki / 20160312-150409-pewter-hacksaw / C 385758 A 385...

32	25	0	12	14	0
Juggernaut	Hard to Kill	Assistant	Glory Hound	Pain Merchant	Soul Preserver
11	10	25	10	25	7
Marksman	Overachiever	Tank	Walking Wounded	Immortal	Controller

Fewest deaths

[ESC] BACK

PARTY - 1/6 PLAYERS
[E] VIEW PARTY

Commendations are a lot like Medals, but only one is awarded per match. Commendations are given to the player who performed a specific action the best out of everyone in the match. For example, the Controller Commendation is awarded to the player who captured the most control points in a Domination match. While all players who capture a control point earn the "Capture" Medal, only the person with the most captures earns the "Controller" Commendation.

TITLE	DESCRIPTION	ICON
Juggernaut	Longest kill streak.	
Hard to Kill	Best kill/death ratio.	
Assistant	Most assists.	
Glory Hound	Highest number of Glory Kills.	
Pain Merchant	Most critical damage.	
Soul Preserver	Surrendered the fewest souls.	
Marksman	Highest accuracy.	
Overachiever	Most damage on your team.	
Tank	Collected the most armor.	
Walking Wounded	Collected the most health.	
Immortal	Fewest deaths.	
Controller	Captured the most points.	
Defroster	Most thaws.	
Marathon Runner	Longest distance traveled.	
Bad Karma	Died the most while taunting.	
Hater	Killed the most taunting enemies.	
Demonation	Most kills as a demon.	

TITLE	DESCRIPTION	ICON
Explosive Expert	Most splash damage.	
Elite Escort	Most time spent in the Warpath Zone.	
Bunny Hopper	Most jumps.	
MVP	All around top performance.	
Clan Leader	Most kills and no deaths.	
Engineer	Most uses of equipment.	
Gadgeteer	Most equipment kills.	
Master Demon Slayer	Most damage dealt to demons.	
Power Killer	Most kills with powerups.	
Bullet Dodger	Longest single lifetime.	
Invader	Highest offensive score.	
Defensive	Highest defensive score.	
Overpowered	Most time using powerups.	
Master Thief	Scavenged the most powerups.	
Hellspawn	Most time spent as a demon.	
Soul Hoarder	Most souls collected.	
Final Blood	Had the final kill.	

Want to make your own version of DOOM? In SnapMap editor, you can! Set yourself up to face hordes of enemies with a few friends, or add some secrets into a multiplayer map, then invite your pals and obliterate them with all the hidden weapons.

With so many available options, the possibilities are endless. Be sure to check out the Featured Maps from the SnapMap community for some good fun.

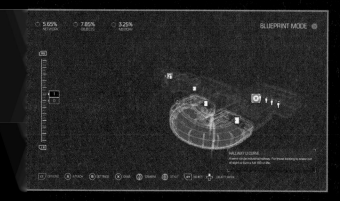

BASICS

After selecting SnapMap from the Main Menu, you'll be greeted by a screen that will allow you to sample maps from the SnapMap community or create your own SnapMaps.

SNAP ACADEMY

Snap Academy will instruct you on everything that you need to know to create great maps for the community. The lessons start out fairly simple, teaching you how to place objects and link up rooms. Later lessons will have you editing longer logic chains and help establish your knowledge of the SnapMap features.

BLUEPRINT MODE

While in Blueprint Mode, you will have access to a staggering amount of room options, allowing you to create a unique experience no matter which game mode you choose.

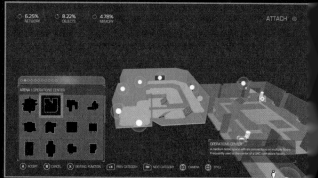

You can use smaller rooms to hide secrets, ammo caches, and even hordes of enemies. Bigger rooms like the Arenas are great for boss fights or a mid-point in multiplayer matches.

To change the appearance of a room, head into Object Mode, then look at a blank spot in the room and press Y/Triangle. You can then adjust the amount of clutter and even add post-processing filters like night vision, or fill the room with smoke.

OBJECT MODE

When you create a SnapMap, you'll likely spend most of your time in Object Mode. Enter Object Mode by pressing D-PAD

UP. Once in Object Mode, you can move freely through the rendered map that you placed in Blueprint Mode.

To place items or level cues, press A/X to open the Object menu. Once you have the menu open, use LB/L1 or RB/R1, and use the Left Stick to switch between the different object choices.

Once you have highlighted an object, press A/X to select the object. Then, press A/X again to place the object. When you are finished placing objects of that type, press B/O to exit the Object menu.

USING LOGIC

Logic chains are used to control how each object interacts with the player, AI, and other objects in the room. For example, a logic

chain hooked up to an explosive barrel and a panel could be set to explode the barrel when the panel is activated.

To set up a logic chain, press A/X on the highlighted object while in Object Mode. After you've selected your first object, a circle will pop up on the screen, showing all available options for that object. Use the Left Stick to highlight the interaction that you would like, then press A/X to select the action.

Move the camera to the next object, dragging the logic chain along with you, and then press A/X. Select the interaction for the second object in the wheel using the same method as the first.

Logic chains can be extended infinitely and through walls. Multiple logic chains can be attached to a single object, allowing you to perform multiple actions from a single action when playing the SnapMap.

FINE-TUNING

All objects and modules have certain properties that you can change. These properties vary depending on the type of object. For example, a demon can have its health and damage boosted to give you a "super version" of that demon. Highlight an object and press Y/Triangle to view or edit its properties.

When customizing an object that you'd like to use more than once in a level, consider duplicating it instead of adjusting each object as you place it. To duplicate an object, hold LT/L2 and press A/X while you have the object that you would like to duplicate highlighted.

TESTING YOUR SNAPMAP

Press Menu/Options, and a small dialog box will pop up. This box allows you to publish your SnapMap for community play, save your SnapMap for more editing later, and exit the editor. Most importantly, though, it allows you to play through your map before you edit it.

Playing through your map is a great way to test out all of the logic chains and other features that you have set up before you publish it for everyone to play.

To quickly revert any changes that you made, hold LT/L2. Then, use D-Pad Left to undo changes and D-Pad Right to redo anything that you've undone. This method makes testing small things in your map a breeze, allowing you to quickly switch between two options.

Select Customize Character to modify your character for SnapMap matches. You can customize your character, weapons, and taunts.

SNAPMAP PUZZLES

SnapMap-exclusive challenges are listed on the SnapMap player profile and earn SnapPoints, which you can use to purchase customized items.

PUZZLE NAME	DESCRIPTION	SNAPPOINTS EARNED
Butcher	Perform 5 Glory Kills on any demon	50
Butcher	Perform 10 Glory Kills on any demon	150
Butcher	Perform 15 Glory Kills on any demon	250
Exterminator	Perform 5 Glory Kills on other players	50
Exterminator	Perform 10 Glory Kills on other players	150
Exterminator	Perform 15 Glory Kills on other players	250
Baron Assassin	Glory Kill 5 Barons of Hell	50
Baron Assassin	Glory Kill 10 Barons of Hell	150
Baron Assassin	Glory Kill 15 Barons of Hell	250
Baron Hunter	Kill 5 Barons of Hell	50
Baron Hunter	Kill 10 Barons of Hell	150
Baron Hunter	Kill 15 Barons of Hell	250
Be the Demon	Transform into a demon 5 times	50
Be the Demon	Transform into a demon 10 times	150
Be the Demon	Transform into a demon 15 times	250
Cacodemon Assassin	Glory Kill 5 Cacodemons	50
Cacodemon Assassin	Glory Kill 10 Cacodemons	150
Cacodemon Assassin	Glory Kill 15 Cacodemons	250
Cacodemon Hunter	Kill 5 Cacodemons	50
Cacodemon Hunter	Kill 10 Cacodemons	150
Cacodemon Hunter	Kill 15 Cacodemons	250
Snap Rivals	Play 5 Competitive SnapMaps	50
Snap Rivals	Play 10 Competitive SnapMaps	150
Snap Rivals	Play 15 Competitive SnapMaps	250
Snap Ops	Play 5 Co-operative SnapMaps	50
Snap Ops	Play 10 Co-operative SnapMaps	150
Snap Ops	Play 15 Co-operative SnapMaps	250
Snap the Demon	Play 5 Demon Player SnapMaps	50
Snap the Demon	Play 10 Demon Player SnapMaps	150
Snap the Demon	Play 15 Demon Player SnapMaps	250
Snap Match	Play 5 Deathmatch SnapMaps	50
Snap Match	Play 10 Deathmatch SnapMaps	150
Snap Match	Play 15 Deathmatch SnapMaps	250
Oh Snap!	Play 5 SnapMaps	50
Oh Snap!	Play 10 SnapMaps	150
Oh Snap!	Play 15 SnapMaps	250
Medalist	Finish 5 SnapMaps under par time	50
Medalist	Finish 10 SnapMaps under par time	150
Medalist	Finish 15 SnapMaps under par time	250
Snap Missions	Play 5 Single Player SnapMaps	50
Snap Missions	Play 10 Single Player SnapMaps	150
Snap Missions	Play 15 Single Player SnapMaps	250
Cyber-Mancubus Hunter	Kill 5 Cyber-Mancubi	50
Cyber-Mancubus Hunter	Kill 10 Cyber-Mancubi	150
Cyber-Mancubus Hunter	Kill 15 Cyber-Mancubi	250
7355608	Destroy 5 C4	50

PUZZLE NAME	DESCRIPTION	SNAPPOINTS EARNED
7355608	Destroy 10 C4	150
7355608	Destroy 15 C4	250
Chain Reaction	Destroy 5 Classic Barrels	50
Chain Reaction	Destroy 10 Classic Barrels	150
Chain Reaction	Destroy 15 Classic Barrels	250
Blue Fire	Destroy 5 Plasma Barrels	50
Blue Fire	Destroy 10 Plasma Barrels	150
Blue Fire	Destroy 15 Plasma Barrels	250
Toxic Spill	Destroy 5 Radiation Barrels	50
Toxic Spill	Destroy 10 Radiation Barrels	150
Toxic Spill	Destroy 15 Radiation Barrels	250
Hell Razer Assassin	Glory Kill 5 Hell Razers	50
Hell Razer Assassin	Glory Kill 10 Hell Razers	150
Hell Razer Assassin	Glory Kill 15 Hell Razers	250
Hell Razer Hunter	Kill 5 Hell Razers	50
Hell Razer Hunter	Kill 10 Hell Razers	150
Hell Razer Hunter	Kill 15 Hell Razers	250
Soldier Assassin	Glory Kill 5 Possessed Soldiers	50
Soldier Assassin	Glory Kill 10 Possessed Soldiers	150
Soldier Assassin	Glory Kill 15 Possessed Soldiers	250
Soldier Hunter	Kill 5 Possessed Soldiers	50
Soldier Hunter	Kill 10 Possessed Soldiers	150
Soldier Hunter	Kill 15 Possessed Soldiers	250
Security Hunter	Kill 5 Possessed Security	50
Security Hunter	Kill 10 Possessed Security	150
Security Hunter	Kill 15 Possessed Security	250
Hell Knight Assassin	Glory Kill 5 Hell Knights	50
Hell Knight Assassin	Glory Kill 10 Hell Knights	150
Hell Knight Assassin	Glory Kill 15 Hell Knights	250
Hell Knight Hunter	Kill 5 Hell Knights	50
Hell Knight Hunter	Kill 10 Hell Knights	150
Hell Knight Hunter	Kill 15 Hell Knights	250
Imp Assassin	Glory Kill 5 Imps	50
Imp Assassin	Glory Kill 10 Imps	150
Imp Assassin	Glory Kill 15 Imps	250
Imp Hunter	Kill 5 Imps	50
Imp Hunter	Kill 10 Imps	150
Imp Hunter	Kill 15 Imps	250
Demon Rampage	Kill 5 enemies as a demon	50
Demon Rampage	Kill 10 enemies as a demon	150
Demon Rampage	Kill 15 enemies as a demon	250
BFG Generalist	Kill 5 demons or players with the BFG	50
BFG Generalist	Kill 10 demons or players with the BFG	150
BFG Generalist	Kill 15 demons or players with the BFG	250
Chaingun Generalist	Kill 5 demons or players with the Chaingun	50
Chaingun Generalist	Kill 10 demons or players with the Chaingun	150
Chaingun Generalist	Kill 15 demons or players with the Chaingun	250
Shotgun Generalist	Kill 5 demons or players with the Combat Shotgun	50
Shotgun Generalist	Kill 10 demons or players with the Combat Shotgun	150
Shotgun Generalist	Kill 15 demons or players with the Combat Shotgun	250
Gauss Generalist	Kill 5 demons or players with the Gauss Cannon	50
Gauss Generalist	Kill 10 demons or players with the Gauss Cannon	150
Gauss Generalist	Kill 15 demons or players with the Gauss Cannon	250
HAR Generalist	Kill 5 demons or players with the Heavy Assault Rifle	50

PUZZLE NAME	DESCRIPTION	SNAPPOINTS EARNED
HAR Generalist	Kill 10 demons or players with the Heavy Assault Rifle	150
HAR Generalist	Kill 15 demons or players with the Heavy Assault Rifle	250
Hellshot Generalist	Kill 5 demons or players with the Hellshot	50
Hellshot Generalist	Kill 10 demons or players with the Hellshot	150
Hellshot Generalist	Kill 15 demons or players with the Hellshot	250
Lightning Generalist	Kill 5 demons or players with the Lightning Gun	50
Lightning Generalist	Kill 10 demons or players with the Lightning Gun	150
Lightning Generalist	Kill 15 demons or players with the Lightning Gun	250
Plasma Generalist	Kill 5 demons or players with the Plasma Rifle	50
Plasma Generalist	Kill 10 demons or players with the Plasma Rifle	150
Plasma Generalist	Kill 15 demons or players with the Plasma Rifle	250
Godlike	Kill 5 demons or players while using any powerup	50
Godlike	Kill 10 demons or players while using any powerup	150
Godlike	Kill 15 demons or players while using any powerup	250
Burst Generalist	Kill 5 demons or players with the Burst Rifle	50
Burst Generalist	Kill 10 demons or players with the Burst Rifle	150
Burst Generalist	Kill 15 demons or players with the Burst Rifle	250
Rocket Generalist	Kill 5 demons or players with the Rocket Launcher	50
Rocket Generalist	Kill 10 demons or players with the Rocket Launcher	150
Rocket Generalist	Kill 15 demons or players with the Rocket Launcher	250
Super Shotty	Kill 5 demons or players with the Super Shotgun	50
Super Shotty	Kill 10 demons or players with the Super Shotgun	150
Super Shotty	Kill 15 demons or players with the Super Shotgun	250
Vortex Generalist	Kill 5 demons or players with the Vortex Rifle	50
Vortex Generalist	Kill 10 demons or players with the Vortex Rifle	150
Vortex Generalist	Kill 15 demons or players with the Vortex Rifle	250
Lost Soul Hunter	Kill 5 Lost Souls	50
Lost Soul Hunter	Kill 10 Lost Souls	150
Lost Soul Hunter	Kill 15 Lost Souls	250
Mancubi Assassin	Glory Kill 5 Mancubi	50
Mancubi Assassin	Glory Kill 15 Mancubi	150
Mancubi Assassin	Glory Kill 15 Mancubi	250
Mancubi Hunter	Kill 5 Mancubi	50
Mancubi Hunter	Kill 10 Mancubi	150
Mancubi Hunter	Kill 15 Mancubi	250
Pinky Assassin	Glory Kill 5 Pinkies	50
Pinky Assassin	Glory Kill 10 Pinkies	150
Pinky Assassin	Glory Kill 15 Pinkies	250
Pinky Hunter	Kill 5 Pinkies	50
Pinky Hunter	Kill 10 Pinkies	150
Pinky Hunter	Kill 15 Pinkies	250
Revenant Assassin	Glory Kill 5 Revenants	50
Revenant Assassin	Glory Kill 10 Revenants	150
Revenant Assassin	Glory Kill 15 Revenants	250
Revenant Hunter	Kill 5 Revenants	50
Revenant Hunter	Kill 10 Revenants	150
Revenant Hunter	Kill 15 Revenants	250
Hero	Revive 5 friendly players	50
Hero	Revive 10 friendly players	150
Hero	Revive 15 friendly players	250
Snap Detective	Find 5 secrets in any SnapMap	50
Snap Detective	Find 10 secrets in any SnapMap	150
Snap Detective	Find 15 secrets in any SnapMap	250
Spectre Hunter	Kill 5 Spectres	50

PUZZLE NAME	DESCRIPTION	SNAPPOINTS EARNED
Spectre Hunter	Kill 10 Spectres	150
Spectre Hunter	Kill 15 Spectres	250
Possessed Assassin	Glory Kill 5 Possessed Workers or Scientists	50
Possessed Assassin	Glory Kill 10 Possessed Workers or Scientists	150
Possessed Assassin	Glory Kill 15 Possessed Workers or Scientists	250
Scientist Hunter	Kill 5 Possessed Scientists	50
Scientist Hunter	Kill 10 Possessed Scientists	150
Scientist Hunter	Kill 15 Possessed Scientists	250
Worker Hunter	Kill 5 Possessed Workers	50
Worker Hunter	Kill 10 Possessed Workers	150
Worker Hunter	Kill 15 Possessed Workers	250
Engineer Hunter	Kill 5 Possessed Engineers	50
Engineer Hunter	Kill 10 Possessed Engineers	150
Engineer Hunter	Kill 15 Possessed Engineers	250
Team Snap	Play 5 Team Play SnapMaps	50
Team Snap	Play 10 Team Play SnapMaps	150
Team Snap	Play 15 Team Play SnapMaps	250
Snap Academy Complete 01	Complete 2 Academy Maps	100
Snap Academy Complete 02	Complete 4 Academy Maps	200
Snap Academy Complete 03	Complete 8 Academy Maps	350
Snap Academy Complete 04	Complete 12 Academy Maps	450
Snap Challenge Completion 01	Complete 2 Challenge Maps	100
Snap Challenge Completion 02	Complete 5 Challenge Maps	200
Snap Challenge Completion 03	Complete 10 Challenge Maps	350
Snap Challenge Completion 04	Complete 15 Challenge Maps	450
Snap Challenge Completion 05	Complete 25 Challenge Maps	600
Snap Challenge Completion 06	Complete 50 Challenge Maps	750
Play 5 Snap Maps	Play 5 SnapMaps	100
Play 10 Snap Maps	Play 10 SnapMaps	200
Play 25 Snap Maps	Play 25 SnapMaps	350
Play 50 Snap Maps	Play 50 SnapMaps	450
Play 100 Snap Maps	Play 100 SnapMaps	600
Play 250 Snap Maps	Play 250 SnapMaps	750
Play 1000 Snap Maps	Play 1000 SnapMaps	1000
Publish 10 Snap Maps	Publish 10 SnapMaps	100
Publish 10 Snap Maps	Publish 10 SnapMaps	200
Publish 25 Snap Maps	Publish 25 SnapMaps	350
Publish 50 Snap Maps	Publish 50 SnapMaps	450
Publish 100 Snap Maps	Publish 100 SnapMaps	600
Publish 250 Snap Maps	Publish 250 SnapMaps	750
Publish 1000 Snap Maps	Publish 1000 SnapMaps	1000
Vote 5 Snap Maps	Vote 5 SnapMaps	100
Vote 10 Snap Maps	Vote 10 SnapMaps	200
Vote 25 Snap Maps	Vote 25 SnapMaps	350
Vote 50 Snap Maps	Vote 50 SnapMaps	450
Vote 100 Snap Maps	Vote 100 SnapMaps	600
Vote 250 Snap Maps	Vote 250 SnapMaps	750
Vote 1000 Snap Maps	Vote 1000 SnapMaps	1000

:X: BLUEPRINT LIST

90 BEND

LAYOUT	NAME	DESCRIPTION
	90 Bend	A standard UAC industrial corridor used in many facilities. First used in Phobos labs.
	90 Climb	A standard UAC industrial corridor intended to connect two floors. Achieved with great success.
	90 Curve	A version 2.0 UAC industrial corridor used to add organic harmony to the original 90-degree bend.
	90 Stairs	A stair corridor intended to connect two floors with human-accessible stairs. The cornerstone of every UAC off-world facility!
	90 Steam Climb	A small hallway filled with steam release valves and a steep climb-up.
	Red Light Zone	A moderately sized room filled with overlapping catwalks and a stark red glow.
	Skylight Nine	An open, multi-floor area where interesting things can happen with light.
	Hub 90	A flexible space with four doors, a set of diagonal stairs, and wide catwalks.
	Simple 90	It's small, it's simple, and it turns 90 degrees.

ARENA

LAYOUT	NAME	DESCRIPTION
	Basement Hub	An expansive space featuring broad catwalks, three stories of hallways, and a lovely pit of toxic slime.
	Operations Center	A medium-sized space with six connections on multiple floors. Frequently used at the center of a UAC operations facility.
	Entrance	A broad loading area downstairs surrounded by a handful of entrances and exits.
	Firing Chamber	A combination space used for both the storage and testing of high-tech experimental weaponry.
	Toxic Flow Room	A medium-sized space intended to allow moisture release from toxic slime throughout the facility. Also contains a cool secret area!
	Machine Room	Filled with complex equipment likely understood by only a small number of people.
	Bunker	Squarish and short, this room offers good cover for interesting combat.
	Hallway H Stairs	A set of halls with mirrored exits. UAC would like to take this opportunity to remind everyone that Disodium-37 is almost definitely not lethally toxic.

ARENA CONT.

LAYOUT	NAME	DESCRIPTION
	Sorting Area	A shipping and storing crossover space featuring high windows and elevated work areas.
	Refining Chamber	A surprisingly hazardous space built to churn molten metals into a hellish steel toffee. No hand railings, so watch your step!
	Small Maintenance Room	A simple space with a 90-degree bend and a small blue nook.
	Repair Bay Overlook	The moderate size and narrow access of this repair bay limits its use to handheld and plasma-powered tools.
	Tall Recharge Room	The recharge room features higher ceilings than most UAC repair bays, allowing for larger tools and equipment.
	Toxic Flow Control	A medium-sized multi-floor space built around a toxic sludge flow. Holding your breath is recommended.
	Disodium-37 Refinery	A central control room flanked by elevated catwalks, floating high above a pool of deadly Disodium-37.
	Thermal Exhaust Access	This medium-sized space is built around a thermal reaction exhaust port for the central power core.
	Sludge Processing	All this high-tech machinery generates quite a bit of nasty toxic sludge. It all comes here to get converted to drinking water.
	Thermal Transfer	A small room built to transfer molten slag from one part of the facility to another while removing impurities.
	Alcoves	A medium-sized space intended to provide easy access to Power Cores, specimens, and other frequently used equipment.
	Security Checkpoint	Provides an isolated safe room for operators to observe foot traffic and glare knowingly from behind bulletproof glass.
	Disodium-37 Overflow	This compact, well-ventilated room pumps Disodium-37 between processing areas.
	Slag Run-Off	This multi-floor transitional space is built around a molten slag run-off trench. It can get really hot in this cramped space.
	Slag Cooling Pit	Long catwalks span a deep, smoldering cooling pit. Watch your step.
	Pinwheel Room	Pipes and stairs dominate this loop-shaped room. Red light casts an eerie glow from the Mixom OneStream plasma core.
	Steam Silo Gamma	Ionization cooling pipes abound in this multilevel space. Never look directly into the outlet!
	Observation	A large, cold space built to spy on subjects from above. A blank canvas for building gameplay.

COUPLER

LAYOUT	NAME	DESCRIPTION
	Coupler Small	A UAC industrial connection created to fix those pesky rounding errors inherent to Mars' architectural designs.
	Coupler Medium	Used to bring together those challenging spaces that fall just short of connecting. Often referred to as "the matchmaker."
	Coupler Long	Used by UAC engineers when all other connections won't do. You'll need it, too.

CROSS

LAYOUT	NAME	DESCRIPTION
	Large Cross	Can connect four of your favorite spaces together, bringing long-lost friends together again.
	Catwalk Crossover	With a short catwalk between and across the entrances, this small crossover features security window access from all four corners.
	Slime Catwalk Crossover	A multi-floor crossover space above a slime pit.
	Steam Vent Cross	A small four-door hallway with steam vents.
	Steam Vent Cross Climb	High doors and low doors, with a climb to get out. Lock it down, and it becomes quite workable as a killing jar.
	Small Cross	A tiny four-way industrial hallway. Simple yet elegant in its design.

DEAD END

LAYOUT	NAME	DESCRIPTION
	Elevator	A standard UAC industrial cargo elevator. Often used to transition from level to level.
	Small Skylight	A small dead-end room. Great for secrets, entrances, and storing industrial waste!
	O of Destruction	This circle of death features some excellent hiding spots for surprise demon attacks and loot caches.
	The Reach	A bottomless pit. A perfect shooting gallery for demons and sunlight that bends at strange angles. There's only one way in or out of The Reach.
	Computer Room	Features four sets of mainframe access terminals, all located at convenient second-floor workstations.
	Armor Hall	A dead end built around a disconnected computer terminal, now used to store body armor and various munitions.

HALLWAY

LAYOUT	NAME	DESCRIPTION
	Hallway H	A multifunctional industrial corridor built to connect up to four additional spaces. Use with caution.
	Hallway S Curve	An essential part of every UAC installation. Featuring not one but two beautiful right angles of industrial hallway glory.
	Straight Hallway	The workhorse of the UAC industrial corridor spaces. Used to connect everything to everything else.
	Hallway Climb	A two-story Straight Hallway with a missing staircase. Better bring your climbing boots.
	Hallway Stairs	It's the hallway everyone is always talking about. Two stories, two doors, and a swanky staircase.
	Hallway U Curve	A semi-circle industrial hallway. For those looking to snake out of sight or turn a full 180 on life.
	Bunker End	A large hallway built to allow for bidirectional egress. When egress efficiency matters, Bunker End is the best choice.
	Bulkhead Observation	Multiple levels of overlapping catwalks, with access to an observation room at the top.
	Wide Catwalk	A maze of twisty little catwalks, all alike.
	Long Hall	A long, narrow hallway with a bump in the middle. Zero visibility between the doors means opportunity for surprises.
	Long Hall Catwalk	A long, straight hallway suspended above a shimmering pool of Disodium-37. I wonder if you can stand on those pipes?
	Straight Large Hallway	This UAC industrial corridor is an upgraded version of the tiny Straight Hallway.
	Heat Exchange S Curve	An S-shaped corridor with a centralized staircase. Think of this as a speed bump in hallway form.
	Disodium-37 S Curve	A short hallway featuring a twist, a climb-up, and 3,600 gallons of Disodium-37 per minute.
	Disodium-37 U Curve	A corridor that really knows its place, the U-shaped hallway with a climb-up does the job and does it well.
	Disodium-37 S Curve Stairs	Under twisting catwalks and over stairs, toxic chemicals have to get from one place to another. This is how.
	Disodium-37 U Curve Stairs	A turnabout with stairs and that romantic purple glow that only Disodium-37 can offer.
	2 Story Hallway Stairs	A short, solid hallway with doors two floors apart.

HALLWAY CONT.

LAYOUT	NAME	DESCRIPTION
	2 Story Hallway Stairs	A longer hallway with three staircases. Does one thing very well.
	Double Hallway	A pair of hallways separated by a thermal cooling pit. Jump, climb, or fall.
	Disodium-37 Vertical Transfer	Vertical Transfer features multiple catwalks for easy access to pipes. Nearly all of the facility's Disodium-37 flows through this room.
	Double Split Hallway	A wide split catwalk with access to four doors. Connect some hallways (may we recommend Simple Hallway?) and add some gameplay.
	Simple Hallway	Whenever you have amazing, gameplay-filled rooms that need connecting, Simple Hallway is here.
	Hallway U	A simple industrial hallway that bends back on itself. Use with reckless abandon.

JOG

LAYOUT	NAME	DESCRIPTION
	Jog Small	Used to connect spaces that have shifted due to unforeseen geological anomalies or simply bad planning.
	Jog Large	Used to connect spaces that are offset by staggering lateral distance. Used by UAC engineers to traverse subterranean hot spots.
	Jog Large Wide	The big brother to the Jog Large, used when lateral shifts just aren't enough to get the job done.

SET PIECE

LAYOUT	NAME	DESCRIPTION
	Foundry	A huge space with tons of ledge grabs, jump areas, and a giant pit of molten lava to wash it all down.
	Prison	This patented open-cell design matches the incarceration needs of any off-world research facility.
	Molten Catwalks	A medium-sized space that continues the UAC tradition of placing an acrobatic apparatus above giant vats of deadly molten metal.
	Transfer Area	A large multi-story space featuring cantilevered staircases intermixed with wide-open sightlines. Great for parties!
	Container Storage Alpha	A tall and wide room featuring curved hallways and catwalks. Can you find the secret room?
	Storage	Various dead ends, climb-ups, and drop holes make this module perfect for puzzle or combat gameplay.
	Receiving	A medium-sized space used to receive large shipments from other facilities to sort and ship elsewhere.

SET PIECE CONT.

LAYOUT	NAME	DESCRIPTION
	Crossover Cargo Station	Storing and moving around cargo is serious business. Here is where the robot's arms meet the heavy cargo containers.
	Warehouse	Tall ceilings, high catwalks, and abandoned cargo trolleys. A useful mix of cover and open lines of fire.
	Engine Room	A small room featuring fuel storage for the backup generators and a control panel or two.
	Steam Junction	Something has gone awry in this steam-venting thermal access corridor. Keep away from open flame.
	The Gap	Dead ends and short hallways, and some of the catwalks are under construction. Mind the gap.
	Superheater Overflow	This large transitional space surrounds two superheated molten flows.
	Slag Control Dam #3	The Dam was quite a tourist attraction when the facility was built.
	Airflow Enclosure	A medium-sized space used to circulate air throughout the facility.
	The Vats	Molten slag flows into the vats, where it is processed and refined before beginning the thermal cooling process. Let's cook breakfast.
	Systems Hub	This hub space is often used at the center of a UAC industrial core. Loads of the tech gear mixed with wide egress corridors.
	Coolant Support Chamber	Designed for an earlier version of the thermal discharge process, this room is hardly ever flooded with super-cooled liquid without warning.
	Disodium-37 Cooling Pit	Keep your head and arms inside the railings at all times. Exposure to Disodium-37 may cause dizziness, insomnia, and loss of appetite.
	Multilevel Storage	A steam vortex on the lower floor promotes thermal cooling. This maze of catwalks features some tricky dead ends and sweet jumps.
	Stacked Slag Cooling Pit	An expansive thermal cooling pit. Lots of room to move, both horizontally and vertically.
	Cooling Core	The underside of a primary power reactor where the cooling rods reside. Some things in here don't react well to bullets.
	The Heatlamp	Nicknamed "The Heatlamp" by prankster engineers, the center charges to 5950 Kelvin in less than 20 seconds. Largely unused after the incident.
	Pipe Overflow Release	Before the advent of the new thermal transfer process, this room was used for spontaneous coolant overflow in the event of a core breach.

SET PIECE cont.

LAYOUT	NAME	DESCRIPTION
	Power Relay Maintenance	When the power relays go bad, they're brought here. And we all know that Power Relay 8623 has been very, very bad indeed.
	Repair Bay 9	UAC offers repair bays of varying shapes, sizes, and application. This one comes with an optional equipment fire.
	Command Overlook	A large multi-tiered space with tons of cover opportunities, ample storage, and a comfortable iceberg-blue hue.
	Molten Vats	A huge metal reduction chamber inside a vast space filled with catwalks precariously placed over spinning molten death.
	Icon of Sin	Is this the end? Is this the opening to Hell? Descending staircases? Belief over science, surely it's too wide and vast.
	Pyramid of Death	Huge pipes and condenser coils converge on a single space, concentrating enormous amounts of energy here.

STAIRS

LAYOUT	NAME	DESCRIPTION
	Red Overwatch	Long staircases wrap around a pair of central security rooms.
	2 Story Spiral Stairs	A short spiral staircase over an open pit of toxic slime.
	4 Story Spiral Stairs	A longer spiral staircase, also over an open pit of toxic slime.
	6 Story Spiral Stairs	Six stories of stairs winding their way to the top above (you guessed it) an open pit of toxic slime.

T-JUNCTION

LAYOUT	NAME	DESCRIPTION
	Small T Junction	A three-way corridor providing the much-discussed fork in the road. This metaphor is literal.
	Double Curve	A tall, curved, Y-shaped hallway junction.
	Y-Split	Stock and industrial, a Y-shaped split room.
	T Incline	A small T-junction with a climb-up.
	Hallway T	A simple T-junction hallway.

TALL

LAYOUT	NAME	DESCRIPTION
	Reheating Furnace	A huge space with two huge molten mixers. The perfect spot for a weekend picnic.
	Climber	One of many large stairwells built for personnel to evacuate in an emergency. This particular space transitions 10 stories.
	Circulation Furnace	Where molten slag is melted to remove impurities at 1300 degrees. Also a great space to jump around with reckless abandon!
	Reactor Core	A mammoth space surrounding a powerful Argent Energy ribbon. Ignore your radiation alarms; nothing to be concerned about.
	Casting Chamber	An enormous work area filled with interwoven catwalks positioned above molten casting vats.
	Loose Screw	Tall and complex, this room features multiple overlapping catwalks and exits at various heights.

:X OBJECT LIST

AI

ICON	NAME	DESCRIPTION
	AI Combat Point	Demons following an AI combat path will move to the last combat point and defend it. You can't stop here—this is demon country!
	AI Conductor – Classic	The Classic AI Conductor will auto-populate a linear level with increasingly difficult demon encounters that do not respawn behind you.
	AI Conductor – Survival	The Survival AI Conductor will spawn an increasingly difficult onslaught of demons until every player is dead.
	AI Path Point	Demons following an AI path will move from point to point until they reach the end point or are interrupted.
	AI Proxy	The AI Proxy is used to apply inputs or gather outputs from demons in your map.

AUDIO

ICON	NAME	DESCRIPTION
	2D Speaker	The 2D Speaker broadcasts sound everywhere. There is no escaping!
	3D Speaker	The 3D Speaker emits positional sounds from locations inside your map.
	Facility Voice Speaker	The Facility Voice Speaker plays words and phrases. It's a great way to hear voices in your head.

AUDIO CONT.

ICON	NAME	DESCRIPTION
	Music	The Music object can control the sweet jams you want players to hear in your map. It's Radio UAC, and you are the DJ.
	Roomtone	The Roomtone object sets ambient sounds within the module.
	VEGA Speaker	The VEGA Speaker plays words and phrases. It's the best way to hear voices in your head. The VEGA speaker includes more dialog options (such as numbers and letters) to help you make custom phrases.

COMMUNICATION

ICON	NAME	DESCRIPTION
	World Text	The World Text object is used to communicate messages to players with the text that floats in world space.
	Message	The Message object is used to send messages directly to a player's HUD.
	Callout	The Callout object uses pre-defined combinations of HUD messages and audio to inform players of game events.
	HUD Settings	The HUD Settings object allows for customization of a player's HUD during gameplay. Remember to activate it once you've changed settings.
	POI Settings	The POI Settings object defines the color, shape, and look for point of interest icons.
	Objective	The Objective object controls HUD text, icons, or progress bars to help direct players to their goals.

DEMONS

ICON	NAME	DESCRIPTION
	Possessed Worker	Possessed Workers are created in a Lazarus Wave event, a phenomenon discovered during Dr. Olivia Pierce's Lazarus Project research operation.
	Possessed Scientist	Posthumous brain activity in Possessed Scientists is limited to primal behavior. They will stand dormant until presented with a live food source.
	Possessed Engineer	Possessed Engineers are created when an appropriate explosive material is readily available. They exhibit self-destructive behavior.
	Imp	Imps, ferocious and agile demons, are found all over Hell and are often used on the front line during concerted attacks in both dimensions.
	Lost Soul	Lost Souls are found wandering aimlessly within the temples of Hell as they search for a host to inhabit.
	Hell Razer	The Hell Razer is an astute and tactical foe that will engage enemies from a distance with a fierce beam of unrefined Hell energy.

DEMONS CONT.

ICON	NAME	DESCRIPTION
	Possessed Soldier	Some Lazarus Wave victims continue to display tactical cognizance posthumously. Combat-trained individuals will become enemy combatants.
	Possessed Security	Possessed Security units exhibit complex battle strategies, including use of a mobile shield and the ability to fire while in cover.
	Cacodemon	The Cacodemon is a monstrous psionic demon driven by the desire to feed. It displays limited intelligence but makes for an intimidating enemy.
	Hell Knight	The Hell Knight is a towering brute bred for combat deep in the bowels of Hell.
	Mancubus	The Mancubus is a lumbering behemoth demon. A foul odor accompanies its presence, and the stench can be overwhelming if inhaled directly.
	Cyber-Mancubus	The Mancubus strain of demon has been manipulated by a team of bio-geneticists led by Dr. Pierce herself.
	Pinky	These demonic animals were colloquially named Pinkies when first discovered by the Lazarus Project's Tethering Operation.
	Spectre	The Spectre is the unfortunate result of an attempt to genetically modify the Pinky. There are no known behavioral differences from the Pinky.
	Revenant	Revenants are UAC operatives that have been transformed through cybernetic augmentation and repeated Lazarus Wave exposure.
	Baron of Hell	The Baron of Hell is the highest demon among the order of the Hell Knights.

EXPLODERS

ICON	NAME	DESCRIPTION
	C4	A C4 explosive that detonates when shot and gets a little touchy when you look at it funny.
	Classic Barrel	This minimally reinforced barrel explodes at the slightest hint of damage.
	Plasma Barrel	This barrel explodes when damaged, spilling hot plasma everywhere.
	Radiation Barrel	This barrel explodes when damaged, spilling radioactive goo. You probably should eat the goo.
	UAC Barrel	The highest UAC safety standards were followed in the manufacturing of this barrel.

FLOW

ICON	NAME	DESCRIPTION
	Player Iterator	The Player Iterator can be used to perform actions on all players in the map.
	Team Iterator	The Team Iterator can be used to perform actions on all teams in the map.
	AI Iterator	The AI Iterator can be used to perform actions on all AI in the map.
	Integer Compare	Compare two integers, and signal outputs based on the results.
	Number Compare	Compare two numbers, and signal outputs based on the results.
	String Compare	Compare two strings, and signal outputs based on the results.
	Gate	The Gate can perform logical operations on Boolean inputs.
	Count	A counter that can signal its outputs when the specified max count is reached.
	Timer	A Timer will signal its outputs after waiting a specified number of seconds.
	Delay	The Delay will hold a signal for a short time before sending it down the logic chain.
	Repeater	The Repeater object will signal its outputs over and over again a number of times or infinitely.
	Relay	A Relay will pass along any input signal to all of its outputs.
	Random Relay	A Random Relay will signal one of its outputs at random.
	Sequencer	A Sequencer will signal its outputs in a specified order. The default order is the order in which the outputs are connected.

FX

ICON	NAME	DESCRIPTION
	Point Light	When your map is without form, and void, and darkness is upon the face of your textures, place a light, and there will be light, and it will be good.
	Spot Light	When a Point Light doesn't provide enough focus, the Spot Light is there to fill your light beam needs.
	Medium Sparks	Light produced by a sudden discontinuous discharge of electricity through the air or another dielectric.

FX CONT.

ICON	NAME	DESCRIPTION
	Small Sparks	A tiny spark effect for use with tiny malfunctions.
	Large Explosion	Develop your own big bang theory with this military-grade kaboom maker.
	Medium Explosion	It may not be large, but it's the second-best explosion you'll ever experience.
	Small Explosion	Amaze your friends and frighten your neighbors with this bite-sized explosion.
	Barrel Explosion	Sometimes, you want the explosion without the barrel.
	Electric Explosion	This is what happens when you stick your entire head into a wall socket.
	Large Fire	When a small fire just isn't enough, go large.
	Medium Fire	If that fire is too large and that other fire is too small, this Medium Fire might be for you.
	Small Fire	Fire! Fire! A Small Fire is just a big fire waiting to happen.
	Flame Jet	Nine out of 10 pyros agree that this Flame Jet is the best! Causes fire damage to players and demons.
	Large Smoke	Where there's smoke, there's a particle emitter.
	Medium Smoke	Fool all your firefighter buddies into getting dressed for nothing.
	Small Smoke	It's illegal in most places to have a Small Smoke indoors.
	Large Smoke Stream	Where is all this smoke coming from?
	Medium Smoke Stream	Don't breathe this.
	Small Smoke Stream	Traveling at the speed of smoke.
	Poison Cloud	Inhale the sweet aroma! Causes poison damage to players and demons.
	Poison Jet	Use a high-pressure jet of noxious death to rapidly insert poison into the atmosphere! Causes poison damage to players and demons.

FX CONT.

ICON	NAME	DESCRIPTION
	Large Steam	A high flow rate steam exhaust. Proximity can result in amazingly wrinkle-free clothes.
	Medium Steam	This isn't your grandma's humidifier.
	Small Steam	A tiny jet of superheated gas. 2,400 PSI never looked so good!
	Plasma	Looks like somebody dropped a cup of superheated plasma. So clumsy! Causes plasma damage to players and demons.
	Radiation	A blob of radioactive goo you can use to decorate any room. Causes radiation damage to players and demons.
	Invisible Hazard	When you want to inflict pain from an unseen force, the Invisible Hazard is for you. Causes variable damage to players and demons.
	Laser	Wield the power of the light! Causes damage to players and demons.

GAMEPLAY

ICON	NAME	DESCRIPTION
	Gameplay Settings	The Gameplay Settings control numerous options for your map, such as revival, loot drops, spawning rules, par time, and more.
	Score Settings	The Score Settings control score point values and multipliers.
	Map	The Map object can signal when the map starts or be used to reveal a secret.
	Module	The Module will apply inputs or signal outputs based on the module in which it is placed.
	End Game	The End Game object defines the victory, defeat, and draw conditions.
	Teleporter Pad	A UAC-i337 Teleporter Pad. Used to teleport humans, demons, and cargo from Point A to Point B with a 95.2% success rate.
	Teleport Destination	Teleport players, AI, and other objects to this destination.
	Camera	Control a player's view with the Camera. Direct your own mega budget Snapchinima.

INTERACTIVES

ICON	NAME	DESCRIPTION
	Munitions Box	What's in the box?! Munitions! Well, not just munitions. Sometimes, there are cool things like health and armor…
	Panel	An interactive Panel, built from the highest quality punch-resistant polymer, can be used by players to signal other objects.
	Power Station	The Power Station is the receptacle for Power Cores.
	Pressure Plate	The Pressure Plate will signal its outputs when a player or demon stands on it.

LARGE PROPS

ICON	NAME	DESCRIPTION
	Barrels 01	A non-explosive UAC containment barrel.
	Barrels 02	Three non-explosive UAC barrels. No human would stack barrels like this.
	Barricade 01	A reinforced portable wall unit.
	Barricade 02	A security barricade unit.
	Barricade 03	A security barricade unit.
	Barricade 04	A security barricade unit.
	Barricade 05	A security barricade unit with warning information.
	Barricade 06	A large multi-panel security barricade unit.
	Barricade 07	A reinforced metal security blockade unit.
	Barricade 08	A retracted security barricade unit.
	Barricade 09	A security barricade scanning unit.
	Box 01	A storage case for laboratory equipment.

ICON	NAME	DESCRIPTION
	Box 02	A general-use storage box.
	Box 03	A shipping crate for laboratory equipment.
	Cart 01	A UAC open equipment cart.
	Cart 02	A UAC environment-controlled equipment cart.
	Control Console Corner Segment	A corner segment for the modular control console.
	Control Console Main Segment	The central unit of a modular control console.
	Control Console Short Segment	A short segment for the modular control console.
	Control Console Tower Segment	A tower segment for the modular control console.
	Control Panel	A freestanding control panel.
	Crate 01	A practical and attractive storage solution for vitrified waste and compacted metals. Available in yellow.
	Crate 02	An industrial storage crate.
	Crate 02 Lid	A lid for an industrial storage crate.
	Crate 02 Open	An open industrial storage crate.
	Crate 03	An equipment container.
	Crate 03 Lid	The lid for an equipment container.
	Crate 03 Open	An open equipment storage container.
	Crate 04	An industrial storage crate.
	Crate 05	An industrial storage crate.

ICON	NAME	DESCRIPTION
	Crate 06	A large shipping and storage system.
	Debris 01	Metal debris.
	Debris 02	Metal debris.
	Debris 03	Metal debris.
	Debris 04	Metal debris.
	Debris 05	Metal debris.
	Debris Pile	A pile of metal debris.
	Director's Chair	Adds an elegant yet powerful touch to any director's office décor.
	Duffle Bag	A rugged and easy-to-use equipment bag.
	Executive Chair	Designed to fit your body like a glove, this office chair is for people who think best off of their feet.
	Exit Sign 01	An inactive Exit sign.
	Exit Sign 02	An active Exit sign.
	Fan	A portable fan.
	Floor Mat	A UAC floor mat.
	Floor Pad	An industrial floor pad.
	Fork Lift	An industrial fork lift.
	Fuel Container	A portable refueling station.
	Generator 01	A portable generator.

ICON	NAME	DESCRIPTION
	Generator 02	A backup power supply with extension cable.
	Generator 03	A backup power supply.
	Hand Light 01	A portable industrial light.
	Hand Light 02	A portable industrial light.
	Hand Light 03	A portable industrial light.
	Hanging Light	A hanging light.
	Hose Reel	A hose reel.
	Hydraulic Hose	A thermoplastic, high-pressure hydraulic hose.
	Kitchen Chair	A chair commonly found in lunchrooms.
	Large Trash Can	A large containment barrier for storing community detritus.
	Locker 01	A personal locker.
	Locker 01 Door	A personal locker door.
	Locker 01 Open	An open personal locker.
	Locker 02	An equipment locker.
	Machine 01	A thermal generator carbon extraction unit for oxygen-depleted work environments.
	Machine 02	A tri-station variable frequency converter rack.
	Monitor 01	A heavy framed industrial monitor.
	Monitor 02	A wall-mounted facility monitoring station.

ICON	NAME	DESCRIPTION
	Monitor 03	A free-standing facility monitoring station.
	Office Chair	A standard office chair.
	Orange Chair	Both orange and uncomfortable, this chair is the perfect working-class seating solution.
	Pallet 01	A warehouse pallet.
	Shelf	A storage shelf.
	Table	A kitchen table.
	Vending Machine 01	A food vending machine.
	Vending Machine 02	A drink vending machine.
	Wall Light	An industrial wall light.
	Warning Sign 01	A Move Up sign.
	Warning Sign 02	A Move Down sign.
	Warning Sign 03	A Watch Your Step sign.
	Warning Sign 04	A Work Zone sign.
	Warning Sign 05	A Hazardous Environment sign.
	Warning Sign 06	An Authorized Personnel Only sign.
	Warning Sign 07	A High Temperature sign.
	Warning Sign 08	An Inhalation Hazard sign.
	Warning Sign 09	A Burn Hazard sign.

LARGE PROPS CONT.

ICON	NAME	DESCRIPTION
	Warning Sign 10	A Do Not Enter sign.
	Warning Sign 11	A Fire Hazard sign.
	Water Cooler	An eco-friendly water-responsible rehydration station.
	Wire 01	Coiled electrical wire.
	Wire 02	A scrap electrical wire.
	Wire Spool	A wire spool.

PICKUPS

ICON	NAME	DESCRIPTION
	Red Flag	A droppable Red Flag.
	Yellow Flag	A droppable Yellow Flag.
	Blue Flag	A droppable Blue Flag, the Red Flag's evil twin.
	Green Flag	A droppable Green Flag.
	Gray Flag	A droppable Gray Flag.
	Red Keycard	A droppable Red Keycard. Grants you access to the cafeteria.
	Yellow Keycard	A droppable Yellow Keycard. Grants you access to the executive lounge.
	Blue Keycard	A droppable Blue Keycard. Grants you access to the research laboratory.
	Green Keycard	A droppable Green Keycard. Grants you access to the armory.
	Gray Keycard	A droppable Gray Keycard. Grants you access to Level 5 restricted areas.
	Red Power Core	A limited edition droppable Red Power Core.

PICKUPS CONT.

ICON	NAME	DESCRIPTION
	Yellow Power Core	A droppable Yellow Power Core. Enjoys being picked up and going on adventures.
	Blue Power Core	A droppable Blue Power Core. Gets a bit lonely when it's away from its Power Station.
	Green Power Core	A droppable Green Power Core. Filled with sustainable, exo-friendly energy.
	Gray Power Core	A droppable Gray Power Core. Supports the Power Station's five-year plan for Mars domination.
	Ammo Box	A box of universal ammo. One round to rule them all.
	Ammo Pack	An Ammo Pack filled with universal ammo. All those UAC research dollars actually produced something useful.
	Armor Shard	An Armor Shard worth 5 points of armor. Just slap it on like an armor-plated bandage.
	Armor Shield	An Armor Shield worth 25 points of armor. Ergonomically designed for less chafing.
	Armor Suit	An Armor Suit worth 50 points of armor. It protects your innards!
	Container	A Container can be filled with health, armor, ammo, or player resources.
	Demon Rune	When picked up, a Demon Rune will transform a human player into a demon player. An unholy marriage of science and the occult.
	Flag Base	This object is used to mark key locations, such as a flag spawn.
	Haste	Haste increases a player's movement speed and firing speed for a short time. Gotta go fast!
	Large Health	A Large Health pack worth 50 points of health. How am I supposed to fit all these fluids in my body?
	Medium Health	A Medium Health pack worth 25 points of health. Helps you walk it off.
	Mega Health	A Mega Health pack worth more health and armor than you can carry.
	Quad Damage	Quad Damage significantly increases a player's damage for a short time. Four times the damage, 20 times the fun.

ICON	NAME	DESCRIPTION
	Regeneration	Regeneration restores a player's health over time. Does not cause immortality.
	Small Health	A Small Health pack worth 5 points of health. A cure for little bumps and bruises.

PLAYER AND TEAM

ICON	NAME	DESCRIPTION
	Player Proxy	The Player Proxy is used to apply inputs or gather outputs from players in your map.
	Team Proxy	The Team Proxy is used to apply inputs or gather outputs from teams in your map.
	Player Start	A spawn location for a player. At least one is required per map.
	Inventory	The Inventory object is used to give or take inventory items from players.
	Vitals	The Vitals object is used to give health and armor to players.
	Player Loadout	The Player Loadout object is used to give weapons, equipment, and skills to a specific player.
	Player Input	When enabled, the Player Input object collects player input that can be used to signal other objects.

SMALL PROPS

ICON	NAME	DESCRIPTION
	Battery	An ancient repository for converting chemical energy into electrical energy.
	Beer Can	A full can of Olympus Mons brewed GRUD LIGHT.
	Boot	A technician's work boot.
	Box 01	A small container.
	Bucket	It's a bucket.
	Cleaning Bot	The custodial engineer's partner in a daily battle against dust and grime.

ICON	NAME	DESCRIPTION
	Computer 01	A computer.
	Computer 02	Another computer.
	Computer 03	The third computer.
	Computer 04	The last computer you'll ever need.
	Drill	An all-purpose tool used for drilling holes and driving screws.
	File Holder	A file holder. It contains files.
	Food Tray	A food tray.
	Fuel Can	A fuel can.
	Glove	A technician's work glove.
	Hammer	A device to amplify the force applied to futuristic construction nails.
	Hard Hat	The minimum safety gear required for anyone entering the facility.
	Mop Bucket	A mop bucket.
	Noodles 1	A box of Dopechan noodles.
	Noodles 1 [Opened]	An empty box of Dopechan noodles.
	Noodles 2	A box of Cheezy Mac dinner in a box.
	Noodles 2 [Opened]	An empty box of Cheezy Mac.
	Office Mouse	A super high-tech quantum-entangled 4.5 quadrillion DPI mouse.

SMALL PROPS CONT.

ICON	NAME	DESCRIPTION
	Plastic Bottle 1	A bottle of Banhar purified water fresh from the terraformed waters of Mars' own Olympus Mons.
	Plastic Bottle 2	A bottle of Grulp Energy Drink.
	Plastic Bottle 3	A bottle of Bubbles soda product.
	Plastic Bottle 4	A bottle of unsweetened Sure Greaf Tea.
	Plastic Bottle 5	A bottle of low-fat generic Milk Chocolate Drink.
	Plastic Box	A box of Grangles Potato Crisps.
	Screwdriver	A handle, shaft, and tip placed firmly into a screw head to rotate it.
	Small Tin Can	A tin can.
	Soda Can	A can of Diet Grulp energy drink. Blargh!
	Tea Can	A can of Bubbles tea approximation.
	Trash Can	A radiation-resistant containment barrier for storing personal detritus.
	Wet Floor Sign	A Wet Floor sign.
	Wrench	A space-age spanner for enhancing rotational torque applied to low-tech devices.

SPAWNERS

ICON	NAME	DESCRIPTION
	Custom Group Encounter	A Custom Group Encounter will spawn a number of encounters simultaneously.
	Group Demon Encounter	A Group Demon Encounter will spawn a single group of demons.
	Single Demon Encounter	A single Demon Encounter will spawn a single specified demon.
	Survival Event	The Survival Event will spawn an increasingly difficult onslaught of demons for the duration of the event.

SPAWNERS CONT.

ICON	NAME	DESCRIPTION
	Wave Event	The Wave Event will spawn multiple waves of enemy encounters successively. The event ends when all waves are vanquished.
	Miniboss Event	The Miniboss Event will spawn a powerful miniboss. The event ends when the boss is defeated.
	Item Spawn Settings	The Item Spawn Settings provide control over global automatic spawning for pickups, Munitions Boxes, powerups, and weapons.
	Spawn Weapon	The Spawn Weapon object will spawn a weapon on demand. Guns. Lots of guns.
	Spawn Ammo	The Spawn Ammo object will spawn ammo on demand.
	Spawn Armor	The Spawn Armor object will spawn armor on demand.
	Spawn Health	The Spawn Health object will spawn health on demand.
	Spawn Powerup	The Spawn Powerup object will spawn a powerup on demand.
	Spawn Droppable	The Spawn Droppable object will spawn droppables on demand.
	Spawn Container	The Spawn Container object will spawn containers filled with the specified items.

VARIABLES

ICON	NAME	DESCRIPTION
	Player Resource	A variable that represents a custom Player Resource type. It can be set to a whole number.
	Team Resource	A variable that represents a custom Team Resource type. It can be set to a whole number.
	Integer	An Integer variable can be set to a whole number and used to control certain properties on other objects.
	Number	A Number variable can be set to a number with decimal places and used to control certain properties on other objects.
	String	A String variable can be set to a text string and used to control certain properties on other objects.
	Boolean	A Boolean variable can be set to true or false and used to control certain properties on other objects.

VARIABLES CONT.

ICON	NAME	DESCRIPTION
	Color	A Color variable can be set to a specific RGB value and used to control certain properties on other objects.
	Custom Filter	Add filters to the Custom Filter to define the who, what, and where. Use the Custom Filter by name, or place it between an output and an input.
	Cached Object	A Cached Object variable will store away an object, allowing the stored object to be referenced later in a logic chain.

VOLUMES

ICON	NAME	DESCRIPTION
	Box Trigger	The Box Trigger will signal its outputs when a player or demon enters the bounding.
	Cylinder Trigger	The Cylinder Trigger will signal its outputs when a player or demon enters the bounding.
	Inhibit AI Conductor Spawning Box	The Inhibit AI Conductor Spawning Box prevents AI Conductor objects from spawning a demon inside the defined volume.
	Player Blocking Volume	The Player Blocking Volume prevents players and projectiles from passing through the defined volume.
	Shootable Trigger	The Shootable Trigger will signal its outputs when taking damage.
	Team Capture Point	It takes teamwork to gain control of the Team Capture Point.

WEAPONS

ICON	NAME	DESCRIPTION
	BFG	Most research regarding the BFG-9000 remains classified. The design was first [REDACTED] by [REDACTED] and [REDACTED].
	Burst Rifle	A selective-fire battle rifle equipped with a reciprocating barrel assembly and three-round burst mode.
	Chaingun	A large drum-fed rotary machine gun with a high rate of fire.
	Combat Shotgun	A pump-action shotgun with a tight spread of buckshot.
	Gauss Cannon	A devastatingly accurate long-range weapon with a noticeable kick that its operator must compensate for.
	Heavy Assault Rifle	Features a dependable mechanical firing mechanism, high accuracy at long range, and an abundant supply of ammunition.
	Hellshot	An advanced semi-automatic energy weapon.
	Lightning Gun	Short-range energy weapon that fires a constant stream of electricity.
	Plasma Rifle	A fully automatic rifle that fires pulses of super-heated plasma capable of dealing splash damage.
	Rocket Launcher	Fires rockets that explode on impact, doing damage over a large area.
	Super Shotgun	A break-action double-barrel shotgun that fires a wide spread of buckshot.
	Vortex Rifle	A precision long-range energy weapon with a magnified optic.

TROPHIES

NAME	DESCRIPTION	MODE(S)	XBOX ONE GAMERSCORE	PLAYSTATION 4 TROPHY
A Gift from Beyond	Earn a Rune	Campaign	15	Bronze
A Toe into Madness	Complete "The UAC" on Ultra-Nightmare	Campaign	10	Bronze
An Old Friend	Acquire the BFG	Campaign	30	Bronze
Argent Fiend	Fully upgrade Health, Armor, and Ammo capacity on a single campaign run.	Campaign	30	Silver
Argent Overload	Fully upgrade Health, Armor, or Ammo capacity	Campaign	15	Bronze
Butcher	Perform 200 Glory Kills	SP, MP, SNAP	50	Bronze
Combat tested, Doomguy approved	Reach Level 5 in Multiplayer	MP	30	Bronze
E1M1	Complete the first mission of the campaign	Campaign	25	Bronze
Entryway	Complete the SnapMap Basic and Advanced Tutorials	SNAP	20	Bronze
Every Nook and Cranny	Find all Collectibles	Campaign	30	Silver
Historian	Find all Data Logs	Campaign	25	Bronze
Hot Swapper	Acquire all weapon mods	Campaign	30	Silver
IDDQD	Upgrade all Runes	Campaign	100	Gold
IDKFA	Earn the Masteries for all weapon mods	Campaign	50	Gold
Into the Unknown	Warp to Hell	Campaign	15	Bronze
IPXSETUP.EXE	Win a Multiplayer match	MP	15	Bronze
Juicin' it Up	Kill 150 enemies while using Power Ups	SP, MP, SNAP	50	Silver
Knee-Deep in the Dead	Complete the campaign on "I'm too Young to Die", "Hurt Me Plenty", "Ultra-Violence" or "Nightmare"	Campaign	100	Gold
Momentum Shift	Upgrade a Rune	Campaign	25	Bronze
No Rest for the Living	Play 5 published SnapMaps	SNAP	20	Bronze
Outnumbered? No Problem	Defeat the Hell Guards	Campaign	25	Silver
Overclocked	Fully upgrade all Praetor Suit categories on a single campaign run	Campaign	50	Gold
Rip and Tear	Glory Kill all common enemy types in the campaign	SP	20	Silver
Shareware	Create and publish a SnapMap	SNAP	10	Bronze
Shoot it Until it Dies	Defeat the Cyberdemon	Campaign	25	Silver
Specialist	Earn the Mastery for a weapon mod	Campaign	20	Bronze
The Circle is Complete	Earn all Runes	Campaign	30	Silver
Thorough Shopper	Complete all Challenges for a single mission	Campaign	20	Silver
Thy Flesh Consumed	Earn all Trophies	SP, MP, SNAP	0	Platinum
Timing is Everything	Use explosive barrels to kill 100 enemies	SP, MP, SNAP	15	Bronze
Tinkering	Fully upgrade a Praetor Suit category	Campaign	15	Silver
Up Close and Personal	Kill 50 enemies using the chainsaw	SP, MP, SNAP	25	Silver
What Else Ya Got?	Complete all Mission Challenges on a single campaign run	Campaign	35	Gold
Who's Next?	Defeat the Spider Mastermind	Campaign	25	Silver

Written by Michael Owen, Doug Walsh, and William Murray
Maps created by Loren Gilliland

DK/Prima Games, a division of Penguin Random House LLC
6081 East 82nd Street, Suite #400
Indianapolis, IN 46250

Standard Edition ISBN: 978-0-7440-1724-3
Collector's Edition ISBN: 978-0-7440-1725-0

Printing Code: The rightmost double-digit number is the year of the book's printing; the rightmost single-digit number is the number of the book's printing. For example, 16-1 shows that the first printing of the book occurred in 2016.

19 18 17 16   4 3 2 1

001-298937-April/2016

CREDITS

SENIOR DEVELOPMENT EDITOR
David B. Bartley

SENIOR GRAPHIC DESIGNER
Carol Stamile

PRODUCTION DESIGNER
Justin Lucas

PRODUCTION
Angela Graef

COPY EDITOR
Angie Mateski

PRIMA GAMES STAFF

VP & PUBLISHER
Mike Degler

EDITORIAL MANAGER
Tim Fitzpatrick

DESIGN AND LAYOUT MANAGER
Tracy Wehmeyer

LICENSING
Christian Sumner
Paul Giacomotto

MARKETING
Katie Hemlock

DIGITAL PUBLISHING
Julie Asbury
Tim Cox
Shaida Boroumand

OPERATIONS MANAGER
Stacey Ginther

ACKNOWLEDGMENTS

Everyone at PrimaGames would like to express our gratitude to the team at Bethesda for your tremendous support and cooperation. Special thanks to Mike Kochis, Sean Bean, Joshua Gillespie, Michael Aubuchon, Greg Barr, Kevin Cloud, Kirsten Dearnley, Chad Eanes, Jon Lane, Kurt Loudy, Tom Mustaine, Peter Sokal, Nels Nelson, and Chandi Abey. Your combined time and talent have helped make this guide great.